DREAMING AMERICA

Dreaming America

Obsession and Transcendence
in the Fiction of
Joyce Carol Oates

G. F. WALLER

Louisiana State University Press
BATON ROUGE AND LONDON

Copyright © 1979 by Louisiana State University Press
Manufactured in the United States of America

Design: Dwight Agner
Type face: VIP Sabon
Composition: LSU Press
Printing: Thomson-Shore, Inc.
Binding: John Dekker & Sons, Inc.

Quotations from the following works by Joyce Carol Oates are reprinted by permission of Vanguard Press: *The Assassins; Childwold; Crossing the Border; Do With Me What You Will; The Edge of Impossibility; Expensive People; A Garden of Earthly Delights; The Goddess and Other Women; Marriages and Infidelities; New Heaven, New Earth; Them; Upon the Sweeping Flood; The Wheel of Love; Where Are You Going, Where Have You Been; With Shuddering Fall; Wonderland.*

LIBRARY OF CONGRESS CATALOGING IN PUBLICATION DATA

Waller, G   F
Dreaming America.
Includes bibliography.
1. Oates, Joyce Carol, 1938–
—Criticism and interpretation.   I. Title.
PS3565. A8Z94   813'.5'4   78–16141
ISBN 0–8071–0478–7

FOR LINDA
who gave me words for feelings
feelings for words

Contents

	Acknowledgments	ix
	List of Abbreviations	xi
One	The Obsessive Vision	1
Two	The Phantasmagoria of American Personality	27
Three	Forms of Obsession: Oates's Fictional Stance	61
Four	*With Shuddering Fall, A Garden of Earthly Delights*	87
Five	*Expensive People, Them*	113
Six	*Wonderland, Do With Me What You Will*	143
Seven	*The Assassins: A Book of Hours, Childwold*	183
Eight	Conclusion	213
	Selected Bibliography	221

Acknowledgments

THIS study of Joyce Carol Oates grew out of a fascination with her work that at times has been as obsessive as that same quality I find in her fiction. I hope that something of the same passion communicates itself in my writing.

I am grateful to a number of persons and institutions for encouragement and help. Joyce Carol Oates herself has been a kind friend and stimulating and generous host. Allen Bevan was kind enough to print an early version of the treatment of *Wonderland* in the *Dalhousie Review* and I acknowledge his permission to reprint the material and would like to record my personal thanks. Valuable help came from a generous grant from the Dalhousie University Research and Development Fund, while useful comments and encouragement came from many friends, colleagues, and students. In particular, Peter Dane many years ago contributed most of my understanding of D. H. Lawrence, and Margaret Witten-Hannah initially helped me to understand something of the experience of the Reva episode in *Wonderland*. Above all, Linda Levine introduced me to the thought of Paul Ricoeur, and especially provided an essential critique of the more facile parts of my comprehension of psychological theory. Her contribution to the whole study is recorded , however inadequately, in the dedication. Other valuable help came from, among others, Andrea Clough, Eric Gould, David and Pamela Kellner, Heather Kirk, Geoffrey Harvey, Rae ·McCarthy MacDonald, Carmen Phinney, J. Bruce Stovel, Kathy Tyler, and Jennifer, Andrew, and Michael Waller. Joan Waller miraculously transformed illegible handwriting into typescript from the other side of the world while Janice Downey typed and retyped the manuscript, often silently (and sometimes not so silently) adding useful corrections and criticisms. To all these, and many others, deepest thanks.

List of
Abbreviations

THE following abbreviations for Oates's works are used in this study. Unless otherwise stated, the edition used is that published by Vanguard Press.

AF   *Angel Fire*. Baton Rouge: Louisiana State University Press, 1973.

AS   *Anonymous Sins*. Baton Rouge: Louisiana State University Press, 1969.

A   *The Assassins: A Book of Hours*. 1975.

BNG   *By the North Gate*. 1963.

CB   *Crossing the Border*. 1976.

C   *Childwold*. 1976.

DWM   *Do With Me What You Will*. 1973.

EOI   *The Edge of Impossibility*. 1972.

EP   *Expensive People*. 1968.

GOW   *The Goddess and Other Women*. 1975.

GED   *A Garden of Earthly Delights*. 1967.

HG   *The Hungry Ghosts*. Los Angeles: Black Sparrow Press, 1974.

LD   *Love and Its Derangements*. Baton Rouge:
      Louisiana State University Press, 1970.

LD-F *Love and Its Derangements and Other Poems*
      (comprising *Anonymous Sins and Other Poems,
      Love and Its Derangements*, and *Angel Fire*).
      Greenwich, Conn.: Fawcett, 1974.

MI   *Marriages and Infidelities*. 1972.

NHNE *New Heaven, New Earth: The Visionary
      Experience in Literature*. 1974.

NS   *Night-Side*. 1977.

PK   *The Poisoned Kiss*. 1975.

S   *The Seduction*. Los Angeles: Black Sparrow
      Press, 1975.

TSM   *The Triumph of the Spider Monkey*. Santa
      Barbara: Black Sparrow Press, 1976.

T   *Them*. 1969.

USF   *Upon the Sweeping Flood*. 1966.

WGWB *Where Are You Going, Where Have You Been*.
      Greenwich, Conn.: Fawcett, 1974.

W   *Wonderland*. 1971.

W-F   *Wonderland*. Greenwich, Conn.: Fawcett, 1972.

WOL   *The Wheel of Love*. 1970.

WSF   *With Shuddering Fall*. 1964.

DREAMING AMERICA

ONE

The
Obsessive
Vision

SINCE the mid 1950s—if we are to believe contemporary criticism—the American novel has expired and been revitalized; fictions have journeyed beyond the wasteland of institution and conspiracy; fiction has been dissolved, fragmented, and dislocated. The once stable world of history has been reviled, re-created, reinterpreted, and transcended; contemporary events have been dismissed by contemporary and postcontemporary fictionists as both banal and unbelievable, dreamlike and discontinuous. Situated somewhere near the center of this frenetic fictional activity of our time, "celebrating darkly the traditional pieties of the novel," [1] as Ihab Hassan puts it in his map of the contemporary fictional terrain, lie the novels of Joyce

1 Ihab Hassan, *Paracriticisms: Seven Speculations of the Times* (Urbana: University of Illinois Press, 1975), 105.

Carol Oates. Since 1963, she has published eight novels, inter-spersed with seven collections of poetry, eleven volumes of short stories, two collections of critical essays, and many uncollected or separately published stories, essays, plays, and poems (as this study has been written, the list has had to be constantly revised). Such an output would be remarkable enough were it not that Oates's work reveals her to be among the most sensitive record-ers of the intellectual, social — and most important of all — the emotional dynamics of our time. She has been awarded many lit-erary prizes, including a special O. Henry award for continued achievement in the short story, and while hardly a darling of avant-garde criticism (Hassan's reference is briefly dismissive for instance), she has acquired a solid literary following. She is frequently anthologized; she is increasingly taught in college courses; she has moved close to the top of the dissertation stand-ings; she may appear in virtually any kind of periodical from the *Southern Review*, *Chelsea*, or the *Journal of Existential Psychol-ogy and Psychiatry* to *Chatelaine*, *Redbook*, or *Family Circle*.

The almost obligatory topic with which to introduce Oates is, in fact, the amount she has published. A survey of her work may suggest a compulsive writer and maybe even a lack of self-criticism. Her poems, collected in *Women in Love* (1968), *Anon-ymous Sins* (1969), *Love and Its Derangements* (1970), *Angel Fire* (1973), *Dreaming America* (1973), *The Fabulous Beasts* (1974), and *Women Whose Lives Are Food, Men Whose Lives Are Money* (1978), are often jagged and metrically uncertain, and sometimes over-packed with superfluous words; but fre-quently they can crystallize with electrifying clarity inexplicable moments of experience on the edge of fear, despair, terror, or joy. Many read, in fact, like passionate footnotes to her stories or novels. Her two collections of criticism, *The Edge of Impos-sibility* (1972) and *New Heaven, New Earth* (1974), also show uncanny parallels with the concerns of her fiction. The earlier collection of essays on tragedy includes essays — especially those on *Troilus and Cressida* and Yeats — which reflect on her fiction written at about the same time; the later collection (which includes a superb study of Lawrence, previously published as a separate monograph, and a fine essay on Kafka) parallels a developing apocalyptic stand in her fiction of the 1970s. As well as overlapping with her fiction, her criticism, it should be noted, is often extraordinarily suggestive, especially in the way it opens up, by analogy or brooding meditation, startling psychological and philosophical perspectives.

It is in the short stories perhaps that Oates's best work is to be found. They have been collected so far in *By the North Gate* (1963), *Upon the Sweeping Flood* (1966), *The Wheel of Love* (1970), *Marriages and Infidelities* (1972), *The Hungry Ghosts* (1974), *Where Are You Going, Where Have You Been* (1974), *The Goddess and Other Women* (1975), *The Seduction* (1975), *The Poisoned Kiss* (1975), *Across the Border* (1976), and *Night-Side* (1977). A novella, *The Triumph of the Spider Monkey*, was published in 1976. Many of the stories are certainly repetitive or trivial. But some — "Where Are You Going, Where Have You Been," "Unmailed, Unwritten Letters," "Accomplished Desires" from *The Wheel of Love*, "The Sacred Marriage" from *Marriages and Infidelities*, to mention a few of the best — are so bewilderingly evocative that they must rate along with the masterpieces of the genre. In this study I have frequently used her stories to illustrate her vision and fictional stance, but it is with her novels that her reputation and importance must rest. It is there that her prophetic urgency, the obsessive desire to "dream America," emerges at its most tantalizing, frustrating, and evocative. To date, her novels are *With Shuddering Fall* (1964), *A Garden of Earthly Delights* (1967), *Expensive People* (1968), *Them* (1969), *Wonderland* (1971), *Do With Me What You Will* (1973), *The Assassins: A Book of Hours* (1975), and *Childwold* (1976). The early novels, although technically more cautious, nevertheless share the same obsessions as the mature works of the seventies, where Oates attempts to dramatize the mystery of the human spirit struggling amongst our personal and shared nightmares.

Critics discussing Oates have usually felt obliged to comment wryly upon this prolificacy.[2] Undoubtedly, no writer can write too much, but it may be true that Oates has published too much and so given the impression of writing "too much, too quickly" and being "too little self-critical."[3] One of the reasons this study concentrates on her novels is that so many of her numerous stories and poems do overlap or repeat each other. Reading a collection of her stories straight through sometimes feels like an encounter with a recurring nightmare. Swept from a storm of little magazines, her stories fall about like leaves, tumbling together, blown by a force seemingly outside the author's control. Together they reveal a desire to classify and order overwhelmed by an avalanche of situations.

But once the almost ritual criticism of the bulk of her work is passed over, something more intriguing may be sensed. Each story, poem, essay, or novel is an experiment, another struggle towards verbal consciousness, part of the articulation of the inarticulate with which a writer must wrestle. Alfred Kazin has suggested that Oates possesses a negative literary personality, continually fascinated with other people's experience (another age and sensibility, of course, might have described this quality as "negative capability").[4] For instance, looked at in terms of the American novel tradition, in approved academic manner, her sources and affinities certainly make up a representative and colorful ragbag. Critics have repeatedly noted how her early novels seem to have affinities with the naturalistic tradition of Crane or Dreiser; her fascination with the interpenetration of religion, sexuality, and violence has placed her for some readers

2 See, for example, Walter Sullivan, "Old Age, Death, and Landscape," *Sewanee Review*, LII (1974), 538.
3 Calvin Bedient, "Vivid and Dazzling," *Nation*, December 1, 1969, p. 610.
4 Alfred Kazin, *Bright Book of Life: American Novelists and Storytellers from Hemingway to Mailer* (Boston: Little, Brown and Co., 1973), 201–202.

with Flannery O'Connor; her interest in the sexual struggles of the American middle class with Updike.[5] Perhaps the most convenient description suggested is that most hospitable of terms, the American gothic, which combines the rational with the romantic, and which perhaps best describes her characteristic sudden upsurges of violence, horror, or intense lyricism through a seemingly naturalistic surface.[6] Oates herself occasionally gives some support to this view of her fiction, and has remarked that "Gothicism, whatever it is, is not a literary tradition so much as a fairly realistic assessment of modern life,"[7] a suggestion I shall take up later. If we look outside the American tradition, we might consider that she herself has alluded to her affinities with Stendhal's romanticism or—more germanely perhaps— with Kafka. One contemporary non-American writer she has admired is Doris Lessing, and we can sense in Oates's work the "audacity" she finds in Lessing of "taking a naturalistic heroine into a non-naturalistic setting" and then "subjecting her to extraordinary experiences." Again, the association, however loose, with the gothic may be most appropriate. Oates comments further on Lessing that, like Norman Mailer, she combines a "complete identification with the era" with a "desire to affect radically the consciousness of the times" and to dramatize herself "as a spiritual representative of the times, and its contradictions."[8] Such a description peculiarly fits her own intentions, as we shall see.

Oates's reviewers and critics have been occasionally irritated by her unclassifiable qualities. Is she a young writer insecure in her medium or rather engaged in a ruthless search for a medium of significance? Christopher Ricks, watching her seemingly flit

---

5 See, for example, Bernard Bergonzi, "Truants," *New York Review of Books*, January 2, 1969, p. 40.
6 See, for example, Geoffrey Wolff in *New York Times Book Review*, October 24, 1971, p. 5.
7 "Joyce Carol Oates: Writing as a Natural Reaction," *Time*, October 10, 1969, p. 108.
8 Joyce Carol Oates, "A Visit With Doris Lessing," *Southern Review*, n.s. IX (1973), 877, 881, 878.

from one fictional mode to another, has called hers "a talent ex-
asperatingly misguided about itself." [9] Alongside most of her
contemporaries, Oates does stand out as a curiously chameleon
figure. "America outdoes all its writers," observes Richard, the
narrator of *Expensive People*, and Oates takes her role seriously
as searching for ways of surviving within the flux of modern
America. At times, as in the story "Double Tragedy Strikes Ten-
nessee Hill Family," told largely through newspaper extracts,
or the much-anthologized "How I Contemplated the World
from the Detroit House of Correction and Began My Life Over
Again," she moves vigorously towards postcontemporary fictionists like Robert Coover or Donald Barthelme, but even in
such stories, "the social and moral conditions of my generation"
are kept consistently in view. Rather waspishly, she criticizes
"new fictionists" and "black humorists" for their refusal to "deal
with the utterly uncontrollable emotions that determine our
lives." They are, she writes, "monastic . . . in the sense of having
castrated themselves in order to perform with more purity — an
asceticism . . . that makes little sense to women and has as much
appeal to them as the self-mutilated priests of old would have
had." [10] She has, further, curtly asserted that "any modestly
gifted writer can venture into 'surrealism.' Few indeed can han-
dle the densities and outrageous paradoxes of 'real' life." [11] We
might recall Joseph Conrad's remark that "the world of the living contains enough marvels and mysteries as it is, — marvels
and mysteries acting upon our emotions and intelligence in ways
so inexplicable that it would almost justify the conception of life
as an enchanted state." [12] *Expensive People* contained some vig-
orous pastiche and some Nabokovian fantasy, and readers might

9 Christopher Ricks, "The Unimaginable Real," *New York Review of Books*, Febru-
ary 12, 1970, p. 23.
10 Joyce Carol Oates, "Art: Therapy and Magic," *American Journal*, I (July, 1973),
18.
11 Cited by Tony Tanner, "My Life in American Literature," *Triquarterly*, XXX
(1975), 96.
12 Joseph Conrad, *The Shadow-Line* (London: J. M. Dent, 1921), ix–x.

have marked it as a new direction in her fiction (as a few critics have done), but she seems wary of the apocalyptic fantasies of Hawkes or Barth, so beloved of a postmodern critic like Ihab Hassan. That ubiquitous influence on so much contemporary fiction, Jorge Luis Borges, receives due praise from her, but her affinities with him are less in mode than, occasionally, in subject. Just as Borges' Buenos Aires becomes an hallucinary prototype of the twentieth-century *urbis*, so Oates's Detroit is what she terms "transparent," a symbol of everything with which contemporary American civilization bombards our sensibilities.[13]

Another line of Oates criticism is, predictably — especially among journalistic treatments of her work — to focus on the relation between the writings and the novelist herself. Literary gossip is of course an easy out for critics. Too many reviewers have constructed the paradox of Oates as a mild and shy woman, an American exile in a small Canadian university, pouring forth horrific and violent stories about the life she sees across the Detroit River. They have pointed to an apparently typical atmosphere of her stories (a concept I will take up more seriously later) which, as depicted by Marvin Mudrick, consists of arson, rape, mental breakdown, "murder (plain and fancy, with excursions into patricide, matricide, uxoricide, mass filicide), suicide."[14] We are given a picture of a slight, fragile, somewhat academic person, abstemious, modest, earnestly researching automobile racing jargon in magazines. This is Kazin's passive, almost invisible, literary personality, peering, as one of her stories, "Norman and the Killer," puts it, "in, there, at the very center of the jostling, to see the exposed bleeding flesh suddenly catapulted out of the usual channels of life" (USF, 125). Because of what is repeatedly presented as her "I'm-not-that-interesting" personality (she is in fact, an intense, friendly, engaging, volatile, and serious person) and her sex, she has been exploited by cloying interviewers focusing on her personal background and

13 Kazin, *Bright Book of Life*, 199.
14 Marvin Mudrick, "Fiction and Truth," *Hudson Review*, XXV (1972), 146.

interests, all oozing voyeuristically over someone who is presented simultaneously as "a tall pale young woman with enormous eyes and a timid little-girl voice," and a writer with a "vision of America as a delusive wonderland of colliding forces, where love as often as hate leads to violence."[15]

Journalistic superficialties present too easy a target. Biographical trivia aside, there is a real sense in which, in Oates's words, "all art is autobiographical."[16] It is initially the record of an artist's psychic experience, an attempt to explain something to himself. Just as in her novels and stories the "real" Detroit becomes "transparent" in her imaginative X ray of the felt experience of living there, so her everyday life as woman, writer, wife, professor, or housewife, provides only a superstructure of a literary personality: quiet, passive, yet fiercely creative, crystallizing not (or not only) her own but her era's deepest, most tangled, obsessions. It is still perhaps irrelevant even after almost twenty years of her writing to ask to see any ultimate direction in Oates's literary career — although it is one intention of this study to open the possibility of discussing some consistent drives and obsessions in the world in which she invites our participation. It is, perhaps, initially tempting to see a development in complexity from her earliest, cautious, most local work, first collected in *By the North Gate* (1963), through the more ambitious work of the mid and late 1970s. We can see that there is an explorative unity in Oates's work; despite its surface variety, like D. H. Lawrence's, the diversity of her writing is already forming itself into what we might term an emotional autobiography, although one that is hardly a mirror of the surfaces of her own life. Looking at obvious affinities, we can set her early writing in a realist tradition, then note the frequent flirtation with the antirealists or fabulators in the late sixties, and see her, in the seventies, tak-

15 Walter Clemons, "Joyce Carol Oates: Love and Violence," *Newsweek*, December 11, 1972, p. 72.
16 Joyce Carol Oates (ed.), *Scenes from American Life* (New York: Fawcett, 1973), vii.

ing up a cautiously experimental but hardly avant-garde place in the contemporary city of words. We might go on to regret, as do Hassan and others, that she retains a faith in the traditional aims of the novel, "a certain faith in the shapeliness of experience," while noting her occasional attempts to "exorcise in vain" the experience of *nada* in many of her fictions.[17]

But a more interesting means of defining the importance and power of her fiction can be achieved by a less academically predictable route. Oates's fictional mode, more than most novelists', has developed as a distinctive state of feeling thrust at her reader. Some of the most compelling writing in contemporary fiction, her stories force upon readers an often frightening sense of our own fears, obsessions, and drives. Indeed, her work operates in terms best described by that increasingly fashionable motif in contemporary fictional theory, the notion of the "implied reader." The "convergence of text and reader brings the literary work into existence,"[18] argues Wolfgang Iser, and in Oates's fiction we have a vivid example of how a writer must rely heavily on the emotional cooperation of the reader. Her geographical landscapes evoke our own emotional or moral dilemmas and allegiances and in reading her we attend not so much to the shifts of plot or scene but to our own changing emotional reactions.

Indeed, in its insistence upon its readers' involvement, Oates's fiction is an excellent test case for the increasingly fashionable phenomenological emphasis on text-as-experience. It has been argued — for instance on the philosophical level by such writers as Maurice Merleau-Ponty and Paul Ricoeur — that our reading of a text is never divorced from a context of feeling. As opposed to a response to a text as an object-in-the-world, in the manner of New Criticism, for instance, reading is described by phenomenological critics as a process in which we are engaged or con-

17 Hassan, *Paracriticisms*, 105.
18 Wolfgang Iser, *The Implied Reader: Patterns of Communication in Prose Fiction from Bunyan to Beckett* (Baltimore: Johns Hopkins Press, 1974), 275.

fronted by a level of feeling, what Merleau-Ponty calls *sens emo-tionnel*, or Heidegger terms *Stimmung. Stimmung bestimmt*: mood determines, argues the sociologist-playwright-theologian Werner Pelz, paraphrasing Heidegger. Without plunging into the middle of this whole critical debate, which seems bound to dominate Anglo-American critical theory for the next decade or more, we might note how well Oates's work fits into such categories. In Heidegger's words, "it is we ourselves" who are "the entities . . . analysed." It is from the midst of our own "thrownness" that we respond to the text before us, and it is our awareness of our felt contingency that opens up Oates's fictional mode to our experience.[19]

"Feeling," writes Paul Ricoeur — arguably the most suggestive theorist of the new criticism — "is the manifestation of a relation to the world which constantly restores our complicity with it." In order for her novels, to use D. H. Lawrence's phrase, to "inform and lead into new places the flow of our sympathetic consciousness,"[20] Oates's fiction plunges us into a distinctively felt atmosphere. All the novels are similarly structured, often as triptychs (with an occasional summary addendum, as in *Do With Me What You Will*), usually concentrating on three phases of a central character's growth to self-awareness. The underlying pattern of discovery in the novels is evoked by the charisma of emotional extremism: actions seem inevitably violent, speech is ejaculative and hostile, underlying fears constantly burst through the surface of the action. Oates's typical imagery reinforces this extremism: imprisonment, shattering glass, bursting and breaking, explosions dominate the emotional field of the action. In *With Shuddering Fall* "music from the jukebox exploded into the room"; in *Them* Jules and Nadine are "locked together," "grown rigid," sensing a "tyranny" in the tension between them which

19 Martin Heidegger, *Being and Time*, trans. J. Macquarrie and E. Robinson (New York: Harper, 1962), 67.
20 Paul Ricoeur, *Fallible Man*, trans. Charles Kelbley (Chicago: Regnery, 1965), 129; D. H. Lawrence, *Lady Chatterley's Lover* (Harmondsworth: Penguin Books, 1962), 104.

makes it inevitable that something will break. As Phyllis Grosskurth points out, *crazy* is a favorite word in the novels, and all
of Oates's important characters live just on the boundaries of
sanity as they clutch and claw at the possibility of momentary
order in the flux of their lives. Her intention is partly to achieve
a shock of emotional extremism which will involve both attention and recognition in the reader's experience. David Madden
notes the consequent difficulty of discussing her writings as "literary fabrications": "If they have form," he notes, "it is so submerged in 'experience' as to defy analysis. . . . Because of her
lack of shape and focus, some of the stories linger on as though
they were real events one wants to forget." Oates's aim, however, is clear: she is attempting to evoke people's struggles to
"order their fantasies, their doubts, even their certainties, into
an external structure that celebrates the life force itself, the energy of life." As well, she writes, "The use of language is all we
have to put against death and silence." The form, or formlessness, of her work, then, is deliberately perspectival as we, her
readers, are driven to create the form, or formlessness, of our
own lives and our own private fictions.[21]

Along with the overriding apprehension that, as Kazin observes, "nothing lasts, nothing is safe, nothing is all around
us,"[22] there is also in Oates's fictional world something of what
she perceives in Lawrence's poetry, where one finds "literally
everything: beauty, waste, 'flocculent ash,' the ego in a state of
rapture and in a state of nausea, a diverse streaming of chaos
and cunning" (NHNE, 41). In Oates's novels such chaos is invariably situated in the emotions, in the convulsive eruption of obsessive feeling, in the pain, anguish, distraught embarrassment,

21 Phyllis Grosskurth, "In Extremis," *Canadian Forum*, LVI (May, 1967), 33; David
    Madden, *The Poetic Image in Six Genres* (Carbondale: Southern Illinois Univer-
    sity Press, 1969), 27; Joyce Carol Oates, "Remarks by Joyce Carol Oates Accepting
    the National Book Award for *Them*," Vanguard Press Release, March 4, 1970, pp.
    1–2. Further remarks about the connections between Oates's works and her own
    inner life can be found, for example, in "Transformations of Self: An Interview
    with Joyce Carol Oates," *Ohio Review*, XV (1973), 51–53.
22 Kazin, *Bright Book of Life*, 202.

and violence of the personality. The anguished narrator of one
of her most powerful stories, "Unmailed, Unwritten Letters,"
ejaculates: "I have never wanted to love anyone, the strain and
risk are too great, yet I have fallen in love for the second time in
my life and this time the sensation is terrifying, bitter, violent. It
ends the first cycle, supplants all that love, erases all that affection — destroys everything. I stand back dazed, flat on my heels"
(WOL, 68). Our understanding of Oates's fiction depends on our
sensing how the "meaning" of such a passage is as much in the
voice as in the words: the reader is asked to respond to an unusual extent to mood, timbre, and modulation of voice. We may,
of course, be nauseated, appalled, fearful, and hostile. But once
seized by that voice, we cannot choose but listen, and to submit
to Oates's world is to enter a realm of psychic violence potentially disturbing to any sensitive reader. Oates has an unusual
ability to bring out the reader's own hidden fears and psychic
nightmares. "Where am I, what am I doing?": Such questions
echo through her work, but the answers do not come satisfac-
torily from external, public events — "I don't know what you
mean by 'events'" protests the confused speaker of ". . . & Answers" (GOW, 154). The real "events" by which Oates's characters are motivated lie deep within the protean chaos of the personality, and her readers are directed back into the depths of
their own inner worlds, perhaps to encounter chaos there.

"I sometimes write as if to relieve my mind of things that haunt
it,"[23] Oates has said, but one outcome of her therapeutic approach to art is to face her readers with their own disturbances,
just as D. H. Lawrence, in shedding his own sickness in his novels, moves his readers (often violently) to an awareness of their
own psychic and spiritual health or destructiveness. Indeed,
Oates's fiction can be tellingly approached through a Lawrentian perspective. Her brilliant account of Lawrence's poetry —
surely, despite its brevity, one of the most suggestive pieces of

23 Joe David Bellamy, *The New Fiction: Interviews with Innovative American Writers*
(Urbana: University of Illinois Press, 1974), 26.

Lawrence criticism in recent decades—speaks of him in terms that strangely reverberate upon her own approach to the artist's role. Lawrence, she writes, "is one of our true prophets," especially in his "moody and unpredictable and unreliable" contemporaneity, speaking from the total engagement of his art to the chaos and disorder and the hope of our era. "He is fascinated by the protean nature of reality, the various possibilities of the ego," and in that openness lies his prophetic relevance, his "deep, unshakeable faith in the transformable quality of all life." Consequently, Lawrence's art may often seem, like Oates's own, slapdash, urgent, repetitive. He "seems to be writing, always writing, out of the abrupt, ungovernable impulses of his soul," which he refuses to shape into perfected and so completed art. In the prophetic flux of Lawrence's art, "aesthetic standards of perfection . . . are soon left behind by the spontaneous flow of life" (NHNE, 42, 43, 45). Lawrence himself wrote of *Women in Love*: "This novel pretends only to be a record of the writer's own desires, aspirations, struggles; in a word, a record of the profoundest experiences in the self."[24] Fascination with flux, with art as prophecy, with the therapeutic exposure of the self—these central Lawrentian motifs are fused and re-created in Oates's work.

In discussing Oates within a Lawrentian perspective—a suggestive preliminary, I believe, to an appreciation of the impact and importance of her work—we should not ignore their differences: the trivial ones of time and place, the more serious ones of stature. Lawrence is one of the greatest writers in English since Shakespeare; Oates is one of the most promising writers of our time. But it is a measure of her potential that we have to look to Lawrence as a measure and a guide, even if by invoking his name we cannot obscure Oates's relative limitations.

In this decade, the seventies, Oates has more and more taken on the role of a prophet, at least in the sense that the writer can

24 D. H. Lawrence, *Women in Love* (New York: Viking Press, 1920), x.

see beyond what we are immersed in. In one of her essays, typically a mixture of rambling abstraction and impassioned lyricism, she quotes Lawrence's poem "Nullus," in which, she says, "he is speaking of the private 'self' that is Lawrence but also of the epoch in which this self exists":

There are said to be creative pauses,
pauses that are as good as death, empty
    and dead as death itself.
And in these awful pauses the evolutionary
    change takes place.

She suggests that the artist must be concerned with the transition through which America—"sensitive, energetic, swarming with life . . . most obsessed with its own history and its own destiny . . . approaching a kind of manic stage"—is passing, "preparing itself for a transformation of 'being' similar to that experienced by individuals as they approach the end of one segment of their lives and must rapidly, and perhaps desperately, sum up everything that has gone before." [25] Writing on James Dickey, she asserts that "a mysterious, unfathomable revolution seems to be taking place in our civilization"; only through the artist laying bare his personal history as representative of the crisis of society can it be "knowable" or "governable" (NHNE, 246).

It is because of the seriousness with which Oates takes the novelist's role as prophet that we might judge her by Lawrence's understanding of "morality" rather than by purely aesthetic criteria, or within the conventional formal terms of fiction. In "Morality and the Novel" Lawrence wrote: "Morality is that delicate, for ever trembling and changing *balance* between me and my circumambient universe, which precedes and accompanies a true relatedness. Now here we see the beauty and the great value of the novel. Philosophy, religion, science, they are all of them busy nailing things down to get a stable equilibruim. . . . But the novel, no." His argument was that only the novel

25 Joyce Carol Oates, "New Heaven and Earth," *Saturday Review*, November 4, 1972, p. 52.

could express its reader's deep awareness of the age's perspectival relativism. "Let us have done with the ugly imperialism of any absolute," he exhorted. "There is no absolute good, there is nothing absolutely right. The whole is a strange assembly of apparently incongruous parts, slipping past one another."[26] Only the novel, the bright book of life, could reflect and direct the dynamism of the age.

Similarly for Oates, the novel is neither just a heterocosm of playful wish fulfillment, as some postcontemporary fictionists might see it, nor a mirror carefully reflecting the passing surfaces of society, as in the naturalistic novel. It has aspects of both verbal delight and social relevance, but if, as one of her poems puts it, "nothing stays/the X of our lives' center" (LD, 34), it is above all the novelist's responsibility to "re-create and reinterpret the world," to provide, even though forced to employ the slipperiness of words, the impetus towards what Lawrence called "the *Deed* of life." Paradoxically, even tragically, the writer "is committed to re-creating the world through language. . . . The use of language is all we have to put against death and silence."[27] The destiny of the novelist is therefore to simultaneously subject himself to and evoke for us the chaos within, exorcising and exhorting at once, providing the reader, one would hope, with the challenge of a profound waking dream. Our dreams offer to show us the deepest roots of our creativity: we hunger for significance and art satisfies that hunger. So the novelist's role, today, becomes that of "dreaming America," an attempt to master in fiction the "chaos outside and inside ourselves," occasionally "winning small victories," then facing the inevitability of "being swept along by some cataclysmic event of our own making." The novelist, she writes, encounters Lawrence's "madness for the unknown," his "diverse streaming of

26 D. H. Lawrence, "Morality and the Novel," in *Phoenix: The Posthumous Papers of D. H. Lawrence*, ed. Edward D. McDonald (New York: Viking Press, 1972), 528; D. H. Lawrence, "Why the Novel Matters," in *Phoenix*, 536.
27 D. H. Lawrence, *A Propos of Lady Chatterley's Lover and other Essays* (Harmondsworth: Penguin, 1961), 118; "Remarks by Joyce Carol Oates," 2.

chaos and cunning" and attempts to render a stasis in his own fiction and, through our receptivity, in the fictions we ourselves constantly create, revise, and re-create.

Oates argues that "the greatest works of literature deal with the human soul caught in the stampede of time, unable to gauge the profundity of what passes over it" (NHNE, 41, 105). At times almost passively and involuntarily, she sees herself as submitting to the flux around her as if, as Kazin puts it, she is "utterly hyp-notized, positively drugged by other people's experiences." Such attitudes seem to regard art as a therapeutic struggle into words. One of her characters broods obsessively: "What were the words for *woman, man, love, freedom, fate?*" (NS, 110). Similarly, Oates's fiction involves an agonizing offer to us to share and ex-tend her fantasy, even while we recognize that, often, "language itself is the primary obstacle to communication" (NS, 198). Fic-tion is built upon an inbuilt, obsessive drive to bring forth. "In the past," Oates has written, "a young woman like myself would simply have baby after baby, would be, simply, helplessly, a kind of machine to manufacture babies, she would have to recognize this other 'self,' this impersonal and rather inhuman self, that exists only to keep the species going. The artist endures some of the same perplexities. But, if he is intelligent enough, he tries to direct the fantasies, the hyperactivity, the visions and disjunc-tions, into external forms that can be of some aid to others."[28]

The emotional and intellectual drives of Oates's fiction grow recognizably from the realities (and irrealities) of contemporary America, but again, we may gain a useful perspective by placing her work alongside Lawrence's. Initially, it might seem odd to compare, say, the grimy, violent, despairing Detroit of *Them* with Lawrence's vision of America. In 1917 Lawrence wrote in a letter: "I feel it is finished in me, with this side of the globe. Now one is like a seed that needs to fall into new soil, under new skies. One needs a new earth and a new heaven." Elsewhere, he

28 "Transformations of Self," 52, 56; Kazin, *Bright Book of Life*, 201.

suggests: "America, being so much *worse*, falser, further gone than England, is nearer to freedom. England has a long and awful process of corruption and death to go through. America has dryrotted to a point where the final seed of the new is almost left ready to sprout." [29] But it is this emphasis on the apocalypse beyond and through corruption, or in Oates's own terms, the transcendence achieved through obsession, that she shares fundamentally with Lawrence. Oates apparently came to Lawrence relatively late, but she must have sensed immediately a genius whose characteristic stance uncannily challenged her own obsessions, leading her to assert that ultimately only someone spiritually attuned to Lawrence could comprehend his work.

The most obvious connection between Lawrence and Oates is their fascination with sexuality. "I can only write what I feel pretty strongly about," he said, "and that, at present, is the relation between men and women. After all, it is *the* problem of today, the establishment of a new relation, or the readjustment of the old one, between men and women." It is doubtful whether Lawrence would have approved what has in fact been established or readjusted, often explicitly in his name, in the last sixty years. We have certainly become, as he put it, more word-perfect. But otherwise . . . ? Like Lawrence, Oates is fascinated with the power and the dynamic of sex. She focuses repeatedly on the numinous aura of sexuality, on how sexuality contributes to, or so often mocks, our attempts to order our lives. John Updike has remarked that what remains perhaps our last uncontaminated act, the sensuous passageway into a woman, gives a unifying and transcendent purpose to our secular lives, but while Oates's view of sexuality acknowledges its embodiment of our hunger for purpose, she also notes that love must be acknowledged as a violent and unstoppable force, not simply an instinctive urge to achieve rest or transcendence. Again, an interesting

29 Peter L. Irvine and Anne Kitey, "D. H. Lawrence: Letters to Gordon and Beatrice Campbell," *D. H. Lawrence Review*, VI (1973), 10; D. H. Lawrence, *Collected Letters*, ed. Harry T. Moore (New York: Viking Press, 1962), I, 481–82.

comparison is with Lawrence. In both writers sexual relations are relations of possibility and power. They may be like the destructive preying of Gudrun upon Gerald, the fierce battle for equilibrium between Birkin and Ursula, or in Oates's work, what she terms "the totally irrational, possessive, ego-destroying love, which can't be controlled and is, perhaps, a pathological condition of the soul,"[30] such as the relationship between the lovers in *Do With Me What You Will* or the tragically unfulfilled desires brought out in stories like "Scenes of Passion and Desire" or "I Must Have You." The most painful and evocative scenes in Oates's work focus on the power of sexual attraction and repulsion and it is in her concentration on sexual desire as an unpredictable and awesome force for change in the personality that her closest thematic connection with Lawrence is found. In love, all we have fixed and made "permanent" (another favorite Oates word, as we shall see) may be suddenly and fearfully shattered. Life becomes fragmentary and unpredictable; where once we had lived by rationality and comfort, in love we become defined primarily by fear and fragility. As in Lawrence's fiction, with Oates's best work we are involved in the affective dimension of the writing. Its rhythmic surges and melodramatic intensification make us face, in ourselves, that same fear and fragility.

As readers we are forced by Oates's concentration upon our feelings to focus on the intense state in which her characters make discoveries about themselves. The typical Oates character, usually a woman, is continually bombarded by sensation — fear, insecurity, a sense of formlessness from within, pursuit from without. In "The Dying Child," Jean, her father recently dead, takes refuge in the ordinariness of her boyfriend or the routine of her widowed mother's home, while "everything she looked at was precarious, mere temporary surfaces upon which she focused her eyes while inside her brain feelings and half-formed ideas demanded her attention" (GOW, 287). Authorial

30 *Ibid.*, 200; Updike, *Picked-Up Pieces* (New York: Knopf, 1975), 473; *DWM*, publisher's jacket note.

directions regularly occur near the start of an Oates story, which
then typically moves inward — or, in terms of its affective power,
outward to the reader. A series of emotionally charged scenes,
often logically disconnected but emotionally integrated, focuses
on the emotional complexity of the initial observation. Jean
"watched blankly the monotonous fields gone dry with fall, the
ugly barbed-wire fences that dropped from wooden posts, part of
the landscape she had been seeing all her life" (GOW, 289). Again,
the author moves suggestively between descriptive setting and
inner revelation, until the violence, which seems somehow repressed by both landscape and characters, wells up. A boy is
killed in a fight: "The child had been nine. Nothing like this had
ever happened, not ever — he had still been alive when found,
dying, but could not talk, was groaning and drooling blood, dying right then, dying right when the other boy found him" (GOW,
293). The boy slowly dies, and the killer remains unknown; the
eruption of violence, the feelings of inexplicable death disrupt
the toughness of the girl. The fearful unpredictability of violence
becomes a liberation for her; all of life — her mother's coming re-
marriage, her boyfriend, her family — suddenly acquires a value
precisely because of newly revealed vulnerability.

Similarly "A Girl at the Edge of the Ocean" starts slowly, with
the reader asked first to observe the central character, Tessa. We
watch her with her aunt, with "the pinched, distracted look of
a convalescent, the intensity that seems to agitate the muscles
around the eyes while the eyes themselves are slightly out of focus, baffled." Gradually, however, we realize that the objective
view we must take initially is inadequate. The external facts of
property, comfort, the "basics of life," the isolated beach house
in which she is convalescing after being involved in a murky mixture of gangland crime, sex, and violence, and where everything
is securely "timed," all represent a shell, a brittle covering which
must be broken through, in classic Lawrentian manner, for any
growth (GOW, 324, 339, 341). Like Ursula desperately climbing
the tree to escape the horses to tumble "in a heap on the other

side of the hedge" and realizing that she is "trammelled and en-
tangled" and "must break out . . . like a nut from its shell,"[31] so
Oates's women characters must make some radical act of the
whole integral personality to discover their true inner direction.

It is perhaps the very totality of both writers' obsession for
the importance of sexual connections that makes them reach for
what Lawrence saw as a dimension of experience found through
and yet somehow beyond sex. Both writers link human sexuality
with the Nietzschean vision of the self struggling to overcome itself. For Lawrence, sexual attraction and repulsion connect with
the most mysterious and vital cosmic movements. In Oates's
"Assault" Charlotte returns to her missing father's old home
and, finding evidence of some lovers in the garden overnight, recalls an earlier sexual assault upon her:

> She recalled the instant of someone's plunging into her, flesh like a fist,
> flesh like metal, and it seemed to her not much different from the act of
> love that had probably taken place out here the night before. Some-
> thing flowed through all these lovers in their contortions, shaping their
> bodies and their straining faces, leaving her pure. It flowed through
> them and through her, leaving her pure. Dreamily she recalled the in-
> stant of her pain and it seemed to her now an empty pain, the memory
> of another person. . . . So her mother had endured pain: all her moth-
> ers, her ancestors. They had endured it and transformed it. . . . *Love,*
> *what did it matter?* Pain or spasms of pleasure or neutrality itself, the
> pure, untrammeled passage of consciousness through her body, what
> did these matter? . . . There was no one to differentiate them except
> Charlotte. And if she refused, they were all one. If she refused to re-
> member the pain, if she chose instead to transform it into something
> else, who could overcome her? Love, hate, pleasure, pain: they were
> identical, descending into the firmest, most stubborn layer of life, a
> vegetative neutrality, and then rearing up again into human life, inno-
> cent even in consciousness. (GOW, 460–61)

So, pain, memory, and fear are transformed as sexuality becomes, in its mystery, terror and joy, part of the neutral rhythm

31 D. H. Lawrence, *The Rainbow* (Harmondsworth: Penguin, 1949), 491, 293.

of the circumambient universe, the life of sensation and emotions by which men and women transcend time, place, and limitation. From such connections, not only do all life-affirming human commitments grow, but humanity is challenged to reach beyond itself. Lawrence's thought here, Oates has argued, "is really revolutionary; it is a total rejection of that dogma of the West that declares *Man is the measure of all things*" (NHNE, 79).

Lawrence's vision of sexual transcendence often strikes readers as paradoxical in a writer so obsessed with sexual attraction and repulsion; but at its strongest, sexual connection was for Lawrence a means of finding a nourishing relationship with nature and the universe: perhaps, he wrote, the human race is dying, but there is "a flame or a Life Everlasting wreathing through the cosmos for ever and giving us our renewal, one we can get in touch with."[32] Fifty years later, less ideologically explicit, but with equivalent passion and evocation, Oates's prophetic vision attempts to define the tragedy of our age, in which individuals yearn towards a new consciousness, sensed through and yet ultimately transcending sexuality, by exploring similarly the way passion and its necessary violence "redeem and may perhaps make a kind of eternity" (EOI, 139).

Oates's aesthetic, in so far as we can talk of one, is so clearly a neo-romantic celebration and evocation of flux and the human potential of unpredictability that it is intriguing to discover the mixture of hostility and homage she has towards Sylvia Plath, perhaps the supreme embodiment of the self-obsessive confessionalism of mid–twentieth-century romanticism. In her essay "The Death Throes of Romanticism: The Poems of Sylvia Plath," Oates makes a compassionate, yet ultimately strongly moralistic, analysis of how Plath exemplifies "the pathological aspects of our era which make a death of the spirit inevitable — for that era and for all who believe in its assumptions." The essay is a sensitive piece of criticism, with curious reverberations back

32 D. H. Lawrence, "The Real Thing," *Phoenix*, 202.

upon Oates's own work. She sees Plath verbalizing her own dark-
est screams and shudders, deliberately exploring the most destructive and troubled aspects of her own personality, and the
inner recesses of her reader's. While she marvels at Plath's living
out her vision and so to a frightening extent making her own life
the testing ground for her art, she sees Plath's poetry as epitomiz-
ing a destructively egocentric phase of civilization. The climax
of the essay prophetically views Plath's sensibility as marking
the end of an era where a "very masculine, combative ideal of
an 'I' set against all other 'I's — and against nature as well — was
necessary in order to wrench man from the hermetic contemplation of a God-centered universe and get him into action." Now,
however, "it is no longer necessary: its health has become a pathology, and whoever clings to its outmoded concepts will die"
(NHNE, 114, 119). Prophetic critical writing is rare today, and
Oates's essay is not only one of the most stimulating written on
Plath, but its tone goes right back to Lawrence's fusion of subjective revelation and prophetic vision in his criticism of Hardy
or his essays on *Lady Chatterley's Lover*. And just as Lawrence's
most passionate literary strictures reflect back on his own fiction, so Oates's rejection of Plath's cultivated, egocentric passivity, and the way "the ego suffers dissolution in the face of the
most banal of enemies" points to the essential robustness of her
own vision of our own age's obsessions (NHNE, 126). Shedding
one's sickness in books must have more than therapy as its end.
Oates says, "I feel my own place is to dramatize the nightmares
of my time" — very much as Plath's poetry does — but she adds,
like Lawrence, "and (hopefully) to show how some individuals find a way out, awaken, come alive, move into the future."
Whereas Plath exclusively cultivated her own potential for destruction, Oates points out how we are struck by how much
Plath leaves out of her poems — childbirth, love, living itself. So
even in the period of terrible transition through which America
is living, she affirms we have the potential to "transform ourselves, overleap ourselves beyond even our most flamboyant es-

timations. A conversion is always imminent."[33] In *Lady Chatterley's Lover* the mechanism of industrialization is a symbol of the repetitive, mechanical forces of human reason and repressed emotion. With the woods increasingly shrinking back from the encroaching mines and factories, for Lawrence it was increasingly urgent to seek the dark flame of human spontaneity, and the deed rather than the word of life. Similarly, from Oates's work we sense just how crucial it is to move beyond the limitations of our isolated self-concentration. We must ultimately open ourselves to the obliteration of the ego and our fixation with its uniqueness. Just as Lawrence saw the fulfillment of the individual consisting in going beyond the individual, to a relationship of star-equilibrium, so Oates looks beyond the guilt-obsessed individuality of our era. "As in Zen Buddhism," she suggests, "the realization of the koan or riddle must be expressed as an event, and not as a puzzle," so our movement beyond our local desires and obsessions occurs, whether in love, or philosophical awareness, or by sudden illumination, "by a sudden obliteration of the ego, a realization of the identity of the finite self with the infinite, a vision of paradise that is at the same time the 'profane' world." But in our radically ego-obsessed world, it may only be through the overwhelming of the ego that a confrontation with something beyond the ego can emerge. In 1915, Lawrence wrote in a similar vein to Katherine Mansfield: "It is one 'I' which is passing from us, one 'I' is dying; but there is another coming into being, which is the happy, creative you . . . there is a rising from the grave, there is a resurrection."[34] Typical of both Oates and Lawrence, here is the radical immanetization of religious experiences, the proving or disproving in the flesh of old words and myths. It is a characteristic Oates also finds in Kafka, in whose work she sees suggestive parallels to Lawrence's. "Dissimilar though they may be on the surface," she writes, they share "a fundamental detestation of the conscious, private, grasping

33 Oates, "New Heaven and Earth," 51.
34 D. H. Lawrence, *Collected Letters*, I, 401.

self," an urge to transcend self-concentration, obsession, old myths, and limitations through an intuited vision of the unity of man and the universe (NHNE, 268–70).

It is curiously suggestive to juxtapose Lawrence's apocalyptic vision, one stressed throughout his work but especially so in his last years, with the similar strand that has lately emerged in Oates's writing, though in most of the novels only by indirection. From within "our fallen, contaminated, guilt-obsessed era," she senses voices of buoyancy and fulfillment, a "tumultuous but exciting close of a centuries-old kind of consciousness" in which poets and novelists "serve to dramatize and exorcise" the nightmares of their society. She looks to the disappearance of an outmoded dichotomous consciousness and an affirmation of a mystical vision of community with the circumambient universe. "Everywhere, suddenly, we hear the prophetic voice of Nietzsche once again, saying that man must overcome himself" to embrace life as a unity. She picks out a diverse collection of artists and scientists—Lawrence, Blake, Whitman, Maslow, Buckminster Fuller, Barry Commoner—and links them, lyrically rather than systematically, with the various movements of mind-liberation in the sixties, claiming that "the idea that through the imagination that mysterious entity 'mankind' is being transformed returns to us in the seventies, in the popular radicalism that declares the revolution to be a matter of individual consciousness."[35] Her collection of critical essays, New Heaven, New Earth, takes its title from Antony and Cleopatra; but this is a recurring phrase in Lawrence, as in this letter written in 1915 to Lady Asquith:

I want to begin all over again. All these Gethsemane Calvary and Sepulchre stages must be over now: there must be a resurrection—resurrection: a resurrection with sound hands and feet and a whole body and a new soul: above all, a new soul: a resurrection. . . There must be a new heaven and a new earth, and a new heart and soul: all new: a pure resurrection.[36]

35 Oates, "New Heaven and Earth," 52, 54.
36 D. H. Lawrence, Collected Letters, I, 372.

Lyrical prophecy is usually irritatingly unanalyzable; it is exhortatory not descriptive, demanding the assent of faith not logic.
But in these two writers there is an accompanying grasp of sensual reality that roots their vision in the world. Lawrence's apocalyptic mysticism was based on a vision of a transformed individuality; Oates speaks of "the potential of normality" and of
the growing contemporary realization "(so clear in imaginative
literature, so muddled elsewhere) that it is here, in the soul, inside the fantastically complex phenomenon of man, that the salvation of the world will take place." She has frequently praised
the work of "third-force" psychologists like Abraham Maslow,
who are concerned with the resacralization of science and with
what Maslow calls the "unnoticed revolution" in understanding
men by their metamotivation, the "resolution of dichotomies in
self actualization" in experiences of transcendence, autonomy,
spontaneity, and "peak-experiences" of love or vision wherein
the universe is apprehended as whole, gracious, or beneficent.[37]
Again, ordinary life is sacralized by the very intensity of joy
through which it is experienced. Although, as I shall show in
the next chapter, her own sensitivity to the personality goes far
beyond the crude banalities of popular third-force psychology,
Oates senses in the work of such thinkers something akin to what
Lawrence found in sexual vitalism, a philosophical basis flexible, suggestive, and intuitive enough to be tested on the pulses
rather than a provable, abstract thesis. There is also, we should
confess, a degree of wistful pastoralism in both writers, a desire
at times to preserve the realm of the imagination from the grim,
violent determinism of history. But at their most evocative and
hopeful, it becomes the writer's crucial role to struggle with that
painful vision of the self and to provide enlightenment through
vision at the point the facticity of civilization corrupts and finally abandons us.

The Lawrentian prophetic mode ultimately rests on an appeal

37 Oates, "New Heaven and Earth," 51, 54.

to the core of spontaneous creativity, the reverence for life which is inextricably a power in the human psyche. It calls forth the reader's own aspirations toward wholeness, which may be overwhelmed by the facticity of life but which are, ultimately, imperishable. It is an exhortatory mode which attempts not to bypass rationality but to transcend the dichotomies of response upon which the rational mind is built. Above all, it looks steadily through pain and violence, confusion and contradiction to a state — achievable, even if only momentarily — of radical conversion and immanent grace. In the poem "New Heaven and Earth" Lawrence asks a question which Oates sees as "parallel with Yeats's famous question in the sonnet 'Leda and the Swan.'" Her own prophetic stance then emerges in her comments: "In the Yeats poem, mortal woman is raped by an immortal force, and, yes, this will and must happen; this cannot be escaped. But the point is: Did she put on his knowledge *with* his power, before the terrifying contact was broken? Lawrence speaks of mysterious 'green streams' that flow from the new world (our everyday world — seen with new eyes) and asks '. . . what are they?' What," Oates asks herself and her readers, lyrically, unpredictably, prophetically, "are the conversions that await us?"[38]

38 *Ibid.*, 54.

TWO

The Phantasmagoria of American Personality

JOYCE CAROL OATES'S fiction combines the Lawrentian view of the artist as prophet with the flexible mode of the American gothic. Oates exploits a heady mixture of melodrama, lyricism, psychological realism, and social or philosophical comment to dramatize and thereby "exorcize" our "current American nightmares."[1] Certain crucial kinds of art, she suggests, are "cathartic, exorcizing, magical" (EOI, 115), both for the artist and his audience. Her most recurrent evocatory technique involves the sudden eruption of fearful or unexpected events through apparently realistic surfaces. She comments that in Dostoevsky "reality is constantly turning into something else"

1 Joyce Carol Oates, "Remarks by Joyce Carol Oates Accepting the National Book Award for *Them*," Vanguard Press Release, March 4, 1970, p. 2.

(EOI, 92); elsewhere she writes on the violent conjunction of reality and dream in the writing of Yuli Daniel, whose writing, she argues, "is ordinary, and yet dreamlike, not surrealistic but faithful to the gentle impregnation of our real lives by our dream lives; and these 'dream' lives are not always interior, but part of a larger fantastic dream, totally out of our control."[2] So her own art may also be described not only as affective, but as instrumental: even if she does not conceive of the novelist as a *stylus dei* in the classical religious sense, she nevertheless at times sees the novelist as dependent on, or a manifestation of, an impersonal, creative process of being within the universe, and the dreams the novelist enacts in his fictions as manifestations of that being.

In diverse guises, the notion of "dream," like that of "myth," has traditionally been part of the American literary experience, from the strangers and pilgrims exiled in the dark regions of the America of William Bradford and Cotton Mather to Thomas Pynchon's Tristero. For most contemporary fictionalists, Americans remain stubbornly caught up in dreams of identity and place; for Oates, ours remains a generation which still seeks "the absolute dream" (EOI, 3), and as with the Puritans forsaking their history to journey to a wilderness, our dream must survive within an environment so aggressively materialistic that to assert the primacy of the unquantifiable seems necessarily to end in the Manicheism which has constantly characterized American experience. This tension between materialism and dream is crucial to the mythos of Oates's work. She described three of her novels — A *Garden of Earthly Delights, Expensive People,* and *Them* — as a trilogy dealing with "social and economic facts of life in America, combined with unusually sensitive — but hopefully representative — young men and woman, who confront the puzzle of American life in different ways and come to different ends."[3] Although the "social and economic facts" of these three

---

2 Joyce Carol Oates, "Fiction Chronicle," *Hudson Review*, XXII (1969), 531.
3 Quoted in Barbara Mackenzie (ed.), *The Process of Fiction* (New York: Harcourt, Brace, Jovanovich, 1974), 517.

novels are vividly evoked, rather than conveying a sense of lo-
cality Oates's settings are "transparent," redolent of more than
social significance. The artist must write out of the specifics of
time and place, but her America is not so much a place as an experience of surging psychic volatility. We might say it is a dream
of fulfillment, not that fulfillment itself. Consequently, her apprehension of "the terrible, unfathomable future" (NS, 253) of
America is of surfaces broken through, eruptions of passion,
violence of unexpected significance. America is a place where
the quest is for significance, for meaning, not for contentment.
Even in the early novels, such as the trilogy just mentioned, she
is attempting to reach through the facticity of economic and social forces to the deeper life of the personality caught in those
forces. Even the most factual descriptions of highways, gas sta-
tions, or motels are part of a mythopoeic rather than a naturalistic world. The smallest details of domestic life may be loaded
with threat; seemingly innocent traits of personality or small incidents will open up fearful significance. Oates's America is an
experience, not a place; it is what our personalities create as
well as what we are thrown into. Airline terminals, the bridge
at Lockport over the Erie canal, icecream parlors, fruit stands,
roadside diners, all participate in a vision of the obsessions of
America, "blessed by God" as Dr. Pedersen orates in *Wonderland*, "and pushing outward, always outward, as we yearn for
another world, we yearn to be assimilated into God as into a
higher protoplasmic essence. . . . There is something magical
about the United States. This is a time of magic" (W, 125).

Whether American life is magically reaching beyond itself or
into a "downward, inward, deathly movement of consciousness," [4] it is a mythopoeic experience. Oates draws her readers
into a world simultaneously jarring, gross, violent, and yet meta-
physically whole. There is a vastness of metaphorical suggestion
that points through surface details of setting, character, and
story to a consistently organized, complex pattern of American

4 Joyce Carol Oates, "The Potential of Normality," *Saturday Review*, August 26,
  1972, p. 53.

reality. She has an awesome ability to show the interpenetration of material or personal detail with significance. She seems, at times, as one reviewer noted, "an inspired medium in contact with characters already formed in the dreamscape of her imagination."[5] She reveals an awesome ability to immerse herself in the phenomenology of the contemporary and to convey the morphology of searching for meaning in a dream-haunted America —writing not only about the feeling of search for meaning itself, but what it feels like to feel that search as a constant, infinitely detailed and surprising experience. Reading the best of her fiction we are struck again and again by how she conveys the mythic significance of the most common or materialistic aspects of America, not in the classic Puritan manner of allegory, spelling out a meaning as Hawthorne, say, does with the garden in "Rappaccinni's Daughter," but through rendering the surface detail symbolically transparent through a constant psychological or emotional intensity, most especially by means of the felt pressure of obsession. In *Expensive People* we experience Fernwood and KRH and Johns Behemoth school through the compulsiveness of a 250-pound eighteen-year-old child-murderer, and the smoothly sculptured suburbs and opulent trivia mirror his distorted, obsessive personality. When deeply disturbed, Oates's characters often walk or drive automobiles frantically, randomly, their restless mobility reflecting back on their inner volatility. Typically, automobiles and highways dissolve into the evocation of an interior landscape, while the speaker's state of mind, thrust at the reader through the breathless ejaculations of the sentence, becomes the primary focus of our attention.

Oates's America is built up as a reverberating symbolic structure from such material commonplaces as highways, automobiles, supermarkets, shopping malls, money, cleanliness, success, marriage, motherhood, all heightened into the fabric of gothic parable. Our experience is consistently revealed as char-

5 Paul D. Zimmerman, "Stormy Passage," *Newsweek*, July 26, 1976, p. 74.

acterized by tragic gaps between word and act, ideal and reality
—not in a trivial everyday sense but almost as a metaphysical
principle, felt all the more strongly just because we are seekers
of meaning, not merely of contentment. In *Them*, for instance,
we sense the painful dislocation between dream or aspiration
with which the personality has been indoctrinated and the oppressive actuality in which those aspirations must be realized.
The Wendall family are all, coherently or confusedly, grasped
by a greater range of desires than their lives can bear. Grandma
Wendall is "baffled at the failure of her body to keep up with her
assessment of herself"; Loretta, living "in an eternity of flesh,"
senses its "sad limits" and yet knows "it was all she had." She
was "locked in flesh. Searching, straining to achieve some permanence" (T, 106). The Wendalls' desires drive them into the
frustration of realizing them only in the sadness of the flesh or
the placid security of houses, jobs, and consumables, away from
the terror of being unsettled. Indoctrinated with the dynamism
of dreams, they find in their materialization a kind of death. The
dream of a modern "wonderland" is similarly realized in the
decorations of a shopping mall "decorated with 'modern' multi-
colored cubes and benches of garish carnival colors," the ersatz
of musak and "square after square of cubes and benches and
potted plants" (W, 445). Materialism seems to provide the only
manifestation of a dream that originated in the pulsing human
spirit.

The basic problem for Oates's characters, living in a world
where the spirit and the dream are so consistently materialized,
is to define their inner selves in any terms other than the merely
external. We reach for the graspable, often out of terror at the
unknown within. Beatrice, the heroine of "The Widows," fixes
on herself as "a face, a body." To go further is to face secrets
which "no one especially cares to know"; "the outside can at
least be contemplated: that was the basis of life" (NS, 33). In
"A Girl at the Edge of the Ocean," in *The Goddess and Other
Women*, Tessa, fleeing from the terrors of past risks and adven-

tures, fights for her psychic survival in the only way she seems capable — by grasping at the predictable basics of life. She conceives of normality in terms of survival, order, and stasis. In her essay on Lawrence, Oates asks in a revealing aside: "*Why* must so much of human behaviour be classified as 'neurotic' when in fact it is simply natural, given certain personalities and certain environments? The impulse to 'make well' may be the most sinister of Western civilization's goals" (NHNE, 13). It may be through apparently pathological behaviour that we come to discover our true possibilities. Certainly, our obsessive concern with material, graspable aspects of life leaves enormous areas of what Oates terms the "night side" of the personality unrecognized. The title story of *Night Side* re-creates, in the style of a Victorian diary, an account of an apparently inexplicable series of spiritualist experiences in nineteenth-century Boston. The narrator, torn between curiousity and fear, mentions discussing the matter with William James, who he says comments that " 'we are at all times vulnerable to incursions from the "other side" of the personality. . . . We cannot determine the nature of the total personality simply because much of it, perhaps most, is hidden from us' " (NS, 20). We may be invaded by this "other side" in strange, inexplicable spiritual experiences, in dreams, in madness, in love, or in the everyday neuroses that much traditional Freudian, and post-Freudian, psychiatry tries to "cure." Another character in the same collection of stories muses over the nature of what he has loosely seen as insanity or hallucination and admits that the term "*pathological* is a mere catchall — a term to explain away what is mysterious and stubborn" (NS, 267). It is from our dreams, visions, and the inexplicable passion of our emotions and desires that our most crucial insights arise. If we fear and repress this "night side" of our lives, then indeed we distort ourselves. In "A Girl at the Edge of the Ocean" the natural instincts thrust through the apparently controlled normality of Tessa's life when a cat claws at her. Tessa looks at herself and sees blood running "from a dozen scratches on her arms and the backs of her hands, a deep slash ran diagonally across her left thigh, through the material of her slacks, blood welled up there and on her face; how could she stop it?" (GOW, 343). Similarity, in *Wonderland* when Jesse Vogel, who has obsessively defined herself by technology and science, encounters Reva (her name itself suggesting dream), she opens up in an urge to find the highest spiritual ideals, but the only medium through which he can realize the dream is limiting, materialistic, and degrading; he too ends his adventure in a bloodbath.

The ultimate degradation of our dream is in our bodies. Like medieval men, we are reminded constantly of death, but our *mementi mori* are not skulls or scenes of judgment but the dirt in our kitchens, our mouths, our bowels. We live by avoiding death, fearing it and keeping it in our consciousness only as unnatural, unnecessary, impossible to reconcile with our dream of the infinite self. Obsessively battling the signs of mortality of course makes us all the more conscious of it. Hospitals, beauty parlors, hairdressers, are shrines of a priesthood designed to spiritualize our bodies in the arcane rituals of cleansing and purifying. Uncleanness reminds us of the basic, natural scent of our dying bodies. Yet "there are those strange, ugly times when your body seems transparent, your skin drawn too tight, something, so that the heightened beat of the heart and the minute hissing of blood through veins seems a concern not just of yourself but of everyone watching you" (WOL, 300); then what Oates terms "the heavy sorrow of the body" (WOL, 308) becomes unbearable, and the repressed fear of decay and disintegration erupts through the frantically cleansed surface of our lives. Beneath the surface at such moments, everything is apprehended as polluted and poisoned.

Indoctrinated with the ideal of cleanliness as a means to immortality or salvation, we see dirt and disorganization as reminders of our repressed fears of annihilation, and as well of the traumas of childhood or adolescence where our childhood security for our own warm flesh, odors, and dirt was systematically

repressed. Fearing that we have only our bodies between ourselves and nothingness, we at once fear and spiritualize the flesh.
As a consequence — and this we find in many of Oates's stories
as well as in *Wonderland* and *Expensive People* — eating is another activity where the dream becomes suborned and betrayed
by material reality. In *Wonderland* meals are presented with
grim comic irony as a kind of religious rite designed to placate
the sense of mortality. Jesse Vogel discovers how food may be
raised to the status of ritual, how the ultimate in material, the
very sustenance by which our bodies live, may become spiritual-
ized — because finally only the material is graspable and real:

Eating. All of them eating around her, at peace. She subsided into that
secret part of her, as if she were the baby growing inside this immense
body, herself the body, nourishing herself. At the outermost level of
her flesh there was activity — she was eating. The jaws moved, the teeth
ground and ground, there was a coarse, sinewy, dance-like motion
to them. It was fascinating, that activity. The lips parted, the mouth
opened, something was inserted into the opening, then the jaws began
their centuries of instinct, raw instinct, and the food was moistened,
ground into pulp, swallowed. It was magic. Around the table, drawn
together by this magic, the family sat eating, all of them eating, glow-
ing with the pleasure of eating together, in a kind of communion, their
hands bowed as they ate. (w, 138–39)

The most important symbolic structure in Oates's fiction
where dream and the material, ideal and physical reality, overlap and confuse each other is the city. America's traditional ambivalence towards the city erupts into her fiction: beneath the
dream that called the polis into existence to civilize the wilderness is the dark undercurrent of human corruption that destroys
it. Life in the Detroit of *Them* is stark, dehumanizing and fearful for the Wendalls. So Jules Wendall cries out to let it burn,
and in "How I Contemplated the World. . ." the blowing dirt of
Detroit becomes a sign of the inner crumbling of the city. But
Oates's cities are also places of meeting, excitement, mobility,
aspiration, and dream. The shopping mall in the story "Year of

Wonders" is like a mandala, a source of wonder, excitement, art, possibility, a place of revelation and purpose. The teenage narrator, Maureen, dances in and out of the "twenty-eight entrances, all equal in size," aware that, although "the 'Main Entrance' is no different from the others—a double thermopane door that opens automatically when you approach it," its significance so impresses itself upon her that it is as if the choice of door "can decide your life" (s, 189). Behind her intuitions is something akin to the intensity of the "so much depends" of William Carlos Williams' red wheelbarrow. We project our inner needs, confusions, or simplicities upon our surroundings.

Oates's ambivalence toward the city is commonplace enough, and in line with the historical American pattern of urgent enthusiasm for urban life and gradual revulsion from the result. What is interesting is that we are faced not with reflections of or evidence for particular sociological patterns but rather with the complexity of the feelings about what Lewis Mumford has termed the fourth migration of America, a period of "flow," caused, he says, not only by new industrial or social movements but by "new wants and necessities, and new ideals of life." [6] Again, Oates's technique is Lawrentian. Just as Lawrence insists on conveying the spirit of place, so Oates works with the felt rhythms, the spirit of energy and frustration beneath the surface of America. In her early novels, especially in *Them*, she conveys the tangled passions, the feel and taste of poverty in both rural and urban America as it becomes more self-consciously an urbanized society and produces a psychology of urban living. The city becomes an overwhelming symbol for the realities into which our time and place have thrown us. Anguish, joys, misery, achievement are inseparable from the city. In *Them*, the destructiveness of the city is felt in Jules's cry to burn Detroit; in *Do With Me What You Will* Jack Morrissey is fascinated but deeply revolted by Detroit; and in *Expensive People*, while Richard rhapsodizes

6 Lewis Mumford, *The Urban Prospect* (London: Secker & Warburg, 1968), 9.

that "if God remakes Paradise it will be in the image of Fernwood" (EP, 146), we nevertheless sense that his mother's judgment is grimly closer to the truth when she protests that "all the
world and all of history is a jungle, when it hasn't been a garbage heap or a graveyard" (EP, 280–81).

A central symbol in Oates's vision is the city of Detroit. Of all
American cities, Detroit must be one of the most powerfully
symbolic, concentrating in its names, nature, and statistics so
many overlapping and confusing myths of America. If we go to
sober sociological surveys of Detroit, we find that a description
of the city seems possible only in terms of mythology. *In Profile
of a Metropolis*, Robert J. Mowitz and Deil S. Wright note: "The
Detroit Metropolis, sprawled on the bank of the Detroit River
in Midwest America . . . is a marvellously complex system of
cultural, social, economic, and political institutions woven together by a network of channels for the movement of people
and goods." [7] "Sprawled," "woven," "movement"—Detroit is
packed with metaphorical significance, a complex of cars, property, jobs, incomes, factories, expressways, the automobile corporations, murder statistics, the affluence of the Grosses (Pointe,
Shores, Park, Farm), race riots. Oates's descriptions of Detroit
are primarily evocations of response and feeling. Her neurotic,
fearful, and self-protective characters take on something of the
emotional reverberation of Detroit, like sleepwalkers acting out
the urgent feelings that erupt through the virulent surface of the
city. Detroit is "all melodrama," she comments, "so transparent
you can hear it ticking." [8] Unlike Theodore Dreiser's Chicago or
Stephen Crane's New York, her Detroit is deceptively solid—its
violent clashes of feelings have their origins and meanings on levels far below the swirling dirt of the streets. "The molecules in the
air of Detroit are humming. . . . Next door to us a boy is out in

7 Robert J. Mowitz and Deil S. Wright, *Profile of a Metropolis* (Detroit: Wayne
State University Press, 1962), 5.
8 Alfred Kazin, *Bright Book of Life: American Novelists and Storytellers from Hemingway to Mailer* (Boston: Little, Brown and Co., 1973), 199.

his driveway, sitting down, playing a drum. Beating on a drum. Is he crazy? A white boy of about sixteen pounding on a drum. He wants to bring the city down with that drum and I don't blame him. I understand that vicious throbbing" (WOL, 61–62). *Do With Me What You Will* evokes the super-material, bustling world of Detroit's social elite—General Motors, Lakeshore Drive, Kercheval Boulevard, Woodward Avenue—but the details are all subservient to a mythology of survival and aspiration, power, and conscience. Detroit stands for a volatility in the human spirit.

Limitation and death haunt Detroit in both *Them* and *Do With Me What You Will*. Detroit is a "hole with a horizon" (T, 264), "a kind of stretched out hole" (T, 232), into which one journeys "deeper and deeper" without "coming to any center" (T, 80). And yet Detroit's unpredictability is exciting, stimulating ("Lots of people die," Jules notes, "and in strange ways"), and ultimately its anonymity and "airless boxed-in streets" may be a means of liberation. We sense from the Detroit novels that liberal reformists like Jack Morrissey or Jules's friend Dr. Mort Piercy may be wrong to think the city must be destroyed "before a new, beautiful, peaceful society can be erected" (T, 501–502). The city and what it stands for in our experience is like the court in a Jacobean tragedy — an omnipresent symbol of the world itself, which we cannot escape and through which we must struggle. In *Do With Me What You Will*, Elena looks across to Canada from Detroit and broods about "the people who might live there, in those houses that looked so distant, so safe, in a foreign country and safe from Detroit — as if anyone could be safe from Detroit, anywhere" (DWM, 382). It is in the center of the city, before the statue of the Spirit of Detroit that Elena and Jack will meet; the energy of the city may have fearful manifestations but that energy may transform the lives that the city has brutalized or distorted.

Driving the dynamo of Oates's America is the fact of violence. The city and its automobiles and freeways, its material and psy-

chic energies, are manifestations of the assertiveness and violence of America, of our desire to conquer and order so that we
may be free to adventure yet again, and the personalities that
create and react to America are driven and inspired by the violence we have set in motion. The centrality of violence to our
lives is a fearful aspect of our personal and social mythoi. Oates
has asked herself: "Am I personally haunted by the fear of violence, the need for violence, or do I reflect everyone else's feelings about it? I sense it around me, both the fear and the desire,
and perhaps I simply have appropriated it from other people?"[9]
But the violence that always threatens to erupt through the surface of Oates's America exists only in part as an acknowledgment of the omnipresence of the struggle, crime, and chaos in
our society. Oates seems fascinated with violence as a symbol of
eruptions in the personality itself, and with our consequent needs
and, too often, inability to express this power creatively. She repeatedly uses concentrations of violence in her fiction to direct
her reader's attention away from the externals of American society to crucial underlying surges in the psyche. She observes in a
critical essay on Yeats that his works are filled with a "violence
[which] is the flooding of the ego by the fury of the veins, a sudden and irrevocable alliance with nature's chaos" (EOI, 6). Such
surges of rage or stark observations on the fact of violence dominate her stories. She devises a rhetoric of violence to direct us to
the highly volatile, nightmarish undercurrents in our psyche,
making us aware of imminent dislocation or disaster in our lives.

   With Shuddering Fall is, for instance, saturated with scenes
and images of destitution, strain, hatred, fighting; ordinary incidents are depicted dramatically, violent scenes constantly heightened. "I was a child murderer" is the opening sentence of *Expensive People*; *Them*'s opening scene is a concentration of
pointless, uneasy malice, murder, blood soaking into a pillow,

9 Joe David Bellamy, *The New Fiction: Interviews with Innovative American Writers*
(Urbana: University of Illinois Press, 1974), 24.

the odor of blood and bodies, crazed fear, rape, and through it all, the relentless determinism of poverty. Life seems primarily a struggle for survival not only with the world but with forces inside the psyche. To battle with oneself and survive is a kind of art—like, indeed, the novelist's own. Art, Oates comments often, is itself built around potential violence, inasmuch as it is an affirmation of selfhood, growing from a desire to establish one's own psychic boundaries and autonomy, a gesture of liberation which may culminate unpredictably in either chaos or order. We risk and strike out in order that we may become. In a society where the instincts are so much repressed, violence may become a gesture of liberation, of purging, or self-discovery. Indeed, violence seems to be at the heart of the dream of America, as we cultivate the palpable risk, the danger of our deepest desires. Some of Oates's most vivid stories tell of women who venture half-consciously, with a felt sense of sensual destiny in their veins, into experiences of violent victimization from which paradoxically they draw strength. Others evoke the deterministic helplessness of being ruled by their inner drives. "I was in love with a man I couldn't marry, so one of us had to die" is the opening of "I Was in Love" (WOL, 388). This story evokes in breathless spurts of masochistic energy the fragility of the personality suffering from love, constantly threatened by physical or psychic destruction. The narrator, in the midst of a guilty affair, is terrified, condemned, fearful, sensing the surrounding violence in Detroit as revelatory of her own fearfulness: "Love is testing. You prick him with a small needle. You reach behind his eyes with your fingernails and give a tug to the optic nerve" (WOL, 402).

Violence therefore must be faced as omnipresent in our society's life; this observation is thrust at us not just as an obvious commonplace but as an urgent insight that our most revered rituals, games, and relationships are necessarily interpenetrated by violence. Rather than trying to maintain standards of civilization in the face of violence, Oates's characters are forced to reaffirm or reassess their values as they encounter violence at the heart of all their most intimate and valuable experiences. Love, the most integral of all, is at once the most fragile:

my skin is rubbed raw
the pigment sucked out
you outline my face constantly
with your thumbs—
I am a wound nursed open
germless in the hot sun

    it is not a baptism
    or a fury from an old god's beak
    but an ordinary violence
    framed by windowsills
    the loosing of fresh blood
    an ordinary violence
    girls strain from windowsills
    to achieve.

The "ordinary violence" of love becomes in Oates a liberating excitement. On the one hand, such violence makes us all victims:

if I could turn outward
into the flat white walls
of the rooms we use
I would witness a body
at its fate tugged by the moon
all the inches of its skin
rubbed raw with the skin
of men.   (LD, 21, 31)

Uniting Oates's dream of America is the restlessness of the human personality itself. Home is where the moving van roams; the paranoid search for material security is the external sign of an inner restlessness born of the dream of an America permanent only in its changes and chances. When Oates says that "the greatest works of literature deal with the human soul caught in the stampede of time, unable to gauge the profundity of what passes over it" (NHNE, 105), it is clear that she is not just concerned with social determinism. Her primary focus is, in fact, on the struggle for autonomy by the personality of which her land-scapes are perspectival reflections. Counteracting the poverty, violence, and mobility of her America is a tone of celebration based on an awareness that the inner landscape — the human personality and its dreams and desires — is what creates the external world. She has described herself as a "psychological real-ist," which she explains as taking "the area of the human psyche, or mind, as the centre of all experience of reality." [10] Nowhere in her fiction do we escape from her concentrated, often obses-sive, concern with personality. Even her doubts about Western philosophy's preoccupation with the uniqueness of the person-ality are, like Lawrence's similar opposition, a tribute to its hold over her — and over our whole age. This concentration is further coupled with an awareness, often suppressed or half-admitted by her characters, that the personality, just because it is so im-portant, is fragile, vulnerable to threats from both outside and inside the self. At our most creative we are at our most vulner-able. The "phantasmagoria of personality" emerges from a dual awareness of the value and the risk of the human soul.

In the novels, the vulnerability and unpredictability of per-sonality is most obviously focused in sex. Oates's most gripping writing is concerned with the struggles of the personality caught in the tensions, betrayals, frustrations, and unpredictable joys of sexual love. It is in love, which is depicted ruefully as a kind of pathological state, that the personality is at its most vulnera-ble, and where preexistent concepts of one's self, roles, and des-tiny are most radically challenged. Love offers us experiences of risk, simultaneously fulfilling, stabilizing, yet alluring, unpre-dictable, and dislocating. Oates frequently uses the phrase "per-manently married" to describe, often ironically, the mixture of apparent stability and constant newness involved in the tradi-tional American fixation with marriage as the means of stabiliz-ing the unpredictable drive of sexuality. She is fascinated by the

10 "Face to Face," *Maclean's*, April, 1974, p. 60.

unforeseeable ways the personality may be imprisoned by its security and yet be challenged to become something new. Contemporary men and women, adrift in the echoing landscape of
America, are "flesh with an insatiable soul" (WOL, 72), and the
bond between them is at best ambiguous when it is not confining, indefinable, and perplexing. One story asks: "Everywhere
on this highway, at this moment, there were men and women
driving together, bonded together—what did it mean to be together? What did it mean to enter into a bond with another person?" (MI, 392–93).

What it means, most crucially, is to be vulnerable. If, as Lawrence puts it, sexuality is always flowing, a never-ceasing movement, then we are caught, protesting, reluctant, often destroyed,
in the obsessive movement of a cosmic drive. We experience sexuality as power—as dominance, violence, spilling over into our
dreams. At its most demanding sexual love is both a pathological condition and a religion, violent and deterministic, which
invades our being, making us aware that our personalities are
insecure, and that if we want to grow, we must accept this insecurity. Love lures us into an unknown, a promise of we-know-
not-what. Falling in love may be an illusion but in its disturbing
our preexistent concepts of self it may be a hopeful illusion. It
demands of us that we badger the future for fulfillment, that we
refuse to take even the wisest, most prudent "no" for an answer.
As Werner Pelz remarks, "It must be a paltry joy which from
the beginning does not thirst for eternity."[11]

But can the human personality, partly formed or unified by so
many external pressures, lost in the not-so-fun-house which is
contemporary America, stand the pressure of living by the fragile hope which love may offer? Many of Oates's stories are about
the struggle of the personality to withstand and create some kind
of order from such situations. Deciding to live by hope rather
than fact, by the power of the possible rather than the appar-

11 Werner Pelz, God is No More (London: Gollancz, 1964), 45.

ently actual, requires a courage that most of her characters trag-ically lack. To desire against the persistent and seemingly omni-present facticity of the world needs a combined recklessness and stability which is rare. Consequently, many of Oates's characters experience their sexuality as derangement or as fate. As Kazin comments, love for Oates appears as "an attraction of person to person so violent that it expresses itself as obsession and takes on the quality of fatality." [12] A desperate craving for satiation is countermanded by a fear of dissolution and pain. The explo-ration of this terrifying power of sex saturates the best Oates stories. Love and terror, ecstacy and dislocation of the person-ality seem inevitably fused in erotic experience, and the radical breakthrough into the final transcendence of *Do With Me What You Will* is a rare note in her fiction. More typical is the depri-vation that the opening of "I Must Have You" communicates. We are instantaneously confronted with a series of staccato ejac-ulations, the obsessive distress of a woman's sexual need:

I saw him. I crossed the street to him. I knew the face because
I had cut his photographs out of paper — once, in a library back
in the States, I had used a razor to cut the photograph out, slitting
back and forth gently, gently.
    I said-
    I stammered and said-. . . .
Pain scattered up my left side, rib after rib electrified the pain.
I hadn't eaten for a while. I felt my hair blowing savage around
my face and I felt the pinched lips, my pale pinched lips.
    "I— I want— I need" (GOW, 167)

Groping amongst the feelings of this America, a landscape we experience as at once fiercely materialistic yet transparently sym-bolic, her characters are manipulated by their obsessions, caught in patterns of biological, social, and emotional determinism they barely understand. So overwhelming are the wider symbolic rit-uals in which they enact their small roles that they take refuge in

12 Kazin, *Bright Book of Life*, 202.

private, more manageable, myths of themselves. Over and over, Oates portrays characters whose experiences burst the bounds of any preconceived conception of the self—and a test of their integrity or plain ability to survive is whether they accept such unpredictability or whether their concepts of the self become a neurotic escape. The very notion of the fixed self, in Lawrence's terms, is "a spurious, detestable product . . . man born out of his own head," static and unadaptable, essentially secure from risk, struggle, and therefore growth. Oates's characters, especially her women, are rigidly encased in their mental ideas of the self, hypersensitive to the fragility of the ego, fearful of their bodies' darker urges, buffeted by and largely formed by others' reactions and desires. They are ruled by the ego in Lawrence's sense, by "a body of accepted consciousness inherited more or less ready-made" and which is "dictating . . . issues which are quite false" to any "true, deeper, spontaneous self," a "creative identity."[13] Caught between the desires of their lovers, the demands of their social roles, or simply others' random expectations, Oates's women are usually vivid exemplifications of Lawrence's attack on the incubus of the false self. They are deeply vulnerable, constantly pursued, stared at, driven by their outside environment but also stultified, trapped inside themselves by fearful and largely mental images of the self.

Amidst the current reassessments of women's sexual roles and the impetus towards a distinctively female culture, Oates sympathetically but pessimistically points to the deep-rooted and fearful determinism of American women.[14] The stereotyped roles of women—goddess, bitch, mother, lover—cannot, it seems, be circumvented simply by our being aware of them. They are apparently deterministically bound into our deepest drives and

13 D. H. Lawrence, *Phoenix: The Posthumous Papers of D. H. Lawrence*, ed. Edward D. McDonald (New York: Viking Press, 1972), 710–11.
14 See the suggestive treatment of love, women, and the family in Oates by Cynthia Charlotte Stevens, "The Imprisoned Imagination: The Family in the Fiction of Joyce Carol Oates" (Ph.D. dissertation, University of Illinois at Urbana-Champaign, 1974).

demands; even when they are social in origin, they seem upon analysis to become inexplicably and tragically rooted in our glandular or hormonal chemistry. However a woman may reject sexual stereotypes, their hold upon her psychological and emotional behaviour remains frighteningly real. Many of Oates's stories are about American women struggling for survival amidst a host of conflicting roles and masks which a sexually deterministic society has thrust upon her. With few exceptions, their greatest achievement is just to survive. Elena, the heroine of *Do With Me What You Will*, is an amalgam of feminine stereotypes — a beautiful model, rich, sexually provocative yet dreamily passive, identified by her husband's wealth, power, and possessiveness — and yet moved to struggle, almost wordlessly, towards some kind of autonomy as she learns to fall back upon and revere a dark reservoir of sexual power in her nature. Elsewhere, such hopeful strength is subjected to much cooler scrutiny by Oates: the myth, so widespread throughout American history, in diverse religious and secular guises, of the greater body-consciousness possessed by women is revealed as a fearful source of psychic confusion, frustration, and violence. Oates's women walk through her world bombarded by sensations and reactions that heighten and isolate their sensuality. The narrator of "Unpublished Fragments" notes how "something in my face must have attracted them, because they glanced at me — that look men give to women, startled, recoiling a little as if looking into a beacon, too much unwanted light" (GOW, 350). Her women are obsessively used by men, fantasized about, virtually invented "to explain the humiliating chaos" (GOW, 358) of a man's life or else victimized by their own half-understood drives and desires. However indignantly we may reject such stifling roles, we are operated upon by urges and motives beyond our conscious control, and even the most intellectually emancipated women are driven by forces that, Oates pessimistically suggests, re-create the sexual roles they try to destroy. Sadly, those characters who have careers are even more defensive and threatened than the women in traditional roles of wife, lover, daughter, or mother. Sister Irene in "In the Region of Ice" is fearful and frigid; Elena's mother, Marya Sharp, is aggressive, exploitative, and incapable of any real commitment, a characteristic she passes on to her daughter. Furthermore, Oates asserts that "the mechanical fact of possessing a certain body must no longer determine the role of the spirit, the personality," for "to be mechanically operated, to have one's body moving along in a process that the spirit cannot control, to have the spirit trapped in an unchosen physical predicament — this is a kind of death." [15] On the other hand, although it may be destructive passion born of many conflicting urges and destructive myths, and therefore a kind of disease, love may yet lead to a transfiguration of self; it is an invitation to enter a new era of existence which is at once a risk and yet offers the possibility of transcendence.

The ambiguous power that exists in women's bodies is one of Oates's major concerns. Like Lawrence, she wants her reader to enter into the experience of the dark mysteries of sexual passion in order, eventually, to be enabled to transcend them and reach what Lawrence regarded as an area of pure stillness, the famous "star-equilibrium" of *Women in Love.* Like Lawrence, too, she sees — invariably compassionately — her female characters unable to achieve such harmony because of the determinism of their social conditioning. Introducing a collection of her stories, subtitled "Stories of Young America," she speaks of the "tragic ... casualties" among young Americans "who sense that their society is an unhealthy one but who have no idea of how to transcend it" and she describes her stories as dealing with heroic struggles to define their identity in a society which radically limits their possibilities (WGWB, 9). Most of the stories are centered on women — not only because she herself is a woman, but because she senses that her sex most clearly displays the essential mythology of confused and destructive feeling that character-

15 Joyce Carol Oates, "Out of the Machine," *American Review*, CCXXVIII (1971), 44.

izes contemporary sexual relations in America. She conceives the most crucial struggle for a women not to be that of finding a satisfying social role but of liberating the creative springs of the personality. Occasionally we apprehend how love may become a miracle achieved, a momentary fusion which points to a new hope of achievement and openness; but tragically often it strikes the personality as a kind of disease. One of Oates's most emotionally affective (and effective) stories on this theme is "Unmailed, Unwritten Letters." The narrator, torn between her husband and her lover, fantasizes her dilemma in a series of imagined letters, factual or superficial to her parents, guilty and anguished to her husband, passionate and urgent to her lover, threatened and vindictive to his ten-year-old daughter. The experience the story records is conveyed by a remarkable intensity of tone. The reader of the story is seized and wrenched by the anguished paranoia of the woman, starting with the surface trivialities that she dutifully allows to occupy her mind—new clothes, dentists, travel. Then, immediately we dive into the emotional chaos of an unmailed, unwritten letter to her lover's daughter, in which the threatened woman demands: "Why do you play these games, why do you pursue me?" In fantasy, lying "here in a paralysis of love, sorrow, density, idleness" she confesses her affair to her husband; to her lover, she is both ecstatic and yet overwhelmed with fear and pain. The woman hovers on the edge of breakdown and confession, sensing her confusion and masochistic anger reflected in her surroundings, the "angry parts of Detroit, all of Detroit angry, white and black, bustling, ominous" (WOL, 57, 60). Caught between her affection for her husband and her craving for her lover, she is paralyzed, dreaming of death, her own, her lover's. She is "a woman trapped in love, in the terror of love. Paralysis of love." The challenge of new growth offered by her love seems too radical, too strong. She bitterly acknowledges "I will die slowly in this marriage rather than come to life in another." "Flesh with an insatiable soul," she lacks the essential courage to seize her deepest dreams.

Aching "with a lust that has become metaphysical," her crazed inner state reflected in the anger and crudity of Detroit, in the flashing knives and grinding automobiles of the city, attached to her husband but unable to stop betraying him, she dare not affirm her deepest wants (WOL, 61, 68, 72).

Her story evokes through the confusion of metaphysical yearning, physical and emotional anguish, the fragility of the personality in sexual love and the tragedy of inner fear, and it is probably Oates's most moving short story. She herself has commented on how many readers have found its evocation of paranoid paralysis disturbingly true of their own relationships. In doing so she asks ruefully what such recognition suggests about American marriages — but, furthermore, we might ask what it says about the contemporary psyche. Love is understood as a surprising reaffirmation of our deepest hopes, and to refuse its fulfillment is to acknowledge that we lack the courage to live except in the shallows of life. What love, even in its fear, violence, and pain, brings to each of us is that through the terror, through the very vulnerability of the personality, we may realize that it is our very openness to change that finally makes for our redemption.

Few of Oates's women — in the novels, only Elena in *Do With Me What You Will* — make such a radical act of affirmation. Oates's women are either suspended between agony and commitment or are driven by their intensity into the tragic security of mechanical, unspontaneous responses, into frigidity and aloofness. Touch (in Lawrence's sense) is feared precisely because it may disturb the secure equilibrium of the personality. The story "In the Region of Ice," in *The Wheel of Love*, sympathetically depicts a Catholic sister teaching in a university who finds her secure role and fixed personality challenged by an immature and yet enthusiastic student who attacks her scholarly and vocational aloofness. "'The humanist must be committed to the totality of life,' he said passionately. 'This is the failing one finds everywhere in the academic world.'" Such claims throw her into an area of psychological risk, where rationality and cool sympathy prove insufficient. When eventually the student kills himself, she is saddened but relieved, as her insubstantial self relaxes into her chosen role:

> Sister Irene could feel a part of herself drifting off, lured by the plains of white snow to the north, the quiet, the emptiness, the sweep of the Great Lakes up to the silence of Canada. But she called that part of herself back. She could only be one person in her lifetime. That was the ugly truth, she thought, that she could not really regret Weinstein's suffering and death; she had only one life and had already given it to someone else. He had come too late to her. Fifteen years ago, perhaps, but not now.
> She was only one person, she thought, walking down the corridor in a dream. Was she safe in this single person, or was she trapped? She had only one identity. She could make only one choice. What she had done or hadn't done was the result of that choice, and how was she guilty? If she could have felt guilt, she thought, she might at least have been able to feel something. (WOL, 20, 32–33)

In another story in the same collection, "Bodies," a similar insight emerges. Oates has in fact written a number of stories about the self-destructiveness of unreturned passion, and brings out the distinct, if unwilled, responsibility that falls as much on the pursued as the pursuer. In "Bodies" Pauline is an artist, cool, withdrawn, "interested only in the human head," her own hair worn "in a kind of crown, braided tightly . . . her face was cool, slow to awaken interest, held always in a kind of suspension." She is approached by an impulsive and clearly disturbed man. Increasingly obsessed by her in a strange way she cannot understand, he follows her around the city, bringing out in her not just the dread of being pursued by a stranger, but a repressed loathing for touch, for any relationship that would put her self-sufficiency in question. Previously she has preferred "safe" relationships with people who don't draw her out, who "could never harm her," whereas the city is an area of risk: "Down here, the city was open. Anything could happen" (WOL, 262, 258, 264,

259). Finally, Pauline's coolness, her fearful inability to become involved, produces a violent reaction in her pursuer, as he strikes out with a knife—not at her but at his own throat. Some of his blood splashes onto her. She shudders, returns home, scrubs herself, confronted with what she fears most, the pulsing vulnerability of bodies. She obsessively washes, reads medical books, believes herself to be pregnant, bleeds, and ends in madness, repressed dreams of bodily contact erupting from her subconscious.

As in many of Oates's stories, the denouement of violence occurs here suddenly yet with a frightening emotional logic. Her characters live in fear of the inner landscape of their psychic and physical existence, their very fear of touch or involvement so often the cause of the violation they most fear. In *Do With Me What You Will*, Elena's passivity is like that of Minette in Lawrence's *Women in Love*: she is a victim, "provoking" a sort of destructive electrical discharge in men around her, "waiting in her separation, given,"[16] her passivity enraging and potentially destroying those who pursue her.

And yet the very role of the seductive, passive victim is one projected upon modern women by generations of conditioning, social and psychological. Oates's characters often grope clumsily among their swirling psychic and physical desires because their personalities are formed to a frightening degree by obscure, unacknowledgeable events or forces. Family, class, religion, and above all the ruthless complexities of the American dynamic have reduced human personalities to bewildered marionettes. Children ("Wild Saturday"), family ("Stigmata," "The Dying Child") nostalgia ("Narcotic"), mass media, marriage, race, all are localized in personal history and the personal present. A miscellaneous collection of stories, *Where Are You Going, Where Have You Been*, has been brought together by Oates to give some focus to her concern with the struggle against this degree of determinism, to achieve what she terms an "energizing divin-

16 D. H. Lawrence, *Women in Love* (New York: Viking Press, 1920), 72.

ity." We are experiencing, she writes, "countless manifestations of the struggle I believe to be common to most young Americans today: the attempt to rescue spiritual values from a society constantly in the process of devaluing itself. . . . These stories deal with human being struggling heroically to define personal identity in the face of incredible opposition, even in the face of death itself" (WGWB, 9). The struggle Oates describes might be taken, in fact, as a dominant theme of all her fiction. The phantasmagoria of the personality is involved in a barely understood struggle for survival which belies the seeming serenity of ordinary social intercourse. We feel safe when there is no risk, and when the public, shared world of facts can control the restless, uncontrollable world beneath the surface.

We might ask: how, in Oates's view, does the healthy personality manifest itself? So many of her stories and novels explore the exhaustion or disintegration of partial, inadequate selves, and yet she is clearly fascinated with a drive towards wholeness. *Wonderland*, as we shall see, dramatizes the tragic substitution of a series of materialistic, scientific concepts of the personality, formed and regulated by external stimuli. Where is the source of the integrated, openly explorative personality? "The organism," writes Carl R. Rogers, "has one basic tendency and striving — to actualize, maintain, and enhance" itself as it grows, a process he terms "self-actualization," characterized by greater differentiation, growth, self-government, self-regulation and autonomy from the control of external forces. Such a view of the personality avers that "the ultimate driving force is the person's unrelenting will to come to grips with himself, a wish to grow and to leave nothing untouched that prevents growth." [17] Life is conceived of as an autonomous dynamic event, and its processes do not merely serve to help the organism "survive," to revert to Oates's own term, but more dynamically, to transcend the momentary status quo, to impose an autonomous determination upon an ever-increasing realm of experience.

17 Carl R. Rogers, *Client-Centered Therapy* (Boston: Houghton Mifflin, 1951), iv.

The "third force" psychologists such as Carl Rogers or Abraham Maslow place great stress on self-actualization and self-enhancement through human-centered experiences such as love, aesthetics, mysticism, creation and insight, what Maslow terms "peak experiences." Such experiences, essentially nonmeasurable, allow us to comprehend our experiences instinctively as whole, mysterious, and self-enhancing. Man, it is claimed, is neither a tension-reducing animal nor a conditioned animal, but is possessed by evolutionary and constructive urges challenging him to realize his potential. "Man," says Maslow, can "create himself in large part . . . from given possibilities. . . . Man *can* solve his problems by his own strength. He never has so far, because he has never yet developed to his full strength. As to the forces of goodness within him, neither have these ever developed fully enough to be seen as the hope of the world—except in rare moments of exaltation. He doesn't have to fly to a God. He can look within himself for all sorts of potentialities, strength, and goodness." [18] Healthy human development is conceived of as a process of self-actualization; unhealthy development as one of self-alienation. Notwithstanding her admiration for Maslow, Oates's fiction expresses what is at once a gloomier and yet a more exalted view of the human personality. Like most twentieth-century psychological theories, third-force psychology is basically need-oriented. For Maslow, let us say, man's psychological development is mainly determined by the structure of individual needs and the degree to which these needs can be gratified. On the other hand, as we have seen, Oates views the human personality as involved rather in a search for significance—a will to meaning rather than a will to satisfaction—and such a process may equally well emerge through pain, anguish, neurosis, and self-alienation as through need-satisfaction. Destructiveness, violence, and alienation cannot, in a Maslovian view, be regarded as creative or healthy; they are the expression of the frustration

18 Abraham H. Maslow, *A Memorial Volume*, comp. by Bertha G. Maslow (Monterey: Brooks/Cole Publishing Co., 1972), 80, 113.

of basic needs. Once these needs are satisfied, the individual can be elevated "to the point where he is civilized enough to feel frustrated about the larger personal, social, and intellectual issues."[19] Emerging from Oates's fiction is an understanding of the human personality which is both more primitive and more subtle. Certainly it is less facile and less oriented towards the optimistic hedonism of such general exhortations.

Many of Oates's characters might be described as dominated by a paralizing horror of self-actualization. But consistently she shows it is through or because of our vulnerability, deprivation, or self-alienation that some of our most creative acts emerge. Elena in *Do With Me What You Will*, for instance, is caught in an undeniably painful experience of self-alienation, but the growing autonomy and confidence which the novel follows occur through her anguish and limitation. Her development is one of positive disintegration as she painfully responds to the challenge to go beyond her limited, externally conditioned and passive concept of self. In other characters, such challenges do, often, result in the paralysis of the narrator of "Unmailed, Unwritten Letters," but sometimes they may be necessary preliminaries to painful but real growth. We cannot live fully by merely repeating the given patterns of our ancestors, families, or society or by satisfying a set of basics or even a hierarchy of needs; it may be in the very vulnerability of our changing experiences where we must discover our potential and embrace it.

The Maslovian concept of a "real self," too, is something essentially alien to Oates's vision — as, indeed, it would have been to Lawrence's. For Oates, vulnerability is the preliminary to growth; any concept of a "real self" as an original or fixed set of healthy characteristics, as favored by many third-force psychologists,[20] is quite different from her insistence that the fearful

19 Abraham H. Maslow, *Motivation and Personality* (New York: Harper, 1954), 119.
20 See, for example, Karen Horney, *Neurosis and Human Growth* (New York: Norton, 1950), 13, 17, 158; Abraham H. Maslow, *Toward a Psychology of Being* (Princeton: Van Nostrand, 1968), 179.

(and yet liberating) paradox of the personality consists precisely of its fluidity and fragility. "Most of my writing," she has explained, "is preoccupied with the imagination of pain. . . . I feel the moral imperative to chart the psychological processes of someone who has gone through suffering of one kind or another, but who survives it (or almost survives)." On the one hand, only by risking our concepts of self and by trusting our vulnerability and volatility can we grow; on the other, that growth may lead us to areas of unpredictability, threat, and destruction. The neuroses of many of Oates's characters emerge as a defense of a concept of the self which is safe, partial, and static. They sense themselves to be vulnerable or limited. As a means of dealing with such insecurity and inner conflict, they protect their concept of a partial self, thus substituting a neurotic view of personality for a fuller, if more vulnerable, openness to change and development. There is a "natural warm flow of common sympathy between man and man, man and woman," Lawrence writes, which keeps us "tender and alive at a moment when the great danger is to go brittle, hard, and in some way dead." Like Lawrence, Oates wants to "restore into life" an openness to this "warmheartedness and compassionateness" as "the most natural life-flow in the world."[21] Yet so many of her characters choose the brittle and hard forms of life precisely because such forms are seemingly invulnerable. Her most intense characters are deeply aware of their fragility and vulnerability. We all carry "ourselves like glass, we are very breakable" says Jules Wendall in *Them*, whose most admirable characteristic is at once recognizing and risking that vulnerability. Visiting his sister in the hospital, "he carried himself . . . like a man carrying something breakable" (T, 223); his sister Maureen, by contrast, is desperately afraid of "breaking into pieces" (T, 202), and she watches people around her survive by freezing their faces "into expres-

21 "Transformations of Self: An Interview with Joyce Carol Oates," *Ohio Review*, XV (1973), 56; D. H. Lawrence, *Sex, Literature, and Censorship*, ed. Harry T. Moore (New York: Viking, 1953), 66–67.

sions of cunning and anger" (T, 136). Elena is similarly taught that she must *"take care of"* her face, *"carry it like a crystal"* (DWM, 79). She too is faced with *"nullity"* and "extinction" (DWM, 410). "I am glass," writes Richard Everett, "transparent and breakable as glass, but — and this is the tragedy — we who are made of glass may crack into millions of jig-saw pieces but we do not fall apart. . . . We want nothing more than to fall apart, to disintegrate, to be released into a shower of slivers and have done with it all, but the moment is hard to come by, as you can see" (EP, 101).

The word which recurs throughout Oates's fiction to represent the safe wholeness the fearful personality seeks — and ironically, the word she uses to describe the temptation of the fixed self — is *permanent*. It occurs most especially in such phrases as "permanently married." In *Them* Faye is "attached permanently to another man" who is himself "permanently married"; in another sense of the phrase Nadine confesses that "there are men who are permanent in a woman's life; everything in them is permanent and terrible . . . there's no choice about it," while Jules feels that their love is "irreparable, a permanent condition, as permanent as his own name" (T, 233, 367, 414). The phrase recurs in many of Oates's stories, as if she had a fixation with both our desire for and temptation of different senses of permanence. Somewhat like R. D. Laing (and, again, very unlike the need-oriented psychology of both the Freudians and most of the third-force psychologists), Oates is concerned with bringing the personality *through* crises, and so making them redemptive by facing and living with them. Autonomy is not something one can will or rationalize into being. It must be fought for, as we accept and explore our divided, neurotic, fluid selves. Hence the ideal of "permanence" is deceptive. A "permanent" commitment may involve an ultimate risk, the recognition of the transcendent gift within the flux of immanence, but it also may involve a fear of the unknown, the acceptance of the confining, the limiting, a legalistic or constrained view of the self. *Do With*

Me What You Will is built upon a contrast between these senses of permanence, between the way of spontaneous, passionate affirmation and the constraints of role and image ultimately sanctioned by law.

Wrestling with their conceptions of duty and selfhood, their desires and insecurity, Oates's characters are grim reminders of the enormous weight that Western, and most especially American, civilization has placed on authentic individuality—indeed on "self-actualization" itself. "Every human being," in Lawrence's words, "must come to the fullness of himself... every man to be himself, to come to his own fullness of being.... Let our ideal be living, spontaneous individuality in every man or woman." Yet, as Lawrence—in whose work the Western emphasis on individuality probably reached its fullest expression— realized, we have reached a point in our civilization where our individuality is "pseudo-spontaneous"; we are "in the toils of helpless self-consciousness... too fixedly conscious," and thus we fall into the curse of automatic self-glorification. Hence the paradox: Lawrence, the apostle of self-authenticity advocating getting beyond personality. On the one hand he can write that instead of "finding our highest reality in an ever-extending aggregation with the rest of men, we shall realize at last that the highest reality for every living creature is in its purity of singleness and its perfect solitary integrity, and that everything else should be but a means to this end. All communion, all love, and all communication, which is all consciousness, are but a means to the perfected singleness of the individual being." On the other hand Lawrence can write of so-called modern individualism as "a cheap egotism, every self-conscious little ego assuming unbounded rights to display his self-consciousness." Consequently he spoke, preached even, of getting beyond personality, or getting beyond sex, to restore the preconscious connection between the vital core of the individual and the cosmos.[22]

Joyce Carol Oates believes that we are seeing something of

22 D. H. Lawrence, "Education of the People," *Phoenix*, 605, 607, 629, 637.

what Lawrence prophesied. Perhaps, she suggests, "we are approaching the end of a traditional ego-centered consciousness," the "death throes of the Renaissance." She suggests that "in many of us the Renaissance ideal is still powerful, its voice tyrannical. It declares: *I* will, *I* want, *I* demand, *I* think, *I* am. . . . *I will exist* has meant only *I will impose my will on others*."[23] Like Lawrence, she looks forward to the conversion of this "I-centered personality into a higher or transcendent" personality. Writing in 1975 in *Psychology Today*, Oates described the "self" as not isolated or autonomous but "part of a larger reservoir of energy." She argues that "as long as the myth of separate and competitive 'selves' endures" then our society will remain "obsessed with adolescent ideas of being superior, of conquering, of destroying." The isolated self is inherently connected with violence, retreat, defensiveness, and brittleness. The pronoun *I*, she comments wryly, "is as much metaphor as 'schizophrenia' and it has undergone the same metaphor into myth process."[24] But in order to achieve "the self's basic impersonality"[25] we must face our conditioning to believe in the uniqueness of the personality so that only through its annihilation can the transcendence of the self be achieved. Her seemingly compulsive return to the same themes and motifs in her fiction might even be seen as a ritual purging of her own conditioning. She writes of Yeats's similar fascination with the Freudian insistence on "reliving certain events in one's past life again and again in order to be purged of them," a process wherein the "dreamer goes back again and again to unsettling memories, in order to master them, to purge them" (EOI, 179–80). Jesse Vogel's daughter tries to purge herself in such a way as she strives to break her father's hold over her. Noel, her lover, tells her that "systematically . . . you dream back and erase yourself . . . step by step, year by year, erasing the monster so that you can be free" (W, 383).

23 Joyce Carol Oates, "New Heaven and Earth," *Saturday Review*, November 4, 1972, pp. 52, 53.
24 Joyce Carol Oates, "The Myth of the Isolated Artist," *Psychology Today*, VI (May, 1973), 74–75.
25 Oates, "New Heaven and Earth," 54.

Many of Oates's stories, essays, and novels published in the mid-1970s have increasingly wrestled with the need for recognizing the sources of such purgation or conversion. Often, change in the personality comes only through violence or unpredictable change from within the "night side" of the self. In *Wonderland* suicide or violent death are ever-threatening possibilities as the fragile ego is increasingly threatened. In *The Assassins* violence is depicted as a means of escaping the burden of individuality and a way of escaping our fear of the final meaninglessness of the ego. By contrast, in *Do With Me What You Will* Mered Dawe offers the lovers what to them — and perhaps still to most of us — is an unrealizable possibility of a nongrasping, nonpossessive acceptance of the contradictions and ambiguities of their love. There are hints, however, even in *The Assassins*, and more strongly in *Childwold* and *Night Side* that she has become fascinated with the roots of religious and mystical experience. For a number of years, she has looked to various Eastern philosophies as a possible paradigm for the conversion towards which she looks, and in her most recent writings, in the mid and later seventies, she has extended this interest to areas of Western experience which our civilization has ignored, distorted, or over-rationalized. In her seminal essay on Kafka in *New Heaven, New Earth*, to which I have already referred, she writes of Kafka's "record of the ego's crisis as it approaches its own transcendence" and of how, like Lawrence, Kafka had "a fundamental detestation of the conscious, private, grasping self." Although her analogy is never fully developed in the essay, Oates struggles to draw a parallel between Kafka, Zen, and Taoism, stressing their analogous attempts to transcend the self. "In Taoism," she suggests, "we come across the very spirit of Kafka himself, the awareness of an absolutely impersonal and incomprehensible Being over the efforts of individuals to influence it" (NHNE, 276–78). As so often with Oates's essays, her insights reflect back on her own fiction. In *The Assassins* especially we are bombarded with the stifling presence of the ego, obsessed with its own threatened disintegration and unable to effect any transcendence of the grimly deterministic material world it inhabits and which is its fragile justification. Like the Pedersens in *Wonderland*, the Petrie family in *The Assassins* represents an horrific extreme of the self-obsessiveness of the Western tradition. What they fear above all else is death, the disintegration of the ego. Only Stephen, the dislocated, mystical younger brother, can conceive of any possible escape from the burden of the ego, and his vision is so alien to the rest of the family and the cloying world of material fact in which he must live that he can find no means of integrating his vision of God with the world. Similarly, in *Do With Me What You Will*, Mered Dawe clearly embodies the serene egoless vision of nonpossessive love, but such a vision can find no roots in the dynamic, egocentric psychic landscape of contemporary America.

Oates's concern with the growth of selfhood, then, so prominent in her early novels and stories, seems to have undergone a radical change in her work of the mid-1970s. The change can be illuminated, perhaps, by another glance back at Lawrence who was at once the passionate advocate of the affirmation of the flesh, the unique and single self, and at the same time of the individual's place in the circumambient universe. Unity of thought, "permanence" of vision, is not necessarily a virtue in a novelist, least of all in a writer like Oates who is so immediately sensitive to the feeling of living in contemporary America. When we stand back from the world Oates draws us into in her fiction, we are made aware of an exciting paradox. The America she evokes is violent, spiritually destructive, and yet hopeful in its fragility; hers is a vision of openness as much as of despair. Oates's dream of America is an enticement to a "new heaven, new earth" by participating in dreaming itself, a celebration of the potential triumph of the imagination that, paradoxically, only America embodies.

THREE

Forms of Obsession: Oates's Fictional Stance

FICTION constitutes a way of looking at the world and in its experimentation and surprises contemporary fiction is in a frenetic process of self-conscious expansiveness, perhaps catching up with and at times absorbing lessons from the increasingly central media of our time, including film, rock music, and even the fine arts. An acceptable if somewhat shallow and question-begging explanation is that it is our world at large, not merely our fiction, which is changing. As Alain Robbe-Grillet put it in his now curiously dated attempt to create a theoretical basis of a new novel in France, "Things have generally been speeding up" and "not only in the sphere of art. . . . If the reader sometimes has difficulty in finding his bearings in the modern novel, it's the same way in which he gets lost in the actual world he lives in, when all the old construction and standards he is used to are collapsing."[1]

Oates's place in the frenetic fictional activity of our time is curiously indefinable. Although her novels are located, as Ihab Hassan maps it, somewhere near the center of the landscape of "POSTmodern" (or postcontemporary) fiction,[2] some of her stories and certain aspects of her novels do seem to be situated in more remote terrain. There are several landmarks in recent experimental fiction which bear some resemblance to some of Oates's outposts. Abandoning Hassan's geographical metaphor for a time, we might ponder over John Ditsky's remark that even in the sixties Oates's fictions were only "superficially similar to realistic fiction" and instead were "tonally aligned with the experimentalists."[3] Whereas Oates occasionally makes scathing remarks about certain kinds of experimental fiction, her work uses a surprising diversity of formal techniques to articulate her vision. In her short stories especially she has shown herself open to experimentation. She seems to have frequently used short fictional modes as workshops, experimenting with a multiplicity of formal possibilities — using newspaper headlines, parallel simultaneous narratives, diary entries, self-conscious literary parody, textbook extracts, collages of reflection and exposition, dislocations of space, time, and structure. Among her earlier novels, *Them* stands out with its distinctive metafictional dimension, in the sense that it constantly reflects upon its own status as fiction and on the relationship between so-called "reality" and "fiction"; *Expensive People* employs a range of comically alienating techniques such as internal commentary, reviews,

1 See Ronald Sukenick, *The Death of the Novel and Other Stories* (New York: The Dial Press, Inc., 1969), 41, David Lodge, *The Novelist at the Crossroads* (Ithaca: Cornell University Press, 1971), ix, and Alain Robbe-Grillet, *Snapshots and Towards a New Novel*, trans. Barbara Wright (London: Calder and Boyars, 1965), 137.
2 Ihab Hassan, *Paracriticisms: Seven Speculations of the Times* (Urbana: University of Illinois Press, 1975), 56.
3 John Ditsky, "The Man on the Quaker Oats Box: Characteristics of Recent Experimental Fiction,"*Georgia Review*, XXVI (1972), 300.

fictions-within-fictions, and frequent dislocations of scene and tone. Finally, in her novels of the mid-seventies, it seems as if thematic and philosophical changes have required a more open-ended articulation, and many of the techniques tried out in the workshops of the shorter fiction have overflowed into *The Assassins* and *Childwold*.

As I have argued, obsession has always been not just part of the emotional landscape of Oates's America but the center of her stance as a fictionalist as well. The core of her aesthetic is a compulsiveness to penetrate into and evoke the drives of an America created by and acting upon personalities. *Expensive People*, in its wry, indirect way, makes something of the same point as Roth's celebrated comment:

The American writer in the middle of the 20th century has his hands full in trying to understand, and then describe, and then make *credible* much of the American reality. It stupefies, it sickens, it infuriates, and finally it is even a kind of embarrassment to one's own meager imagination. The actuality is continually outdoing our talents and the culture tosses up figures almost daily that are the envy of any novelist.[4]

Expensive People, *Them*, and many of the stories such as "The Dead" and "The Turn of the Screw" announce themselves as fiction. That is, they are not simply concerned, as Raymond Olderman puts it, with doing "what the novel has traditionally sought to do — bring some order and form to the chaos of human experience"[5]; the stories comment on the process by which fiction does (or, maybe, fails to do) this. Oates's explicitly metafictional concerns tend to comment ironically on the fictionist's assertion of control in the face of chaos. She alerts us to the disorder around and within us and points to fictions (hers and our own) as temporary and inadequate attempts to grapple with it. We are obsessed with order and find ourselves overwhelmed by chaos. Even this degree of metacriticism in Oates's fiction, then, devel-

---

4 Philip Roth, "Writing American Fiction," *Commentary*, XXXI (1961), 224.
5 Raymond M. Olderman, *Beyond the Waste Land: A Study of the American Novel in the Nineteen-Sixties* (New Haven: Yale University Press, 1972), 26.

ops out of her vision of obsession. She writes, she herself claims, "out of an interior compulsion, hoping that it will add up to an artistic statement of some worth,"[6] with all matters of form and structure being directly determined by that compulsion. Her fiction aims to make affective claims upon its readers; and plot, incident, character, and other elements of the novel are usually subordinated to the creation of that response. Rarely are her plots anything but episodic, their direction or endings determined by violent accident (such as Shar's death in *With Shuddering Fall*) or by deliberate authorial manipulation of our awareness of events (such as the gradually and painfully disclosed realization of the events at the end of *Childwold*). *The Assassins* deals with what in realistic fiction might be considered a world of shared factiveness, but the focus of each of the novel's three parts is on the subjective consciousness—sometimes overlapping, sometimes independent, sometimes contradictory—of the main characters. The result is a blurred focus and the fearful realization that material phenomena are arbitrary, their meanings ambiguous and threatening. Alfred Kazin comments, correctly enough but clearly trusting to the traditional novel's emphasis on harmonious unity and clarity of form, that Oates's fictions "are not the deeply plotted stories that we return to as perfect dramas; her novels, though they involve the reader because of the intense connection with her material, tend . . . to fade out of our minds. Too much happens . . . we miss the perfectly suggestive shapes that modern art and fiction have taught us to generate." Reviewers of the novels have frequently commented similarly on Oates's apparent indifference to form within what, especially in the earlier novels, looked like a traditional allegiance to it. Reviewing *Wonderland*, for instance, Peter S. Prescott commented irritably that "a chart of one of her novels would look like an electrocardiogram gone beserk: a plateau or two and a few longueurs scattered among a dozen or so more hor-

6 Joe David Bellamy, *The New Fiction: Interviews with Innovative American Writers* (Urbana: University of Illinois, 1974), 26.

rendous, superbly dramatic set pieces, self-contained episodes so securely crafted that they often appear elsewhere as short stories — which is not entirely salutary." Indeed Oates frequently publishes pieces which are not merely part of a novel-in-progress but seemingly discrete stories which at a later date are welded together within a novel.[7]

Of course, today, Kazin's phrase "modern art and fiction" is distinctly archaic. We have become attuned to dislocated, open-ended fictional forms in the past decade or more (even if we might want to qualify Jerome Klinkowitz' whimsical choice of the 1967/68 publishing season as the watershed); we move comfortably amongst metafictions, surfictions, postcontemporary fictions of various kinds and, as well, amongst an intensely introspective criticism of such fictions, in a variety of writers — Barth, Barthelme, Sukenick, Wurlitzer, Coover, and many others. Rarely is Oates as self-consciously experimental as these writers. Indeed, her theoretical pronouncements on contemporary fiction are either directed back to questions of artistic motivation or out to the writer's philosophical insight. She can be cuttingly critical of what she sees as the escapism of her fellow writers, as in the following:

For many years our most promising writers have lined up obediently behind Nabokov, Beckett and Borges, to file through a doorway marked THIS WAY OUT. How eagerly they have taken their places! If they glance around at the rest of us, who are holding back, they are ready with mechanized scorn: X is too bourgeois; X is too suburban; X is not experimental; X is *being read*!

She is, in fact, most perceptive about both her own and others' fiction when she is not explicitly concerned with (or, as here, defensive about) questions of form. She typically argues that fiction should give "coherence to jumbled experience" or should bring its readers to a "sense of the mystery and the sanctity of

7 Alfred Kazin, *Bright Book of Life: American Novelists and Storytellers from Hemingway to Mailer* (Boston: Little, Brown and Co., 1973), 204; Peter S. Prescott, "Everyday Monsters," *Newsweek*, October 11, 1971, p. 96.

the human predicament" or should "show us how to get through and transcend pain." When we turn to her detailed comments on work by other writers, we find the same emphases: an eager response to the affective power of a work, a subordination of form to vision, a search for the author's surprising or dislocating vision breaking through the naturalistic, a blurring of our sense of reality, and a sensitivity to recording "those brief, wondrous moments when the human seems to touch upon something bigger than or different from itself."[8] She rarely comments favorably upon formal experimentation displayed for its own sake; "the intellectual concept of unity is impossible for the artist to achieve, except at great cost to his art" (EOI, 158), she writes. Vision determines; atmosphere, mood, tone, and insight are primary.

It may be that Oates's apparent indifference to self-conscious and explicit metacritical concerns in both her criticism and her novels (with the exceptions of *Expensive People* and *Them*, which have occasionally caught the interests of postmodernist critics) obscures the great range of fictional experimentation that is, in fact, to be found in her work. It is therefore interesting to look carefully at her affinities with the concerns of other fictionists and theorists of the past decade or so. In the first place, her obsessiveness constitutes an aesthetic stance that connects her interestingly with many of the deconstructive emphases of contemporary critics, like Harold Bloom, who trace how an artist must struggle against the weight of both an inherited literary tradition and the society from which he writes. The role of the novelist, in Oates's view, is that of accepting his own insecurities and vulnerability and of conceiving writing as a resistance to both the structure of our age and the linguistic limitations which threaten to overwhelm us all. "I have come to the conclusion that all writing is a matter of psychological and even bio-

8 Walter Clemons, "Joyce Carol Oates: Love and Violence," *Newsweek*, December 11, 1972, p. 77; "Transformations of Self: An Interview with Joyce Carol Oates," *Ohio Review*, XV (1973), 53; Joyce Carol Oates, "Love Story," *Canadian Forum*, May, 1976, p. 35; Joyce Carol Oates, "Whose Side Are You On?" *New York Times Book Review*, June 4, 1972, p. 63.

logical responses" to a "demonic" experience, Oates writes frequently. Novelists are "so violently driven, so excited, that *what*
they create is not at all important to them." The novelist is "celebrating art itself, creativity itself, as it flows through" the personality.[9]

Harold Bloom has spoken of the anxiety of influence, as a
writer attempts to overcome the burden of an inherited literary
tradition. Indeed, he has mentioned Oates within his argument
as an "ambitious ephebe of Dreiser,"[10] a view of Oates's affinities which I have (I hope, successfully) dismissed. Oates may
be more fruitfully seen as feeling, instinctively and obsessively,
for appropriate vehicles of articulation provided by a great diversity of writers of both the past and the present. There is, for
instance, the closely linked group of stories in *Marriages and Infidelities* which variously imitate, extend, or parody well-known
stories by Joyce ("The Dead"), Chekhov ("The Lady with the
Pet Dog"), Kafka ("Metamorphoses"), and James ("The Turn
of the Screw"). In each case, characters are regrouped, perspectives shifted, thematic concentrations developed, or form and
tone parodied. Oates seems not merely aware of the debt or
burden a contemporary writer owes to great predecessors, but,
more importantly, of her role as an articulator of the great,
shared mystery of human sensitivity. As she puts it, discussing
the strange possession through which she claimed to present the
stories in *The Poisoned Kiss*, if we allow the possibility (and
even if we resist it) we are able to "dream about and to sense,
while awake, some other life, or vision, or personality"; it may
be the expression of a part of the personality that had been sti-
fled, but to accept the participation of the self in the complexities
of the world is both an articulation of the self and what Oates
terms "an almost impersonal function" to which the writer lays
himself open (PK, 187–89).

9 Joyce Carol Oates, "The Myth of the Isolated Artist," *Psychology Today*, VI
(May, 1973), 74; "Transformations of Self," 51.
10 Harold Bloom, *A Map of Misreading* (New York: Oxford University Press, 1975),
164.

In these stories, Oates speaks of being "possessed" by an imaginary author, one Fernandes de Briao. Although "he has no existence," she writes, without his guidance "I would not have had access to the mystical 'Portugal' of the stories" (PK, 15). We may want to express some skepticism about her account, but it does in fact point to something crucial in her approach to fiction. Possession is an explanation for the intensity — what I have called the obsessiveness — with which she experiences and is forced to articulate her vision. The stories collected in *Night-Side* show a similar fascination with the irrational invasion of the personality by alien, unpredictable forces. "Famine Country" evokes the impact of strange dreams which highlight the banality of the personality's everyday, material life and a strange, neglected area of the personality traditionally represented by religious or mystical experience. Ronnie, the central character, is invaded by two dreams: one, a "student-dream," concerned with incomprehensible examinations and buildings, the other, the terrifying, alienating "God-dream" which confronts him with a radical and unprepared-for invasion of his life. In "Further Confessions" a Portuguese nobleman (related to the persona of the Fernandes stories) is similarly disturbed by dreams and visions. Starting as a man "far more than most, *attuned* to the world," he is horrified by the intensity and alienation of his dreams — of his own death, of his father — so much that he is cut off from all his former life, and made to face the primacy of the nonhuman, "the vast indifferent spaces of the world itself — the 'world' as it exists emptied of the human and of all human values" (NS, 310, 311). These stories remind one of Borges, and while there is a genuine continuity with Oates's earlier work — violence, dream, and vision have always been means of shock or recognition in her work — it seems that, like Borges, Lawrence, and in some ways like Doris Lessing, she is pushing her work toward the mystical and prophetic, grappling with areas of experience traditionally regarded as beyond fiction making.

Her fiction is built, therefore, upon what I have termed "obsession," and its goal is akin to mystic transcendence. Once we have grasped this, then we can see how her fiction is experimental in the most radical way — by entrusting the enactment of its meaning to the reader's responsiveness. Her fiction operates by evoking the reader's own dilemmas and allegiances. "It is we ourselves" — Heidegger's words fit Oates exactly — "who are the entities analyzed." It is not only the craft of fiction making for its own sake that motivates Oates. She is not concerned with the prescriptive or self-reflexive nature of language. Her structural devices are not her fictional subject, as with Barth or Gass. It is her, and our, shared "psychic clamor" which makes her "*want* to be an artist, to make the right and well-fitting structure," to quote Kazin. We may also be able to excite the interest of fictionists who miss the technical resourcefulness of Oates's stories. Robert Scholes may be right when he argues that "fiction is about other fiction, is criticism in fact," but only if his notion of "fiction" can be extended to include all of mankind's fiction-making capacities, including his wish, ability, and failures to create private fictions of order from the flux of his ongoing life. Even Scholes recognizes the problem inherent in his argument when he confesses that "all fiction contributes to cognition . . . by providing us with models that reveal the nature of reality by their very failure to coincide with it." Oates's fictions are, usually, unself-conscious about their metafictional dimension and more explicit about their "contribution to cognition." But frequently they are built on the tension between the apparently overwhelming factitiousness of so-called real life, lived from one discrete moment to the next, and our chaotic, contradictory, but nonetheless real desire to find pattern or order in it. In that sense she is as "public" a writer as Saul Bellow, and her overall quest is, as Hassan comments on Bellow, how man may "survive as a creature fully possessed of his humanity . . . in a tangled world."[11]

11 Kazin, *Bright Book of Life*, 203; Heidegger, *Being and Time*, 67; Robert Scholes, *Structural Fabulations* (Notre Dame: University of Notre Dame Press, 1975), 1; Ihab Hassan, *Contemporary American Literature 1945–1972* (New York: Frederick Ungar, 1973), 25.

Nevertheless, if we look carefully at Oates's work we can see how the articulation of her vision has consistently called for a variety of forms and techniques, some of which are interestingly antimimetic. Her early stories are, predictably in a young writer, carefully crafted accounts of incident and character. They grow out of the same fictional concerns that interested the major writers of the fifties and early sixties—O'Connor, Bellow, Roth, Updike—where the effects of realism are highlighted by insistent thematic concerns—the search for identity, the threat of psychic and social entropy, and failure of communication. Mythical and anthropological parallels are continually used to penetrate the surface of society. Memories, especially of childhood, provide ways of exploring the pain or surprise of individuality in a restricted or deterministic environment in *By the North Gate* and *Upon the Sweeping Flood*. A child's fantasies will enable us to sense the passions of a struggle for identity; family tensions show us a consciousness of guilt or failure in individual, social, or communal life. Similar concerns with the determinism of sexual, family, or communal life are prominent in *With Shuddering Fall* and *A Garden of Earthly Delights*, and both novels are reminiscent of Flannery O'Connor in the way a traditional fidelity to accuracy of setting and character is displaced by shifting viewpoints, upsurges of random violence, and elaborate mythical parallels. Her most insistent technique is the use of unexpected violence, to create the feeling of tensions forcing their way through the surface of life from sources deep in the psyche. Even the most commonplace actions may be heightened by violence. Music explodes, glass shatters, irreal characters burst through the commonplace. Oates herself has often expressed her admiration for O'Connor who, she has said, celebrates the "fact of mystery" and reveals "a transcendental world of absolute value beyond the cheap, flashy wasteland of modern America."[12] But the world beyond the wasteland that Oates's

12 "Ritual and Violence in Flannery O'Connor," *Thought*, XLI (1966), 547.

early fiction opens up is one of primitive psychic struggle rather than a transcendental or religious realm. An apparently solid and immediate world is heightened to reflect the torments and tensions of the human drama enacted in it and so intensify the affective manipulation of the reader.

These early stories and novels contain a great deal that is typical of the early sixties. Raymond Olderman's depiction of the age's fictional expectations is relevant when he speaks of "the explosion of the ordinary by the fabulous; the protagonist's sense of helplessness even as he proceeds to a confrontation; the mystery of some *They* who have an irrational hold on things," and, above all, "the movement away from the realistic novel toward a contemporary version of romance."[13] Oates's early fiction is clearly in the dominant American fictional tradition of romance, derived from Hawthorne and beyond, with European analogies in Stendhal, Dostoevsky, and Lawrence. It insists predominantly upon atmosphere and action, and upon a constant use of allegorical, mythical, and symbolic devices to point the reader beyond the surface action. When we turn to the novels and stories of the late sixties through about 1977 — especially the stories collected in *The Wheel of Love* and *Marriages and Infidelities*, along with *Expensive People* and *Wonderland* — a significant increase in fictional sophistication can be observed. We may survey Oates's employment of the mechanics of traditional fiction — plot, character, and setting — and, although we can see her work within the same hospitable romance or gothic modes, an increasing amount of the fiction of this period is formally open-ended and elusive. "How I Contemplated the World from the Detroit House of Correction and Began My Life Over Again," for instance, uses the form of a delinquent high school student's composition as the outline of a story of a child's attempt to find order in her constantly metamorphosing world. The story is subtitled "Notes for an essay for an English class at Baldwin Coun-

13 Olderman, *Beyond the Wasteland*, 5.

try Day School; poking around in debris; disgust and curiosity; a revelation of the meaning of life; a happy ending" (WOL, 170). A neatly juxtaposed mixture of expectation and randomness within the framework of the essay, the story occurs in twelve disconnected fragments, each with its own heading, and subsections under each head. The headings are: I Events; II Characters; III World Events; IV People and Circumstances Contributing to This Delinquency; V Sioux Drive; VI Detroit; VII Events; VIII Characters; IX That Night; X Detroit; XI Characters We Are Forever Entwined With; XII Events. The list is a juxtaposition of essay notes with fantasy and memory. It would be possible to rearrange the story chronologically and retell it mimetically but the dislocatory perspective provided by the reclaimed delinquent girl sitting in her pink room in Bloomfield Hills, Detroit, and making notes for her composition while she fantasizes, remembers, and is simply aware of her recent traumas as a shoplifter, prostitute, and delinquent, is far more effective — and also draws our attention to the metafictional dimension of the story. The divisions of the essay dealing with the world outside the girl's repetitive and disjointed consciousness have virtually no content. Sections III and IV, divisions imposed obligatorily upon her by her teacher and, presumably, the police, have the one word, "Nothing." The "events" she records in a jumbled, dispersive fashion contain the essence of what she has gone through; the "characters" merge in and out of each other, their identities shifting constantly; the settings (affluent Bloomfield Hills, chaotic and dirty downtown Detroit) never seem to inhabit the same planet. The girl's memory focuses on these parts of the traditional well-made essay (or story, or novel) but there are only arbitrary connections between them. Oates forces us into providing what order we can in the story. Like the girl's parents, teacher, or the police, we get snatches of disorganized impressions, gaps in the story, refusals to provide information, and general incoherence.

As well, Oates is manipulating our response to the intensity

of the girl's situation by image and tonal changes. Bloomfield
Hills has "many mild pale lights," its streets are "slow," its po-
licemen "quiet," its automobiles "heavy . . . big . . . long and
black" (WOL, 176, 173). Detroit, by contrast, is "falling out the
bottom . . . . breaking up into dangerous bits of newspaper and
dirt" (WOL, 179). In Bloomfield Hills all is calm; "the weather
vanes, had they weather vanes, don't have to turn with the wind,
don't have to contend with the weather. There is no weather."
In Detroit, the "temperature is always 32°. Fast-falling temperatures. Slow-rising temperatures. . . . Negro gangs, restless cloud
formations, restless temperatures aching to fall out the very bottom of the thermometer or shoot up over the top and boil everything over in red mercury" (WOL, 176–77). Other devices rein-
force the dislocated subjectivity of the story. In her brooding, the
girl recalls the junkie who seduced and prostituted her. "Would
I lie down with him in all that filth and craziness? Over and over
again." Then immediately a one-inch space occurs on the page,
and without the conventional upper-case letter, a random sentence shoots into our consciousness as she is reminded of being
exploited, like Clarita, the prostitute–surrogate mother of the
street: "a Clarita is being betrayed as in front of a Cunningham
Drug Store she is nervously eying a colored man who may or
may not have money" (WOL, 181). Randomness, irreconcilable
juxtapositions, collages, a shifting sense of narrative self all are
used to show up the girl's unwillingness or inability to order her
experience. Sometimes events are described in schoolgirl jargon;
at other times the diction becomes harsh, evocative, and ejaculative.

   Philip Stevick has suggested that the ending of the story is uneasily ambivalent. The girl returns home, it seems, glad to be
back, and Stevick asks: "Having been encouraged to feel the narrator's scorn for the shallow opulence of her suburban world,
shall we now understand the ending as a symbolic statement of
reconciliation to the cashmere and chrome of Bloomfield Hills?"
He suggests that the girl has learned, "with difficulty, that com-

fort is better than pain, civility is better than rudeness, health is better than illness, warmth is better than cold, soft is better than hard, clean is better than dirty." [14] Maybe so; but the dislocating form of the story as we read it, rather than the way we might piece it together, rather encourages us to regard the girl's "happy ending" as a dutiful and desperate attempt to organize and order the randomness of experiences which defy such an easy solution. The story's impact comes from its chaos, not its pathetic attempts at order, from the image of destruction ripping through our flimsy attempts to construct a comforting pattern to our lives. In Bloomfield Hills, "heavy weighs the gold on the back of her hairbrush and hand mirror. Heavy heavy the candlesticks in the dining room. Very heavy is the big car, a Lincoln, long and black, that on one cool autumn day split a squirrel's body in two unequal parts" (WOL, 173).

I am giving such examples of Oates's variety of fictional techniques to show something of her affinities with contemporary experimentalists. But, of course—and this is a matter the more iconoclastic metafictional theorists of our time sometimes overlook—such open-endedness in fiction is a traditional part of the development of fiction. To stress the point, and to connect with my earlier argument, it is instructive to place Oates's fictional mode alongside, once again, Lawrence's. When we once again consider the traditional verities of setting and character, we see how Lawrence's search for a significant medium grows out of his obsessive vision, and the same is true, I am arguing, for Oates.

Both Lawrence and Oates, for instance, are only superficially novelists of place and landscape. "Landscape," wrote Lawrence, is "*meant* as a background to an intenser vision of life." [15] So Oates's Detroit in "How I Contemplated . . . ," like her Eden County or her California, like Lawrence's Derbyshire or Swiss

14 Philip Stevick, "Remembering, Knowing, and Telling in Joyce Carol Oates," in Barbara MacKenzie (ed.), *The Process of Fiction* (New York: Harcourt, Brace, Jovanovich, 1974), 496–97.
15 D. H. Lawrence, *A Propos of Lady Chatterley's Lover and Other Essays* (Harmondsworth: Penguin, 1961), 26.

Alps, exist not as settings in their own right but are created through the leaps of lyrical, passionate feeling with which they are experienced by the characters and the reader. Throughout Oates's fiction, details of setting are habitually chosen for their associations of feeling. In "Ruth," from *The Goddess and Other Women*, the incipient violence within a decaying marriage is evoked by the deceptively realistic opening description:

Across the road a field sloped abruptly to a great mile long swamp; it was overlaid with scum and gray, cobweb-like moss that hung dispiritedly from trees that were dying or already dead. At one time there had been a woods there, mainly oaks and elms, but construction of a new highway to the north had somehow blocked off its drainage — a process so utterly mysterious that it could not be explained to people in the area — and out of nowhere a rich, thick scum had risen, slowly, and for some inexplicable reason the trees had begun to die, dying from the inside, choked. A few were still living; most were trunks from which bark had fallen, as if peeled by hand. At night a vapor hung over the swamp and thousands of insects and frogs sang — in a way, it did seem alive. During the day it appeared sullen, ugly, dead, as if its secret life had retreated beneath the gray scum and could wait. (GOW, 81 – 82)

The concentration of natural surroundings — the original wood, the swamp, the dying trees mysteriously connected with the highway — not only set a mood, they provide the reader with an initial emblem, a moral focus for developments later in the story. Similarly, although evoked tactilely, at times almost photographically, Oates's Detroit in *Them* particularly possesses the vivid significance of an X ray rather than the gaudy realism of a Kodakchrome print. In a not dissimilar way, Lawrence's Derbyshire in *The Rainbow* or his Australia in *Kangaroo* are imbued with the spirit, not the pictorial details of place. "Every continent," he wrote, "has its own great spirit of place . . . a great reality . . . a wonderful terrestrial magnetism or polarity of its own." [16]

Oates's vision of places like Detroit similarly arises from her concern with the city as symbol. She is obsessed not merely by

16 D. H. Lawrence, *Studies in Classical American Literature* (London: Heineman, 1924), 17.

the social profusion of America, but by the ways eddying, brooding currents of feeling tie our society together, and her fiction evokes the city as a revelation of psychological rather than social realism. Here again she is very unlike Dreiser and the naturalistic tradition. The sense of victimization, the rootless bewilderment and paucity of relationships are all rooted in the psyche, and they emerge in our involuntary movements, or cryptic, frustrated ejaculations of command or insult. Likewise, the autonomy or transcendence that may liberate us in the city is possible only from within ourselves. Detroit is everywhere. We cannot escape its pressure upon us, but we may transcend it through the resources we discover within our inner lives.

Predictably enough, a recurrent and emotionally reverberating symbol in Oates's America is the automobile. Dreaming America, we extend our gesturing hands to the unconquered land and find ourselves tormented by frustration, as described in the poem "American Expressway":

5:30
Detroit empties out
men's knuckles close with love
        on their steady steering wheels
traffic rises familiar and conversational
seams in the roadway are melting.

the pulse of the dance is discernible
in the lower backbone
the speedometer needle rises
        and pauses
and rises white and firm again
the breaths of engines are humid

tonight the expressway will be relived in sleep
in the sleep of its constant drives
relived with the repetition of love.   (LD, 41)

Does the jarring of the psyche echo the "pulse of the dance" on the expressway outside? Or are the two mutually interdependent expressions of the same internal dynamic? Speed, mobility, the choice of highway routes or of brands of gas — the spiritual detritus of American postindustrial affluence — are all heightened and transfigured in Oates's fiction, and thus made to become revelatory of a spiritual state. Sometimes the glittering material surface of our civilization becomes symbolic of our attempts to transcend the material by a more intense slavery to it; at other times it evokes a sense of limitless excitement and spiritual autonomy.

Highways, for instance, open up space, "leading off to Mars or the moon, unhurried." They become symbolic of man's struggle with nature and his own limitations:

And there are animals, the designs of animals, mashed into the highways! The shape of a dog, a dog's pelty shadow, mashed into the hot, hot road — in mid-flight, so to speak, mid-leap, run over again and again by big trucks and retired people seeing America .... protoplasm being drawn off into space, out there, out in the West, with no human limits to keep it safe. (WOL, 56)

This description, from one of Oates's most suggestive stories, "Unmailed, Unwritten Letters," is a quintessential passage in her evocation of America. It evokes the symbolic struggle not just between man and nature but within man himself. It conveys in surging obsessive prose rhythms both the adventure and the near-hysteria of the struggle for identity in America. Many of Oates's stories are dominated by such freeways sweeping endlessly across America. A freeway perhaps does not have the deterministic circles and threatening walls of a racing track, like those in *With Shuddering Fall*, but nonetheless it embodies the same extremity of idealistic striving and brutal determinism. The very term "freeway" is, of course, both mythic and heavily ironic. Lewis Mumford comments upon "the most compulsive and tension-producing avenues of locomotion, our 'freeways'" and upon how we "boast of the freedom"[17] of compulsively driving at sixty miles an hour upon the pulsing, deterministic

17 Lewis Mumford, *The Urban Prospect* (London: Secher & Warburg, 1968), 9.

ribbons of interwoven highway, hundreds and thousands of miles of limitation, compulsion, threat, and tension. Ironically, the freeway is as compulsive as the racetrack. But as with the city itself, Oates uses the automobile and the freeway not as symbols of the social oppression of America but to reveal the complexity of our inner drives, our determinism and dreams. A journey may be a quest for transfiguration or it may end in death; its essence is movement and risk. Like life itself, it may be planned for but never understood in advance. Thus the automobile and the highway become symbols of our inner restlessness and indecision — and our possibilities. The drivers in "American Expressway" are living out a ritualistic pattern of urgency, power, and choice. The pattern may be momentarily shattered, exploded by a wreck, by "oil and gas and blood" seeping over the pavement, but it inexorably reassembles itself, nobly reconstituting the dream, intermingling the mechanical, sinister freeway with the human:

vessels gleaming and solid in a dream
unhurrying at seventy miles an hour
at 5:32 PM
the column reassembles itself like a backbone
of detachable vertebrae   (LD, 43)

As with setting, so with character. Lawrence's famous letter to Edward Garnett outlines a view of character which has been strikingly influential in subsequent fiction and psychology, and it is, I suggest, as helpful a key to many of Oates's characters as the American romance-gothic tradition into which she more obviously fits. "You mustn't," he wrote, "look in my novel for the old stable *ego* of the character. There is another *ego*, according to whose action the individual is unrecognizable, and passes through, as it were, allotropic states which it needs a deeper sense than any we've been used to exercise to discover are states of the same single radically unchanged elements." We respond to his characters, in their violent, rhythmical lyricism, as states of feeling, as vivid, personified intuitions of human potential, attracting or repulsing other centers of feeling (including the reader's). The very concept of a fixed self was for Lawrence a disastrously over-conscious conception of being, not only in fiction but in life, a solidification of experience that ignores the risk and chaos in the personality.[18] Oates comments on Lawrence that "it is the 'pulsating, carnal self' he wants to isolate, not the rational self, activity of the personality-bound ego he came to call the 'self-apart-from-god'" (NHNE, 53). In a similar way, and despite her careful attention to surface detail, to the social trivia of the farm, city, hospital, or university, Oates concentrates on the moving, shifting surges of the personality that not only respond to but create their surroundings. Her most significant characters curiously combine, in the way romance characters do, heightened cliché and symbolic vividness that resound back upon their surrounding world — and then out to the reader's own world. The horrendous Dr. Pedersen in *Wonderland*, the dead Andrew Petrie in *The Assassins*, the ambitious Clara in *A Garden of Earthly Delights* are all evoked as centers of passionate consciousness, not depicted in the clear objectivity of the "stable ego" of personality. We fix on insignificant objects or incidents and project our inner urges upon them. Thus, minor details of setting, incident, or surroundings are heightened by and are reflections of the personality's obsessive subjectivity. The heroine of "Extraordinary Popular Delusions" panics when she discovers loose hairs on herself after taking a shower; the woman in "Unmailed, Unwritten Letters" takes up a can lying in the street and intently presses its sharp edges against her skin. Tiny details of life suddenly, terrifyingly seize upon us and become obsessions.

Something further of the characteristic tone of Oates's approach to her characters may be sensed in a comment on Shakespeare's *Troilus and Cressida*. She suggests in passing that it is "the limitations and obsessions of humanity" which "define the real tragedy of this play." *Limitation* and *obsession* are, as we

18 D. H. Lawrence, *Collected Letters*, ed. Harry T. Moore (New York: Viking Press, 1962), I, 282.

have repeatedly seen, two key, linked terms in Oates's world. Her characters are seized upon by obscurely motivated, inexplicable urges which frequently erupt obsessively, turning apparently solid reality into something else, forcing us tragically to confront our limits and battle unsuccessfully to transcend them. *Obsession* is a word Oates constantly applies to her characters and subjects, from Maureen Wendall, who as a "terrible obsession with her personal history" (T, 5), to Shakespeare who is depicted as "obsessed" with certain ideas in writing his tragedies (EOI, 18, 35, 36). Oates's art itself is a form of obsession. She speaks of her addiction to recurring psychological situations. "At times," she says, "my head seems crowded; there is a kind of pressure inside it, almost a frightening physical sense of confusion, fullness, dizziness." Discussing her writing habits, she will speak of being "in a state of spiritual exhaustion" after completing a novel, and of the relief that everyday trivia "keeps us from spinning completely off into the dark, into the abstract universe" — occasions when the world of placid fact dissolves and questions too fearful to face are thrust at us.[19]

One effective manifestation of obsession is found in another story from *The Wheel of Love*. "What is the Connection Between Men and Women?" is organized by a series of questions containing such obsessive self-revelations. "How does it feel to lie awake all night?" is juxtaposed with the strange sense of the speaker's body as obsessively and deterministically out of control. "How does it feel to be waiting for a man?" "What does a woman feel while a man makes love to her?" Feelings, fears, thoughts swirl around, astonishing, shocking, dredging up her husband's death, her frustrations, her past, her fearful separateness from her actual and possible experiences, the fear of sexual awakening:

What are the things a woman might do?
    All things.
How does it feel to be a woman?

19 "Transformations of Self," 53; Bellamy, *The New Fiction*, 26, 27, 30.

Passing through a crowd of men a woman feels something stab in her, in her loins. A fever, a heat like a knife. She makes her way through the mysterious flow of time, as if swimming, as if pressing herself forward into the wind, angry and impatient and frightened. She feels a desire that is not for one man but for a crowd of men, their faces impersonal and threatening; she puts out her hand accidentally and seizes someone's arm, her fingers closing hard around the wrist.

In love there are two things: bodies and words. The words go along with certain bodies, sometimes the names of those bodies, their "names," and sometimes the words those bodies exclaim. (WOL, 436)

This mixture of memory, question, and commentary builds up with extraordinary intensity the dislocated, disorganized sensibility of obsession.

Because Oates's characters tend to exist as the foci of such obsessions, not as case histories of social or political development, they are frequently depicted in stereotypical form. Elena, the heroine of *Do With Me What You Will*, is presented to the reader (who may at first be puzzled or irritated by her explicit conventionality) in terms of heightened beauty and sensual passivity; her role is less that of a heroine than a figure in an allegory of the conflicting demands of love. As a "character" in the traditional sense, she barely exists; as the embodiment of dreams, urges, aspirations present in the American psyche, she is tantalizing, vivid, and emotionally rich. Oates has written that "'characters' really dictate themselves to me. I am not free of them, really, and I can't force them into situations they haven't themselves willed. They have the autonomy of characters in a dream. . . . I am really transcribing dreams, giving them a certain civilised, extended shape." Jesse Vogel, Elena, Jules (in *Them* and a number of later stories) also exist as symbolic projections of their author's insight, not as conventional characters, despite their seemingly recognizably factual surroundings. Many of Oates's reviewers (still, sixty years after Lawrence's remarks!) irritably miss the "stable ego" of character. "In any great novel," he wrote, "who is the hero all the time? Not any of the characters, but some unnamed and nameless flame behind them all. . . . In the great novel, the felt but unknown flame stands behind all the characters, and in their words and gestures there is a flicker of the presence."[20]

The middle period of Oates's work, approximately 1966–1970, then, shows a much greater range of fictional modes and techniques than her earlier period; her fiction since 1970 has shown a similar diversity. Following the publication of *Wonderland*, it will be recalled, Oates spoke and wrote of her changing conception of her own role as a novelist and we might ask whether the increasingly prophetic stance she has adopted is reflected in the formal characteristics of her work. John Gardner has commented, as a fellow novelist, on the change he has observed in Oates. "She's thirty-five," he noted, speaking in 1973, "she's gotten the National Book Award, she's published novel after novel, millions of stories — but it was always the same Joyce Carol Oates. In her fiction the world seemed terrifying; she dealt with this feeling by recording it and eliciting sympathy. Suddenly she has flown up above that world and has begun to look at it from very high up. She sees more beauty, more compassion among characters, and she's turning quasi-mystical. Joyce is a model of the writer who is finding a different attitude, a more heroic and responsible approach."[21] Gardner's emphasis on "heroism" and "responsibility" perhaps reflects more on his own fictional concerns than Oates's, but his remarks do reflect on the change in her work. She has become fascinated by the ways the personality may be invaded by mysterious and unpredictable moments of vision, insight or inspiration, and with the dislocations such invasions cause in the texture of so-called everyday life. Many of the stories published since *Wonderland* hark back to earlier modes: many are wry social satires, often set in universities; but more frequently, she has concentrated on experiences of dislocation and irrationality — and the fictional mode she chooses becomes appropriately dislocated and open ended.

20 Bellamy, *The New Fiction*, 30; W. Y. Tindall (ed.), *The Later D. H. Lawrence* (New York: Knopf, 1952), 193.
21 Bellamy, *The New Fiction*, 183–84.

The Triumph of the Spider Monkey (1976) is an instance of
the increasing experimentation of her recent work. It purports
to be an account, in part confessional, of a maniac killer, Bobbie
Gotteson, who seems reminiscent of, say, Charles Manson or
the vivid Perry Smith as evoked by Truman Capote. It takes the
form of a mixture of narrative, poetry, diary entries, speeches,
fragments, dialogue, interview, authorial comments and footnotes, and newspaper headlines. There is a radical contrast main-
tained between the objective dismissive explanations of the madman's violence and criminality and Gotteson's own analysis,
which is savage, amoral, and desperate. His insanity is a multiplicity of survival techniques, "forms of sanity that keep moving
and eluding definition." The acts and articulations which society regards as "the graphic workings of a sick mind" are radical
challenges to the cloying, material, stereotyped judgments of
that society. "Love," Bobbie broods, "does us all in. . . . We fal-
ter, stumble, stoop over, steal fire . . . and are punished, mocked,
picked to death by tiny painted nails, ooooh'd and aaaah'd over
by tiny button-like lips" (TSM, 16, 34, 47). His rapes, muggings
and brutal killings are nonetheless fearful assertions of self. Like
the experiences of Jules in *Them*, "passion and its necessary violence" (EOI, 139) becomes a route to transcendence — and Oates's
rendition of Gotteson's violence is calculated to evoke a sense of
threat, confusion, and revulsion on her reader's part. The dark
violence of the psyche represented by Bobbie Gotteson is embodied in a self-mocking attempt at ordered presentation of what
is essentially fragmented and inexplicable.

Even though Oates's work in the seventies shows more experimentation, her choice of form continues to be determined by the
material of the story; she is not interested, it seems, in simply
playing with fictional forms. She once criticized Donald Barthelme for his reliance on fragments, quoting a remark in one of
his stories, that "fragments are the only forms I trust."[22] It is
therefore ironic, and perhaps heartening, to see the skill with

22 Joyce Carol Oates, "Whose Side Are You On?" *New York Times Book Review*,
June 4, 1972, p. 63.

which she too can employ fragmentary, open-ended fictions even if she uses fragments without the playful panache of Barthelme or Sukenick. Her last two novels, *The Assassins* and *Childwold*, show just how she has developed in her longer fictions. *Childwold*, in particular, presents us with a polyphony of dislocated epiphanies — scraps of dialogue, isolated memories, written and unwritten fantasies, long naturalistic scenes, few (and sometimes no) transitions, ritual chants, diary entries, quotations from philosophers, snatches of action, long Faulknerian sentences, blocks of space, disjointed paragraphs. Paradoxically, behind the randomness of the novel's surface story is not only an impressive intensification of conflict and self-discovery but a deeply pessimistic story of moral consequence and fearful accident. Rather than producing an atmosphere of cosmic randomness, the formal incertitude of the novel reinforces Oates's grimly coherent vision. The spaces, dislocations, and frayed ends of her fiction invariably point to the apocalyptic state of contemporary America. There are inevitably echoes of her earlier novels — Laney and her brother Vale recall Maureen and Jules Wendall, while Kasch is another brooding intellectual like Jesse Vogel and Hugh Petrie — but her technical control and experimentation and control are startling. Probably never before has Oates handled such a difficult fictional form so effectively, especially the transition she achieves at the novel's end, as an apparent, if complex, order dissolves into chaos and randomness.

Surveying Oates's development, then, from her first stories published in the early sixties through her work in the late seventies, we may observe quite clearly an increased confidence and a much wider range of formal techniques. There is, however, something more important. Oates has searched, often repetitively and restlessly, for forms which will be appropriate vehicles of her vision. The world around us appears material and trustworthy, rational and comprehendable — and she sees our salvation as lying in the gaps between the material things and the rational thoughts of our world. Dislocation, fragments, and evocative incoherence may be the way her vision is articulated, but in a sense, her vision chooses her. As Norman O. Brown commented, "our real choice is between holy and unholy madness: open your eyes and look around you — madness is in the saddle anyhow."[23] Whereas we cannot see Oates in the forefront of the explorers of the postmodernist terrain, her recent work especially shows her capable of leading bivouacs over the most difficult areas of that terrain. When we pick up a new Oates story now, we may expect anything, modernist order or postmodern open-endedness, naturalistic surface or shifting subjectivity, well-crafted incidents or dislocating fantasy. And as we survey her novels, in their historical development, we can see both the unfolding unity of her vision and the growth in her skills as a fictionists. It is to the elucidation of the novels, as her career has taken shape since the early 1960s, that I shall now turn.

23 Norman O. Brown, "Apocalypse," *Harper's*, May, 1961, p. 47.

FOUR

With Shuddering Fall, A Garden of Earthly Delights

R EVIEWERS of Oates's earliest novels, *With Shuddering Fall* (1964) and *A Garden of Earthly Delights* (1966), felt vaguely about for affinities with Dreiser, Faulkner, or Willa Cather. Dreiser's remark in *The Financier* that "we suffer for our temperaments, which we did not make, and for our weaknesses and lacks, which are no part of our willing or doing"[1] might seem to lead straight to her heroines' continual struggles for their survival in repressive social surroundings, while the maze of streets, hotels, railroads, restaurants, and tenements of Dreiser's Chicago have certain affinities with the carefully accumulated details of Oates's Cherry River or (in later novels) Detroit. Reviewers also pounced upon her intently academic

1 Theodore Dreiser, *The Financier* (Cleveland: World Publishing, 1940), 271.

research into the world of automobile racing in *With Shudder-ing Fall*: all the details were, she let slip, drawn from *Hotrod Magazine*. The novel thus seemed clearly within the tradition of literary realism, and it was treated as an impressive, if some-what old-fashioned, melodramatic thriller. Certainly, parts of the novel are reminiscent of the literary thrillers of Capote or Dwight Macdonald. But what reviewers did not notice was how Oates's obsession with realistic detail was held together by a pe-culiar atmosphere that, however timidly in these earlier novels, was pointing her fictional mode beyond the bounds of realism. Looking back from her later work, we can also see how even the stories that predate *With Shuddering Fall*, and first collected in *By the North Gate* (1963) were similarly concerned with evoking underlying currents of subjectivity, not mere detailed descrip-tions of place, event, and story. As it developed, the characteristic atmosphere of Oates's fiction became dominated by her desire to reach the feelings that underlie and link together the details of the given, factitious world. Hence, even in the early fiction, the label of realism does not stick. The America for which Oates was searching was not that of Dreiser or Howells, but far more akin to that of Hawthorne or Fitzgerald or O'Connor. The cabins, swamps, canals, and rural poverty of Eden County, the gloomy hills and the land, all reflect the emotional poverty and psycho-logical confusions of her characters, and attempt, however fit-fully, to set up reverberations of discomfort and alienation in her readers. Eden County — the setting of these stories and much of the action of both the early novels — has probable affinities with Oates's own early life in Erie County, New York, and re-flects her familiarity with the countryside around Lockport (where some of the action of *Wonderland* is set) or Buffalo and Rochester (the setting of parts of *The Assassins*). But no less than William Gass's Indiana (the heart of the heart of the coun-try), Oates's Eden County is (perhaps a little obviously in the early stories and novels) mythic; its main town, Tintern, is clearly a reference to Wordsworth's world of innocent, unself-conscious pleasure, its details carefully chosen to evoke the brutality, violence, or struggle not so much in its streets but at the heart of the characters' lives. As Karen and her father walk towards the crude cabin where a man lies dying, what Oates thrusts at us are details of place which convey the pent-up fear, the inculcated desire to repress feelings that threaten the girl's insubstantial self. In the melting creek where "the ice was broken away an inch at a time," she senses the sinister "thick muddy water" churning "with uprooted bushes, propelling sticks and trunks and parts of boats before it." She recalls a few weeks earlier when she was walking on the ice. Now "the creek had changed entirely — it looked luring and sinister, and the rapids gurgled as if they gloated over its violent metamorphosis" (WSF, 16–17). It is as if entropy is the most complete and fulfilling human state and only violent change or challenge can disturb the suffering psyche of the men and women caught in a sinister process of disintegration.

It is easy to see how, considered in isolation from Oates's other fiction, such descriptions could be related to the tradition of fictional realism. But increasingly, even in this first novel, Oates bombards the reader with detail, not merely for picturesque or local color effect but to convey meaning and evoke feeling. Her descriptions are rarely just for background: the details of the scene are at once clearly outlined and redolent of symbolic significance. A pattern of meaning is translated into visual images, and at moments of psychological crisis a gothic strain of parable or allegory, or a surge of powerful, ugly, or disruptive feeling will erupt through the detail of place or action. In other words, it is the emotional landscape — an interiorized Eden County — which constitutes the real setting of the novels. John Ditsky's remarks on her later work, where the figurative or parabolic sense is further intensified and certainly more obvious, are true even of this early fiction. She is, he writes, "superficially similar to realistic fiction, yet tonally aligned with the experimentalists."[2] The experimental affinities are muted in her early novels, but the

2 John Ditsky, "The Man on the Quaker Oats Box: Characteristics of Recent Experimental Fiction," *Georgia Review*, XXVI (1972), 300.

drive towards what she calls "transparency" is present from the start. The symbolic structures of *Wonderland* or *Do With Me What You Will* are here less formally and richly developed; the symbolism may be fitful or mechanical, but the book's tone points towards her intention. Essentially, the Oates of *With Shuddering Fall* is one with the Oates of *The Assassins* and *Childwold*.

II

Written while Oates was still a student, *With Shuddering Fall* is a powerful, if never fully realized work. Like Lawrence's *The Trespasser*, it simplifies or never fully develops themes that later fiction expands in a more relaxed, detailed, and suggestive fashion. Its relative immaturity can be demonstrated in a number of ways. The symbolic structure is desultory; the book's crises are occasionally weakened by a melodramatic reliance on violence either unrelated or else too obviously related to the book's on-going meaning. What saves the novel from being merely an exercise in melodrama is what it promises — a mode of fiction designed to break down the reader's passivity. Oates is moving towards an evocation of obsession in the reader, relying on emotions of fear, anxiety, insecurity, and threat to convey an impression of the doomed struggle towards self-understanding in the emotional wasteland of contemporary America.

A fully expressed fiction of transcendence through obsession never really develops in *With Shuddering Fall*. But we should nevertheless note the careful way Oates tries to move beneath the setting to reveal intense emotional currents. The book is structured precisely, with two contrasting emotional worlds represented by a dual setting. The frozen land, featureless sky, and the low hills of Eden County reflect the limiting frustration and incipient violence of a world of sour innocence, sexual and social expression, guilt, and death. A little reminiscent of the back-country settings of Faulkner and O'Connor, Eden County is nevertheless clearly meant as a psychological landscape. It is ordered, patriarchal, and repressive. In its apparent pastoral simplicity it contrasts with urban noise and heat, and the confrontations of metal and men of the other world of motor racing. The atmosphere of Synerdale and Cherry River is that of noise, chaos, the violent disintegration of order. Away from the protective repression of Eden County, we confront another world of greater freedom of action, but one that represents an equal deterministic and destructive threat to self-discovery and fulfillment. If the central symbol of Eden County is Karen's stern and repressive father, the world of racing is presided over by the obese entrepreneur Max, whose wealth and sleazy voyeurism reflect the personal conflicts and relationships around him. Where the country is slow and frustrating, the cities are continually threatening to erupt into murder or riot; the collapsing stands, racial violence, prostitution, and murder of Shar's world show it to be equally threatening. The ritual of the automobile race is a counterbalance to the religious ritual of Karen's childhood home: it is a mock communion, involving sacrifice, vicarious participation, risk.

Using this simple, melodramatic contrast, Oates concentrates on a struggle for survival, mastery, and autonomy between her two central characters, Shar and Karen. She focuses on them through a concentrated series of brief, violent scenes characterized by a heightened repetition of physical detail so concentrated as to take its emotional effects beyond the story's realistic bounds. In intention, *With Shuddering Fall* is an exploration, not of motor racing, urban violence, or rural prejudice but of the emotional landscape which these settings body forth.

The mythic intention of the book is set by the title. The "shuddering fall" carries an obvious theological suggestion. Oates herself has spoken of the place of religion in the novel. "I think of religion as a kind of psychological manifestation of deep powers, deep imaginative mysterious powers which are always with us. And what has been in the past called supernatural, I would prefer simply to call natural. However, though these things are natural, they are still inaccessible and cannot be understood, cannot be controlled." Her remarks are especially interesting as they were made some five years after the novel and look as much forward to later novels like *The Assassins* as back to *With Shuddering Fall*. It is debatable whether her concern with the inaccessible and uncontrollable forces in nature is evoked successfully in this first novel, but its outline is clear enough. Karen leaves her childhood home in Eden County for the corrupt, brutal outside world and returns; she seems to undergo a moral fall from innocence into the complexities of adulthood. She vaguely senses that the ugly events which precipitated her departure were somehow caused by her "violating her role" and that "the rejection of her child's bed would lead, after a series of insane, vivid scenes, to the picture of her father lying in the cold mud, bleeding, staring up at her" (wsf, 78). But more to Oates's point, Karen's fall is one from the level of dream to material reality — and a final return to a tragically narrowed world of escapist dream from which she seems unlikely to emancipate herself. Oates has also commented on this more narrowly religious level of the novel with some effect. She speaks of "working out of the religious phase" of her own life, and points to the mysterious pattern in the novel as a reenactment of a biblical pattern, "where the father was the father of the Old Testament who gives a command as God gave a command to Abraham and . . . how we obey it or not obey it."[3] Karen experiences a tragic distortion of Blake's insistence that the redeemed soul — we might say the fulfilled personality — moves from innocence through experience to a final reconciled state of mature innocence. For Karen, both her desperate grasping at maturity and her final capitulation to her family, church, and childhood are movements not toward a more complex maturity but toward repression and death. Never as explicit about her ideals as Flaubert's Emma Bovary, Karen

3 Linda Kuehl, "An Interview with Joyce Carol Oates," *Commonweal*, December 5, 1969, p. 308. A stimulating reading of the novel from a ritualistic-mythopoeic viewpoint can be found in Alice C. Martin, "Toward a Higher Consciousness: A Study of the Novels of Joyce Carol Oates" (Ph.D. dissertation, Northern Illinois University, 1974), Chap. 2.

nevertheless similarly looks for excitement and power within a wider reality than that of her family, and yet cannot escape its repressive determinism. Even at the start of her attempted emancipation, she feels that her father was right "to judge her, to find her guilty! She understood his judgment and accepted it" (WSF, 78). Her self-preserving escape after Shar's death, a miscarriage and madness, the return to her father, the church, the family home and the traditional pattern of repentance, self-sacrifice, and familial obedience from which she had originally fled is a grimly pessimistic conclusion to what is a basic pattern of Oates's work — the obsessive striving of a character to transcend the limitations of American reality and the despair when the dream collapses in the bitterness of disintegration. Most of Oates's characters hurl themselves frantically against their limitations in the way Karen does; their lives are tangled, despairing battles for survival against entrapment and threat. *With Shuddering Fall* therefore sets out a clear and repeatable pattern for her fiction.

Karen's initial battle is to assert herself against an innocence induced by her religious upbringing but which she finds puzzlingly unreal and stultifying. Yet her desire for an authentic self is undermined by a lack of any compelling reason to accept or form more robust modes of self-discovery. Shar Rule, returning to the primitive, isolated area of his boyhood, offers her a violent contrast with her protective, limiting family life. Once merely a big, dirty, aggressive boy, he is now a man of thirty who "belonged to neither world — not the dim, safe past or the static present." He appears to her as "a creature of another species," "a stranger from lower land, the region of paved roads and cities and, far away, the sea itself" (WSF, 46). She escapes the hold of her father by running away with Shar, but she brings a predatory, death-directed passivity to her passion for him, and the relationship ends in death for him and emotional ruin for herself. Indeed, there is a real sense in which Karen conceives of her relationship with Shar as a struggle to the death. When her father is beaten up by Shar, the father, out of a mixture of sexual jeal-

ousy and family resentment, vindictively instructs her not to return until she has killed him. Thenceforth, Shar feels haunted,
trapped, hunted by something in Karen. But she has no active
desire for any kind of revenge. Karen turns to Shar almost passively, hypnotized by him. It is because of this passivity, born
of an insufficient reason for affirmation, that death haunts all
of Karen's strivings for realization and eventually overcomes
Shar as well. The world appears to her as a succession of accidents, riots, brutalities, and murder, out of which she can affirm
nothing.

The exception in all her experience is, in fact, her father. Unlike Shar's father, whose dying body nauseates Karen, her father
seems serenely deathless. He has survived two wives, and in her
feelings embodies an immortal protectiveness. In his eyes, Karen
remains a child, protected and sheltered, "his good girl" (WSF,
315). Similarly, she feels enveloped by the protection of the
church, feeling the communal power of the mass and the family
Bible readings where she learns of the "strange dignity" of fulfilling "one's destiny . . . forever bound . . . manipulated by God
Himself" (WSF, 53) as in the story of the obedient sacrifice offered by Abraham to God of his son Isaac. Karen will become a
type of this story, a sacrifice to a powerful childhood deity by
the customs and conventions of her personality and upbringing.
Even Shar's passion for Karen provides an insecure refuge by
comparison with her father, who grimly receives Karen back into
her childhood world when, finally, Shar is killed. Like the church,
with which he is so intimately associated in Karen's mind, he
seems invulnerable, seemingly proving that security is prefer-
able to risk. The extremity of her love has revealed in her a vulnerability and necessary fear that she is ultimately unable to bear.

When Karen, passively, almost instinctively, goes with Shar,
she does not do so with any hope of positive growth. She flees
from death, reaching out to Shar in fear and guilt. When they
have become lovers, she endures his passion and her parasitic
passivity frustrates and infuriates him. She resists him at the

same time as she gives herself to him. Consequently he can only feel mocked, as if she is using "his infatuation to degrade him" (WSF, 119). Such mockery produces only irritation and frustrated violence in him. Nor can he understand why he is driven back again and again to her: "He was tortured by the fact that he wanted to do it; he could not understand." Karen accepts his violence and anger "as she accepted everything—not bravely but only silently, innocently, as if everything he did were normal," as if such extremity were normal for two lovers. Thus sexual passion, something for which Shar has had an innocent enjoyment, is felt as "indecent—dirty . . . it was dirty, dirty, he had made himself dirty in doing it, yet he enjoyed it, he loved it, he was obsessed by it!" "Exhausted by his energy" in making love, she lies "really untouched by him: he could not reach her" (WSF, 119–20).

The violence Karen evokes in Shar is a result of her passivity —and an insidious knowledge of the power that passivity generates. She knows that when Shar leaves her for another woman, "he would not be free. . . . The fact that she thought of him would force him to think of her." She knows, from her father and her religion, "the value of forced, feigned calm" (WSF, 157), and she believes also that any experience that might leave her vulnerable, at risk before uncontrollable forces, must be kept in control. Karen is the first of a long and frightening series of Oates heroines who cannot face the challenge of sadness, risk, or fear as experiences which call out the strength of the self. Karen's dependence, her lack of integrated responses to her surroundings, her unwillingness to face the pain and anguish of breaking from her father and childhood, all make her relationship with Shar disruptive and predatory. Not only does she bring demands of a complex passion which divert him from the "simplicity of vision, and simplicity of emotion" (WSF, 124) of his own career, but her essentially absorbent passivity creates in him a fury of self-loathing. He comes to feel drained of any moral direction and commitment by her parasitism. He will wake at night from dreams of her "so vivid he could smell the rich perspiring warmth of her body and remember her expression: frank, innocent, brutal in its simplicity." But in fact, Karen is not voluptuous or openhearted — it is only in Shar's imagination that she lures him; in herself Karen "did nothing, or seemed to do nothing" (WSF, 117). Giving herself so dutifully to him (as she had given herself to her father and the church) she finally commits nothing of herself.

Shar's passion for Karen therefore becomes continually deterministic in its demands upon them both. We are caught up increasingly into a grimly fated atmosphere as the lovers quarrel and struggle. From the start, indeed, we sense that it is the seemingly weak, passive Karen who will remain inviolate, undefeated, and who will eventually escape back to the security of her childhood surroundings. Near the beginning of the story Karen visits her family graveyard. The graves foreshadow the inevitable end of the book's action, and the coldness of the stones reflects something of Karen's own passivity and death-directed instincts. Her first boyfriend, Jack, yells at her that she is "as cold as all your family up in the graveyard, might as well be dead! Might as well be dead right now!" and she muses that "deep inside her brain, like a sliver of glass suddenly uncovered in the dark, secret earth, was the knowledge that much of what Jack had said was true" (WSF, 52). Throughout the novel Karen is associated with death. Rule's death, her father's vindictive command to kill Shar, the family graves, her desire to be buried with her family and not with a husband, the atmosphere of confusion and passivity with which she distracts Shar's concentration on escaping death on the racetrack — all characterize Karen's death-centered personality. Such connections between setting and the book's affective level are a little mechanically made at times but we can see how Oates is trying to convey that the subtlest forms of determinism are not the economic or intellectual limitations of family or social background. The very struggle of the personality itself for autonomy locks it more and more grimly into an inescapable pattern of which successive material environments are emblematic. Beneath her temporary rebellion Karen accepts the straight-jacket of her personality as inescapable and given; her rebellion against her family and religion possesses no genuine depth or movement towards self-enhancement. Beneath, she accepts a definition of her self in terms of determinism, duty, and surrender, and her lack of commitment destroys Shar along with any hope of achieving any sense of autonomy and joy.

The book's three sections entitled "Spring," "Summer," and "Fall" stress the deterministic patterns the characters are acting out. In "Spring" seventeen-year-old Karen is restless, sullen, frigid, on her father's farm; in "Summer" she escapes with Shar; in "Fall," after Shar's death and her own miscarriage and an attack of mental illness, she returns to the farm, a recluse from the world, to be sheltered by her father and the church. Then, as a counterpoint to this overall pattern, there are the sudden, un-predictable surges of violence—assault, rape, attempted murder, arson, suicide, riot, vandalism, and above all the enveloping atmosphere of automobile racing. Shar's career as a driver is built upon both patterns of movement which structure the book—the firm, repetitive circling of the racing track which provides an apparent control of the power and violence of the men and machines, and the seemingly unmotivated and unprepared surges of anarchic violence, as a crash occurs, or an automobile explodes. Shar's manager, Max, interprets all of life in terms of the pressures of the racetrack. As in a race, he explains, there are "two pressures," one pushing in, the other pushing out. "That is how our lives are. . . . The pressures are opposed, they fight each other. . . . two forces, one to live and one to die" (WSF, 140). We are forced to battle violently and ultimately to the death, caught between these two forces. Karen not only seems to share instinctively the same beliefs but also to harness something of the forces themselves—at least this is how Shar experiences her presence. She senses something "unnatural—almost mystical" as she watches a race, with Shar moving seemingly hypnotically onwards to victory or death. Uncannily, the lust to dominate him which possesses Karen at such moments seems to explode on the track:

As if in answer to the crowd's secret desire, the car spun suddenly out of control. Out of the invisible ring of pressure it flew, and as Shar and the lead car sped away, the red car traded ends, dust exploded up like a bomb, the volume of the crowd's delight swelled to bursting. All eyes followed the stricken car as it headed for the retaining wall. For an instant it looked isolated: it seemed to hang against the dirty wall, a little off the ground. Then it jerked back into motion and, bursting into flames, scraped along the wall, like a discarded toy, farther and farther along the wall, perhaps for a hundred feet, skidding, with its yellow flames almost obscuring it. What was left of it slammed finallly against a concrete jutting and stopped. (WSF, 138–39)

Like the race itself, Shar's affair with Karen is one of increasingly destructive and compulsive movements, and it can end only in victory for one and death for the other. Love and motor racing seem to be antipathetic and yet betray uncanny similarities. About the time Oates was writing *With Shuddering Fall* she published an article on Shakespeare's *Troilus and Cressida*, and just as the play juxtaposes war and sex to show with fearful clarity the corruption of each by the other, so here sexual passion, instead of being a relief or escape from the mechanized brute violence of the racing world, in fact reinforces its destructiveness. Like Cressida's, Karen's seductive passivity — her "queer love" — hopelessly locks and entangles Shar. When Karen asks whether he loves her, he instinctively reacts to her question by thinking of the "relentless dirt track." In both racing and his love affair he feels a "force — drawing at him, luring him into the center, to death, but he did not understand what it was." He understands both Karen and his role as a driver as pressures upon his inner self. Death for a driver, he knows, comes not "through the center, but through surrender to the outside — to centifrugal force, a sudden careening off the track." When he sleeps with her, he will often wake from a nightmare of crashing, waking "upon the moment of impact, drenched with sweat, his fists clenched on an invisible wheel, his legs and feet straining to keep him in, keep him in" (WSF, 118). He cannot understand why he is unable to escape her; despite his power and sense of masculinity, it is she who is dominant and who eventually does, as if in accordance with her father's wishes, destroy him.

Karen was Oates's first lengthy study of the passivity of a woman whose acceptance of her role as a sex object eventually destroys her lover. She is a prototypical Oates heroine, passive yet destructive, and here all the more intense because motivated by an underlying intensity of will. A suggestive comparison might be with Lawrence's Gudrun, possessive and yet derisive of her lover, and unable to enjoy sex except within a predatory relationship. On the rare occasions when Karen becomes conscious of her hold over Shar, she fears only "the fear of losing him, greater than the fear that he might die" (WSF, 135), and gradually, in the face of her concentrated will, he becomes radically self-divided. Making love, "Shar would seize her and press his face against her and tell her he was sorry. . . . She felt how precarious was his strength and how tormented he was by her quiet assurances that he had not hurt her, she was all right" (WSF, 159); this quiet impenetrability tortures him more and more. The sadomasochistic tinge to their relationship brings him guilt even as he enjoys it, whereas she merely accepts it as a means to controlling his will. Giving her body while denying the commitment of passion, she overcomes his will until one or other must die. Like Lawrence's Gerald Crich, Shar eventually kills himself out of sheer despair that sexuality has become nothing other than a victim-destroyer relationship. His death is the outcome of a struggle to be released from the intolerable pressure he experiences with her.

Like most of Oates's novels, the book's climactic chapters bring out in physical terms the explosive psychological violence that has surged amongst the characters in the early chapters. Temporarily separated from Karen, Shar once again becomes a man with an uncomplicated vision, enjoying his simple aims of winning races, pitting himself against the racetrack and his rivals. Like Gerald Crich, he is at his happiest in uncomplicated physical relationship with himself, other people, and nature. When Karen returns, he becomes increasingly depressed and, as if he had succumbed to something within, he asserts he loves her. It is both a declaration and a capitulation. Once again, Shar feels "his bitter rage . . . absorbed and defeated by her, mocked by her" (WSF, 244), and capitulates further when, after her miscarriage, he promises first that they will have a child and that he will marry her. He has become completely subservient to her will:

Karen felt her heart begin to pound, slowly and gravely and yet with a pleasant nervous anticipation, as if her entire life led her irreparably to this moment.

"What do you want me to do?" Shar said.

With the knowledge of his love, she faced him as if in that instant she had somehow forgotten about him—Shar with his suspicious narrowing eyes, the tiny lines on his forehead that would soon turn to creases if he lived to be as old as her father. He had been a stranger and now he was familiar to her; she could not have said precisely when this happened. The finicking nervous strength suggested in his fingers had been transmitted to her. She felt, gazing at him with the mild unhurried look of the possessor, that her tingling fingers would have been capable of touching him, fumbling against his chest, reaching inside his chest to stroke his sweating, pumping heart. Yet she wanted at the same time to embrace him, simply and utterly, as she had imagined she would someday. . . . But she said in the calm, ordinary voice she had despised so in her sister, "You make me sick." (WSF, 256–57)

In the race that follows, Shar seeks through the only instrument he can control, his automobile, the annihilation which alone can free him from Karen. He drives straight for a wall and kills himself.

The final section of the book attests that Karen's final fate is ever more tragic than Shar's death. She emerges from the shock of Shar's death to return to her home, her family, her church, and her father. "Fall" is tragically ironic: having sought salvation through the intimacy and self-offering of sexual passion, Karen has been unable to reach beyond the determinism of her heredity and family conditioning and now it is her turn to be haunted by the obsessiveness of her lover's commitment to her. "Her frenzy turned to thoughts about Shar—she would cry aloud at the memory of this body, his muscles and sweating back, his clenched teeth, his strong thighs" (WSF, 296), but her instincts for security take her back to her childhood. She listens to the priest saying the mass, "and the sound of the persistent, cracked Latin somehow reassured Karen. Now I am home, she thought" (WSF, 310). Her final transformation, however, is tinged with a terrible irony. On the surface, she has repented, and her relatives see her suffering as proof of the justice of the universe and so forgive her. But beneath the surface of her reassumed role of "Herz's youngest, spoiled daughter," she determines that "I can continue with it, with what I have become" (WSF, 311–12)— and what she has become is a ruthless, destructive woman, conscious of her own power to distort and kill. She broods about how she can set her sister and her fiancé at each other's throats and how she can harry her father to death; she knows, as part of her revenge, that "there are men enough for me to feed on until I lose my youth" (WSF, 313). It is a grim ending to a tragedy of determinism that contains few alleviating notes of hope.

The faults of *With Shuddering Fall*, notwithstanding its power and concentration, are obvious enough. The juxtapositions of passionate revolt and family determinism, personal autonomy and predetermined psychological roles, are crudely developed considering the subtlety of Oates's later works. The constant violence which gives the book its heightened, melodramatic atmosphere is usually connected only generally to the more important level of psychological exploration. The parallels between violence in the psyche and the automobile, for instance, are perhaps too simply obvious and are never developed in detail in the way that politics (in *The Assassins*) or law (in *Do With Me What You Will*) will be. Nevertheless, as a first novel, *With Shudder-*

ing Fall is a powerful anticipation of Oates's later works. Like many of her stories of the early sixties, it now allows her readers to clarify themes which will make more complex emotional and intellectual demands upon them in later books. Developing an ability to create a striking atmosphere of fear and violence, her task was clearly to develop techniques whereby this world could be turned inward, to reflect the soul, not merely the gaudy exterior of her dream of America.

III

As we have seen, *A Garden of Earthly Delights* has been described by Oates as one part of a trilogy (along with *Them* and *Expensive People*) to reflect a series of representative American environments. Like *With Shuddering Fall*, it treats of violence and determinism, madness and death, and above all it connects the narrowness of its characters' rural upbringing with their psychological limitations. Alongside the earlier work, *A Garden of Earthly Delights* is a much more leisurely conceived, fuller portrayal of similar themes, and to set it beside the earlier novel enables us to see Oates's developing search for appropriate forms for her vision — and how, in fact, her dream of America points her far beyond the tradition of realism with which her earliest fiction seemed to have affinities.

Once again the setting, especially in the opening scenes, seems to promise a naturalistic exposé of the stultifying conditions of rural poverty. Indeed, if a case were to be made for Oates's affinities with the realists, evidence would come predominantly from this novel. Here, we are among the human dregs of rural itinerant workers, surrounded by wrecked automobiles, rotting vegetables, and the garbage of subsistence itinerant drudgery. In such a setting, Oates's novel might be seen as an indictment of American capitalism, its exploitation and brutality, but through the detail of the novel's setting emerges a parable-like pattern hinted at in the novel's title. As a number of Oates's critics have suggested, the title is derived from the second panel of Bosch's triptych *The Millenium*, which depicts a vision of hell as a chaotic world disintegrating into its human, organic, and spiritual elements. Oates's characters, in their frenzied search for self-realization, seem motivated by the same crazed disintegration and self-destructiveness, and the intensity of the book's setting is intended as a manifestation of a whole spiritual disintegration. Rose Marie Burwell has suggested that structurally the novel and the painting correspond even more precisely — the tripartite structure of the book commences with Clara's birth, follows her adolescence, ambition, and worldly success through Eden County, and ends with her family destroyed and Clara herself in a living hell, having gone mad and with all her ambitions destroyed.[4] As well, as in Bosch's painting, there swarms through the work a variety of characters and emotions which make up a dark emblem of a doomed struggle for survival which is emblematic of a whole civilization.

Each of the three parts centers upon a man involved with the book's heroine — her father Carleton, her lover Lowry, her son Steven (or, as she prefers to call him, Swan). Each man enters into a complex, but ultimately mutually exploitative relationship with Clara, who sees this as part of a struggle to achieve selfhood, respectability, and power. As we shall see, it is significant that Revere, her husband, is not singled out amongst the book's characters in this way. He is merely an instrument of Clara's struggle.

Clara's father, Carleton Walpole, is an itinerant fruit picker struggling through the Depression to repay debts, support his increasing family, and eventually, somehow, regain his family farm. He resents bitterly both his status and his forced association with hillbillies, blacks, and Mexicans. He is especially frustrated by the futile determinism of poverty and transience. Along with the rest of his children, Clara grows up molded by this sense of deprivation, victimization, and a feeling of being driven by

4 Rose Marie Burwell, "Joyce Carol Oates and an Old Master," *Critique*, XV (1973), 48–58; see also Martin, "Toward a Higher Consciousness," 81 ff, for a similar reading of the novel.

complex movements within society beyond her control or understanding. Carleton, brooding and bitter, is aware there are many complex facts he never understood which have poisoned his relationships and his sense of personal dignity. He is therefore dominated by "a moody, doughy look of dissatisfaction," "a restless boredom," which may erupt, unpredictably, in violence and madness. In introducing her characters in this novel, Oates's authorial comments are often too explicit but Carleton's deep-seated frustrations are, as well, evoked through the grim squalor and ejaculations of angry violence which dominate the first part of the novel. Again, we might see the careful build-up of detail as the start of a realistic analysis of men caught in economic deprivation, but Oates's main concentration is not chronicling a family history set against the Depression and the war. The social and economic facts swirl around confusedly, often contradictory and never analyzable in a systematic way, reflecting how they are puzzlingly apprehended by the characters themselves. What matters more than the dimly understood economic and social forces of Carleton's world are the forces that lie beneath: the intimacy of family ties, the confusion of sexual drives and, as we see her grow up, Clara's own burning (and eventually tragic) desire for security, self-fulfillment and power. Oates carefully distinguishes between the impersonal pattern of public history and the less ordered, more intense surges of private or personal history, a mixture of desire and memory, instinctive ties and conscious obsessions. Although the book's action covers forty years and three generations, the psychic realities cannot be computed by historical time: the lack of psychological roots and the identification of personal fulfillment with material security remain fearfully unchanged throughout Clara's life, from her bewildered girlhood to her final lonely madness.

Oates's second novel, then, is another attempt to use the violent flamboyance of American society as symbolic of psychological turmoil. The first part of the book concentrates on the fatalism of Depression life and the erosion of Carleton's manhood from his family prosperity to the frustrated feeling "as if the air had turned hard and heavy above him, pushing him down" (GED, 15). Victimized not just by economic repression but by an accompanying "restless boredom," he turns to violence as his most immediate means of self-assertion. Carleton's rage and frustration push him into killing a friend when a drunken scrap gets out of hand. His own life subsides into final meaningless death when Clara, his favourite daughter, runs away. With the dogged energy she, as we will see, has inherited from him, he pursues her in revenge, increasingly ill, deliriously confusing her with her long-dead mother, and finally dying alone, in a strange city, almost without reaction or sense to the personal or public causes of his tragedy:

Everything—everyone—the whole world—was joined in him, only in him. . . . He was the center of the world, the universe, and without him everything would fall into pieces. . . . It terrified him that people and places and dates should fly off into nothing, as if into the shadowy church ceiling, belonging to no one and making no sense. (GED, 126–27)

As a child, Clara senses that escape is the only means to avoid being crushed by her father's world. She has sensed other, gentler, less persecuted, and, especially, more powerful worlds in the occasional school she has attended, in the five-and-dime store she explores with a friend, in a church, and gradually through her sexuality. Fulfillment seems to her to depend on her control—of self and especially of others. She is offered an escape with Lowry, a gentle and protective whiskey runner she has met; he drives her away from her family, finds her a job in Tintern (Oates's Eden County again), and helps her to set up her first home, a room over a store furnished merely by crates but providing her with a first hint of selfhood and autonomy. Her initial break from her father leads her to grit her teeth and affirm her wants:

"I want somethin' more," Clara muttered. She wanted to seize his arm and make him look at her. She wanted to sink her nails into his arm. "You better listen to me, mister."

"What?"

"You better listen. . . . I want lots of things an' I'm goin' to get them. . . . I want more things than just babies like my ma and Nancy and everybody else! (GED, 137)

In its initial stages, Clara's struggle again resembles that of the classic model of female frustration, Flaubert's Emma Bovary. She is initially enticed by glamor, romantic love, and economic power. But unlike Emma — and, eventually, even more grimly — Clara becomes coolly and ruthlessly clearsighted about her aims. Her first naïve mistake is almost her last. Jealous of Lowry's girls, she eventually seduces him, and as they become lovers she drifts into a romantic — and quite unpractical — dreamworld. "All he said was not to 'make any mistakes.' It was clear what not to do, but it was not clear what she should do." "When Lowry had said, as early as that first day, 'You sure as hell don't want to get pregnant,' Clara had heard the word clearly enough but had dismissed it at once" (GED, 147, 159). Events occur rapidly: Clara becomes pregnant, Lowry is threatened with arrest and is forced to run for Mexico; faced with a future abandoned by him, she wonders "how she would live out the rest of her life" (GED, 213). The accidents which had victimized her father and mother are now threatening her own material security and the small but real freedoms she has achieved. Her friends, Caroline and Ginny, have fallen into loveless marriages. Another friend, Sonia, is killed by her lover.

At this point Carleton's determination, thwarted in his own life, emerges in his daughter. From her childhood, Clara has instinctively possessed a sense of the need for power through autonomy — "I'm not a child, I never was," she has shouted at Lowry at their first meeting — and now she realizes that she must clutch at the only autonomy she knows, through the only means she knows: "It would be done the way Lowry would do something, thinking it through, calculating on it, and then going ahead. All her life she would be able to say: Today she changed the way her life was going and it was no accident. No accident"

(GED, 223). Although "she did not know up until the last moment exactly how she would bring all those accidents into control" (GED, 213), she has sensed what she needs to transcend the sordid fates of her family and friends. She has already met Curt Revere, a wealthy local landowner, whose wife is reputed to be ill or deranged, and who has seemed mysteriously attracted to Clara. She sees his car and seizes her chance. When he offers her a ride, she decides to act: "In the next moment she would know, she thought: it depended on which way he turned the car. If he drove back into town (the car was headed in that direction) she would have to start thinking about getting out of this place, but if he turned around and went the other way, she had a chance" (GED, 221). He turns the car; they go to an empty house he owns and she allows him to make love to her. Clara becomes his mistress and lives in the house he provides.

Unlike Emma Bovary, Clara is determined not to be destroyed by the irreconcilibility of dream and surrounding material fact. She is coolly aware of the value of her body purely and simply as her only means of control over Revere, who sets her up in the house and supports her and the child who he assumes is his. Whereas Lowry has been "dancing forever out of her grasp," Revere appears to Clara as solid, considerate, prosperous — he embodies values her father had lost, envied, and been unable to regain. In accepting him as her lover and some years later marrying him, however, Clara must rigorously repress what she knows is her real desire for Lowry. It is he who has taught her not only her erotic needs but also the more rational lesson she will ruthlessly apply throughout her life — that she must control, manipulate, and plan. She notices the characteristics of men who have power, who seem to triumph in life. They have "turned-away secret indifferent eyes. They knew. They could see. They did not live in a world made up by someone else, controlled by someone else" (GED, 139). Clara seems to be learning the lesson which Karen, at the end of *With Shuddering Fall*, had seized upon. In a world motivated by struggle and domination, a woman's survival depends on the cool and fierce manipulation of her power. It is not Clara's beauty or her vulgarity but her appropriation of stereotypical male behavior that makes her so destructive, even to the point that she annihilates Revere and his potency. Throughout, she forces herself, by the application of the sheer concentration of her will, to become indifferent to her status as a kept woman, where her only company is Revere or his cousin and, as he grows up, her son Swan. Only twice do the strong, anarchic sexual urges she discovered with Lowry emerge — once with a gas-station attendant who reminds her of Lowry and then, crucially, when Lowry himself returns. Clara's life reaches its climactic decision when Lowry drives out to offer her a life with him:

> "I didn't forget anything," Lowry said. "That's why I'm here."
> Then the trembling started in her, a rigid violent trembling that began far down on her spine and passed up her back to her shoulders and arms, a feeling she had never known she could have. All those years with Revere were being swept out into sight and considered and were maybe going to be swept out the back door. . . . He was the same man and she wanted him just as violently; making love with him cost her everything, every agonized straining to give life to that kernel of love he would always keep inside her. She would never be free of him. But she knew what she was going to say just the same.
> "No. I guess I'm not going with you," she said. (GED, 265, 277)

Rather than risk her security, she is prepared to deny her love. She persuades herself that she refuses Lowry because of the child, and when he leaves she feels Swan as "the one thing she had to hate, the only thing that had lost her Lowry" (GED, 281). But there is something more fundamental at risk, and even Lowry mistakes her reason. He looks at Swan and snarls: "I can see in your face you killed something already and you're going to kill lots of things. . . . I can see it right there — all the things you're going to kill and step on and walk over" (GED, 281). While Clara appears forceful and determined, what holds her back is her fundamental terror of risk, an inability to sacrifice the material power which has given her security and self-respect. Eventually she will have her will: she becomes Revere's wife, the mother of his large family, prosperous, even a little genteel — and carefully she eases Lowry's son into the control of his apparent father's property. She has called him Swan because the birds seem cold and hard and dangerous. On her wedding day, Clara tells her frightened son: "You're going to take everything away from them someday and kick them out of this house. . . . Remember that" (GED, 300). But, despite her iron will, the guilty memory of Lowry haunts her, and it eventually transfers itself to Swan and ends in destroying them both.

The final section of the book, "Swan," is remorseless in its intent but is somewhat less gripping than the first two parts. The emotional conflict diminishes, the parabolic suggestiveness turns to rather obvious, moralistic allegory as Clara, the Eve-figure, having refused her true Adamic companion, finds her nature thwarted and her ideals distorted. Her garden turns into a hell. Clara's success and her final frustration are drawn out in a somber but somewhat anticlimactic fashion. Swan grows up as the bearer of his mother's fiercely possessive and ambitious will. Persecuted as a frail boy and a bastard, he is caught among conflicting loyalties to his mother, Revere, and a strange memory of his real father. He inherits his mother's watchful passivity and his father's opportunism and gradually takes on a central place in Revere's affections. Revere's son Robert is killed in a hunting accident; a second son Jonathan disappears from home after a scene in which he beats up a girl who reminds him of Clara; the eldest son, Clark, is tormented and teased by Clara into making a drunken pass at her and must leave home to escape his father's anger. Clara has successfully removed Swan's rivals, but in doing so she has poisoned her son against her. He is caught between an instinctive love for his mother and a passion for his adopted family and their land which motivates his quiet accumulation of influence over Revere. Like Clara's and his own real father, Swan instinctively turns to violence as an outlet for the conflicting demands he feels within himself. He sees himself torn between one kind of garden, "tended and tortured into a garden so complex one might need a lifetime to comprehend it" (GED, 397), and a newer garden, one neither his parents nor grandparents could comprehend, "that vast systematic garden of men's minds that seemed to him to have been toiled into its complex existence by a sinister and inhuman spirit" (GED, 412–13). He takes refuge in introspective withdrawal, reviling his mother for her strange conspiracy to mold him, her rank physicality, and her despising Revere. Steven has developed a confusing admiration for Revere himself, and eventually the confused energies which have been repressed and distorted emerge, typically in an act of radical violence that reminds us of Carleton. He confronts Revere and Clara with a gun, drunkenly searching for the conflicting truths which are destroying him. Clara's final confrontation with her son recapitulates the goading pressure and urgent ambition of his whole life. She screams out what has been the terrifying truth of her self-sacrifice, that "all my life was for you — all of it — You crazy fool!" Then she taunts him with what she sees as his real father's weakness, the level of vulnerability she has never allowed to emerge in herself: "That's my secret about you — you're weak just like he was. . . . What did it get him? Nothing! Nothing! You're just like him!" She taunts him to pull the trigger. The gun goes off and, as Swan pulls it aside at the last minute, accidentally — and all the more horrible because it is an accident — Revere is killed. Swan then shoots himself. With Revere and Swan dead, Clara collapses, and ends up deranged in a hospital, perpetually in front of a television set:

She seemed to like best programs that showed men fighting, swinging from ropes, shooting guns and driving fast cars, killing the enemy again and again until the dying gasps of evil men were only a certain familiar rhythm away from the opening blasts of the commercials, which changed only gradually over the years. (GED, 440)

Swan's sense of frustration and lost identity marks an ironic return to the fate of his grandfather. His shooting of Revere instead of his mother is both a mistake and a misplaced and confused act of revenge for his real father—while Clara's struggle to control her life and her son's ends with her as powerless as her mother. She lives on, a mindless body, psychologically exhausted, with no sense of social context or psychic continuity.

Unfortunately, the novel attempts to pack just too much thematic material into its final section to be totally comprehensible intellectually or satisfying emotionally. The main line of psychological development is clear enough but there is surprisingly little tension in "Swan"—indeed, it reads like the slow-built beginning of a further saga of the Revere family. The result is labored and low-key, except in the crucial scenes of confrontation where, as in *With Shuddering Fall*, the emotional impact of the work is heightened by the intensity of violence. With the book's major climax already reached in Clara's rejection of Lowry, too much new material has to be brought in to maintain the level of emotion which the fierce concentration of the first two parts achieved. We become distracted by the details of Clara's married life and the representative meaning of her history is lost. Nevertheless, the book shows how Oates is developing an impressive ability to build a suggestive atmosphere. She shows she can use intimately detailed settings and action to reveal the underlying psychic forces which are her main interest. She has acknowledged that the novel, like *With Shuddering Fall*, had something of an autobiographic, cathartic intention, saying that Swan was a "rather autobiographical" character onto whom she projected her own metaphysical doubts. Indeed, she seems to have considered the final section of the novel as a "Freudian romance," with the emphasis on the mother-son relationship.[5] But too much is packed into the end of the novel that is not made explicit or adequately evoked for such an intention to become fully realized.

A Garden of Earthly Delights marks both a development and a regression in Oates's career. It is richer symbolically, more in-

---

5 Kuehl, "An Interview with Joyce Carol Oates," 308.

tensely detailed, yet it lacks the structural clarity of *With Shuddering Fall*, and at times falls back to a kind of realism which her best fiction was already starting to grow out of. Its prose style is often too mannered and self-conscious, with gobbets of sociological analysis tending to over clarify and simplify the surges of feeling the work attempts to evoke. Yet it has great moments and an overall intent which possessed enormous potential. After *A Garden of Earthly Delights*, Oates's basic problem as a novelist had become how to combine her intellectual intentions with the suggestiveness of her world of surging and unpredictable emotions.

FIVE

Expensive People, Them

EXPENSIVE PEOPLE appeared in 1968 and marked a new direction in Oates's career — an apparent shift in fictional mode from O'Connor to Barth, as it were. It is true that there were obvious thematic continuities with Oates's two earlier novels, and the author herself, dutifully echoed by some early reviewers, encouraged a view of the novel as part of a trilogy dealing with a spectrum of American social and economic patterns. Seen in the context of the earlier fiction, there is in *Expensive People* a continuing concern with "personal" as opposed to "public" history, with stifling family ties, and with the fragility of the human personality caught up in oppressive social environments. But the sophisticated black comedy contrasts with the solidity and relentless earnestness of the earlier novels and stories, and the rhetorical fireworks (which don't by any means all explode) cannot hide a radical break with the mode of much of Oates's previous fiction. The different setting, in affluent suburbia, partly accounts for the difference in tone. Superficially at least, suburbia is a more amenable setting for comedy than rural labor camps or motor racing circuits and the new tone is partly a reflection of a different milieu.

With Shuddering Fall and even more obviously A Garden of Earthly Delights certainly have affinities with a central tradition of American realism. That by means of parable, melodrama, emotional heightening, stylization of setting, character, or names, Oates was attempting to move beyond that tradition might arguably be seen — indeed was seen as such by most early reviewers — as distracting and aberrative.[1] But Expensive People made it very clear that Oates was, in fact, exploiting just those aberrative aspects of her fiction. It is as if, like Barth or Brautigan, in trying to get behind the surface of American society, she encountered the unpredictable absurdities, contradictions, and paradox of dream. "No story is really fiction," she has written; "the aim of a serious, respectful art is to externalize personal, private, shapeless fantasies into structures that are recognizable to other people."[2] What Expensive People shapes into recognition is the self-consciousness that has, both historically and mythically, created the America it reflects.

It would be possible, but difficult, to see the setting of Expensive People merely as an attempt to depict suburban life. Of course, the affluent suburbs of the American metropolis — Updike's television aerials and abortive friendships, marriages, conversations, or Riesman's suburban sadness — remain a parlour-game obsession for both sociologists and novelists. But Oates's technique is not to analyze but to distort and caricature. She

---

1 See, for example, Granville Hicks, "What is Reality?" Saturday Review, October 26, 1968, pp. 33–34.
2 Quoted in Jack Hicks (ed.), Cutting Edges: Young American Fiction for the '70s (New York: Holt, Rinehart and Winston, Inc., 1972), 543.

chooses if not the most delectable and luxurious rich upper crust, certainly the middle layers of the proliferating tundra of American affluence. Fernwood Heights, with its Vastvalley Country Club and Johns Behemoth Private School, is a heightened and darkly humorous reflection of the Shaker Heights, Lake Forests, or Grosse Pointes of contemporary America. In *Them*, the city will become ugly, violent, and destructive so that Oates's hero, Jules Wendall, will yell that it be burnt down or blown up — "The hell with Vietnam, what about right here? I mean Detroit! Right here, Detroit, this crap-pile, it stinks to the sky, what about blowing up Detroit!" (T, 457). Here, however, we are in a different world; there is genial satire but, more important, it is an exercise in titillation of Oates's audience. In Fernwood and Cedar Grove we are harmoniously seduced with yellow cadillacs, the Continental Market Basket, the security of "fresh, crisp cash" and pedicure rooms, "suburbia's public heaven." As Oates's narrator explains it ecstatically, "everything, everything, is lovely in Fernwood!" He rhapsodizes over the lawns, shrubs, chandeliers, elegant automobiles, courtyards, and sweeping driveways, the fishponds, occasional and discrete glimpses of "colored maids at windows, washing windows that are already clean." To tell us of these things, to tell us, that is, of the gross materialism in our dreams, "would be to write another *Paradiso*. . . . Before the rare beauties of the wealth of America a writer can do nothing. . . . Fernwood is Paradise and it is real!" His celebration reaches mock-ecstatic heights: "If God remakes Paradise it will be in the image of Fernwood, for Fernwood is Paradise constructed to answer all desires before they are even felt." Above all, in this material paradise, "there is never any contrast between what is said and what is done, what is done and what is intended, what is intended and what is desired — everything runs together" (EP, 145 – 46).

The description itself, with its melodramatic, ecstatic tone, is wry and witty, but as such outbursts continue through the novel, they start to become threatening and grotesque. *Expensive Peo-*

ple is related by Richard Everett, a 250-pound eighteen-year-old child murderer ("I don't mean child-murderer, though that's an idea. I mean child murderer, that is, a murderer who happens to be a child" [EP, 3]), who is obsessed with his parents, especially his beautiful, wayward mother Natasha ("Nada"). His story operates on two interrelated levels, merging the macabre with the farcical, sinister comedy with broad satire. Richard's obsessed broodings include brutal vignettes of his mother and of affluent suburban life, amusing pastiches of literary reviews he anticipates for his memoirs, and, above all, a running account of his own distorted, obsessive personality. He gives us a number of amusing satirical portraits of common enough suburban fetishes and neuroses. Oates skims over the prestige, tension, and pretension, the mobility and consumerism of the suburban snakepit. The Everetts move from Brookfield to Fernwood to Cedar Grove and discover that there is a family "on the other street, who had apparently moved at the same time we had; and not one mile away was the same house we had lived in for the last three years in Brookfield, present here in Fernwood like a miracle" (EP, 19). In one particular scene of grotesque pastiche, Nada calls a succession of suburban services on her plastic princess phone — the Cedar Grove Employment Services, Cedar Grove Plumbing, Cedar Grove Green Carpet Lawn Service ("Yes, fungus prevention, everything, edging, thinning, rolling, flattening. The usual. Everything"). And so on — the gas company, the insurance company, the Cedar Grove Garbage Disposal Service, the Sanitation Department, the Good Will ("all that junk in the basement") a school, the Cedar Grove Bank of the Commonwealth, Dr. Bellow the dentist, the Cedar Grove Eye Clinic, a skin doctor, the Roman Wall restaurant, the electric, water, and telephone companies, the grocery store, the drugstore ("Send over some aspirin. The most expensive kind"), a television and phonograph repair shop, Maxwell Voyd the lawyer, the Cedar Grove House of Beauty, the Cedar Grove Key Makers, repairmen for the windows, chimneys, roof, and chandelier, and finally the Continental Market Basket (EP, 186–89). We laugh benignly enough, recognizing the familiarity of the setting and the point of the satire. We smile at the rather obvious allegory of Oates's vacuous characters' vacuous names — Howie Hanson the real estate man, Dr. Hugg the psychiatrist, Dr. Bellow the dentist, the Everetts' friends the Bones, Bodys, Veals, Spoons, and Voyds. The corporations for which Elwood Everett works are OPP, BOX, BWK, and GKS. Beneath the plastic surface, such a world is less amusing: dogs have nervous breakdowns, children become alcoholics at thirteen, status is estimated by the number of one's garbage cans, Richard's mother insists that her son's I.Q. be remeasured when his result seems too low. "Every gesture," ruminates the neurotic victim of this world, "was as phony as hell" (EP, 79).

Our recognition of the phoniness is made more complex by the disarmingly jovial tone through which Richard's satire is conveyed. Many of us, after all, live within a world recognizably like Richard's and many of its comforts and conventions might well be our own. Like Richard himself, we recognize the phoniness while perpetuating it. Hence we may give uneasy assent to both the satire and also Richard's sly celebration of what he is satirizing. "If God remakes Paradise," Richard muses, "it will be in the image of Fernwood, for Fernwood is Paradise constructed to answer all desires before they are even felt" (EP, 146). But, to round off our expectations, Oates provides a delicate ingredient without which no American suburb would be complete — violence, first hinted at comically in Nada's hairdresser, whose "cool indifference" and "flippant razor" reminds him of the possibility that even she, protected and cosseted by this world of beauty, "might die? Some day die? That her lovely blood might be spilled" (EP, 116).

Later Richard's terrors are made real in what for the reader is also an oddly titillating, comfortable way, as he sneaks into the neighborhood and, emulating his mother's fictional creation, fires his mail-order rifle into the living room of the family lawyer. Then after three successfully undetected raids, the macabre fun mounts as, "ladies and gentlemen, another sniper stepped out of the light and into the darkness, following my lead" (EP, 285). Finally, Richard caps his imitators' creations with his own final masterpiece, and shoots his mother. Not only (as Richard has gradually discovered) does she despise her husband and sleep around in chic literary circles but in a sense Richard too is a part of her personal fiction. Indeed, she is an interesting character obsessed with the transformation of her domestic life into obsessive violent fiction, which is, amusingly, rather like Oates's own. Nada is the one person in Fernwood (or Cedar Grove) who wishes to expose the violence beneath the harmonious surface of suburban paradise. On the one hand, she fights for freedom from her husband, her child, her role as suburban hostess; her restless anarchy gives her the insight into the new material of her fiction. But as well, she immerses herself into that same world. She carefully cultivates her image of affluent if slightly eccentric suburbanite. Her most characteristic action on this level of her life seems to be the perpetual cocktail parties to which she invites local acquaintances, businessmen, lovers, and out-of-town intellectuals. One aspect of her is an amusingly fictionalized portrait if not of Joyce Carol Oates herself, at least of some recognizable aspects of the public persona of such a writer. In the course of his own narrative Richard retells a story by his mother, "The Molester" (again, amusingly, a story which Oates herself had published), and finally he starts to act out another of his mother's stories, "The Sniper," culminating his attempt to create in his life a fiction of equal significance to her writings by shooting the author of both. He has rivaled her by acting out her "idea for a short novel" and has become a triumphant creator of his own fiction.

Richard's story is told with great verve and a self-conscious eye for the melodramatic, and Oates adds to the fun by stressing the obsessive personality of her narrator. He fusses over the narrative details of his memoir and (in a macabre parody of Van's and Ada's loving review of incestuous lovers in Nabokov's *Ada*) considers the precedents of child murderers through history: "I have compiled an alphabetical list of child criminals, beginning with Ajax, Arnold, and proceeding through Mossman, Billie, and ending with Watt, Samuel. . . . Oh yes, I should mention Lilloburo, Anjette, the only girl on my list: she put insecticide in the grape drink she was selling on the sidewalk before her parents' modest frame house" (EP, 8–9). With such details, Oates is exploiting her reader's taste for the expected mixture of social satire, titillating violence, and sufficient *angst* to kindle our liberal skepticism of social hypocrisy and indirect brutality, without disturbing our reliance on their comforts. In this way, *Expensive People* does mark an apparent development in Oates's technique as her manipulation of the reader's responses becomes an important (and explicit) dimension of the book's thematic continuity. Richard is what he is partly because we expect him to be so.

There is a further interest in *Expensive People*, however, which points to its greater sophistication. Oates encourages our cooperation in Richard's narrative in order, finally, to focus our interest upon the very nature of fiction making — or more specifically, upon the ways life and art entangle. Who is to say which is the more significant fiction — Richard's earnest striving to pass the Johns Behemoth entrance examination or the elaborate play of flirtation with which his mother smoothes his entry? Nada's story "The Molesters" or the molesting that (as Richard perceives) is going on all through Cedar Grove and Fernwood? Finally we perceive the irony of his successful emulation of his mother as in his life's most significant fiction he shoots her, both imposing his own sense of an appropriate ending on his own (and a number of her) fictions and also improving upon her original story of the sniper.

In order seemingly to distract us from taking such issues too seriously, we are entertained by some amusing pastiche and parody. Richard reads some "dog-eared copies of *The Writer* with earnest articles that will see you through crises of mental blocks, third-person narration, limerick verse" (EP, 104); he lists the steps he has taken to keep reader interest — knowledge of characters, reader identification, emotional preparation, and so on, and speculates on the appropriate kinds of critical response: "I wouldn't mind a hesitant essay called 'Rousseau and Everett: Liars or Saints?' or 'Stendhal and Everett: Incest and Inscape,' for instance" (EP, 107). Some of the jokes don't work quite as well: Richard speculates on the reviews he will receive from *New York Times Book Review, Time, New Republic,* and so on, but the pastiche is just a bit heavy-handed. Because of Richard or Oates herself? We are not entirely sure, but our insecurity before the dismissiveness of such literary parody is, as with our response to the book's social satire, designed to titillate us with its apparent ultimate encouragement of our own cultural sophistication.

Where the book scores heavily and where (if we see it in the context of Oates's other novels) it marks an important development in her fiction is in the way it provides a theoretical perspective for many of the seemingly more realistic settings and issues of the previous novels. Playing with the fictiveness of art, we may become aware that we are all engaged in making fictions from our lives, our gestures at communication, or self-assertion. "My memoir," claims Richard, "will not end in any . . . convenient way; it isn't well-rounded or hemmed in by fate in the shape of novelistic architecture. It certainly isn't well planned. It has no conclusion but just dribbles off, in much the same way it begins. This is life" (EP, 4). Later he remarks that "most novels, which are fiction and therefore limited, have to build up characters slowly and don't dare allow them to be eccentric or surprising unless this is planned; but my memoir [is] dealing with real people, who are already alive and quite ordinary living but who may then do things that seem out of 'character'" (EP, 26). So the events and traits of character are accumulated in a haphazard way, partly revealed, taking on huge but momentary significance, unpredictably structured, united only by the relationship assumed between the narrator and his audience.

We may become aware, however, that the sense of being overwhelmed by the unpredictability and fierce anarchy of one's inner desires is a theme we have encountered before in Oates's fiction. *Expensive People* is more revealing than its narrator knows. Art becomes a temporary refuge, an attempt to will order out of chaos. Just as Karen or Clara stepped back and, partly consciously, partly possessed by their experiences, imposed a temporary order upon their lives — temporary because as every novel's battle for order is transcended by the writer's next — so Richard's apparent stasis is overwhelmed by the flux against which that stasis has been defined. "This memoir is a hatchet to slash through my own heavy flesh and through the flesh of anyone else who happens to get in the way" (EP, 5). Somewhere beneath the outer layers of fat and self-deception there lies a "true" Richard. Just as the novelist believes, even momentarily, that under the swirling events of personal history lies the "true" significance of an era or a theme, so beneath the trivia and randomness of a personal history, whether lived in Cedar Grove or Eden County, there is a fiction of significance waiting to become self-aware.

Viewing *Expensive People* in this context, we may see the characterizing of the narrator's mother as a novelist herself as more than an amusing echo of Richard's preoccupation with his memoir. Richard's own explanation is naïve. He judges her repressive domination of him as an attempt to manipulate and partly live vicariously through the life of another, and his destruction of his school files and the eventual writing of his own memoir are attempts to assert his autonomy against her novelistic control. But the reality he attempts to assert — arson, sniping, and eventual murder — are themselves a series of fantasies. He acts out his mother's "The Sniper" and then becomes upset when another sniper invades and distorts his fiction.

What Richard does not sense and what emerges only indirectly from his mother's stories is that she too is threatened by the chaos of life invading her attempts to achieve artistic stasis. Her background as the daughter of an immigrant family, born in North Tonawanda — "a small town in upstate New York with a ludicrous name" comments Richard — her incompatible marriage with a rich but bumbling husband, her introspective son, her friends and lovers, may all be the richly satisfying material for her art but they are also the threat to that art (and, eventually, to her existence). The more conscious the novelist's attempts to impose a pattern on the unpredictability and contingency of life, the more distorting and dangerous the process may become to the person who is also the artist. Art thus becomes a threatening therapy, a necessary expression of unfulfillment. Fiction is what we all, consciously or not, use as a means of surviving reality; but our reality itself consists of other people's fictions. Approaching the end of his own fiction, Richard comments that "whatever I did, whatever degradations and evils, stupidities, blunders, moronic intrusions, whatever single ghastly act I did manage to achieve, it was done out of freedom, out of choice. This is the only consolation I have in the face of death, my readers: the thought of my free will. But I must confess that there are moments when I doubt even this consolation . . ." (EP, 307–308). Here, of course, he is echoing or, since Oates clearly has the parallel in mind, parodying Sartre. The freedom of choice Nada acts upon to achieve her authenticity as an artist is, as Alice Martin has argued, related to Sartre's *Nausea* (1938).[3] Richard includes in one of his imagined reviews the remark that "Everett sets out to prove that he can out-smartre Sartre but does not quite make it" (EP, 160). Richard's rebellions against his school, his mother's art, and her chaotic and hypocritical life, are all attempts at authentic acts, culminating in his purchase of the rifle and the willed violence he perpetrates. His actions bring about a

3 Alice C. Martin, "Towards a Higher Consciousness: A Study of the Novels of Joyce Carol Oates" (Ph.D. dissertation, Northern Illinois University, 1974), 133.

strange, frenzied joy, a sense of coming alive which makes him feel isolated yet free, lonely yet authentic. Earlier Richard had realized that when his parents' "stage props were ripped away, they always showed that they needed no fresh reasons to hate. They simply hated" (EP, 99). Now he similarly has deliberately chosen to break through the factitious world that surrounds him. Violence has become an affirmation of his freedom. And yet, while the murder of his mother is a free, liberating act, once it is completed, there is no rapturous discovery. His confession is not believed, the surfaces of suburbia close over the deed. He is denied the world's recognition of his terrible freedom; his fiction making is a failure. Even as he writes, the apparent reality he has so carefully ordered has slipped out of his grasp. We laugh at the comic gothic Oates has cleverly created for us, but we laugh as we do at Barth or Barthelme, because there is nothing else to be done.

II

Oates was awarded the 1970 National Book Award for *Them*, and it is a remarkable work as much for what it revealed about the novelist's development as for itself. In it Oates combines for the first time the rich, dramatic energy of the first two novels and the formal sophistication of *Expensive People*. As well, *Them* anticipates in important ways the richer vision which makes the following phase of her fiction (*Wonderland, Do With Me What You Will, The Assassins, Childwold*) so astounding in its fearful intensity. In 1972, she admitted that if she "could live long enough, I would like to write novels touching upon and including every person who lives in the United States,"[4] which sounds jejune (and was probably misquoted) but which does point to the prophetic stance her fiction was starting explicitly to take. The very act of creating fiction was in itself becoming an act of faith.

4 "Transformations of Self: An Interview with Joyce Carol Oates," *Ohio Review*, XV (1973), 53.

In the comic gothic of *Expensive People* we have hints of the invasion of fiction by the brutality of a reality, which in turn is an amalgam of other peoples' attempts to create significant fictions. In its metafictional self-consciousness, it seems to stand slightly aside from Oates's earlier novels, but in its perplexing interrelations between fiction and reality it not only makes explicit something of the theory behind the earlier novels, but it points forward to an important aspect of *Them*, which is built upon one such, quite specific, realization. In the "Author's Note" which prefaces the work, Oates speaks of the particular invasion of her own consciousness in which the story originated. The "Maureen Wendall" of the work was, according to the note, a former student whose "various problems and complexities overwhelmed me, and I became aware of her life story, her life as the possibility for a story, perhaps drawn to her by certain similarities between her and me.... My initial feeling... was 'This must be fiction, this can't all be real!'" Oates goes on to comment how "it is to her terrible obsession with her personal history that I owe the voluminous details of this novel... temporarily blocking out my own reality, my personal life" (T, 11). Reviewers made various skeptical remarks about Oates's claims, pointing out the rather remarkable coincidences between the author's style and the letters of "Maureen Wendall" incorporated into the text, and between the author's obsessions and those of her characters.[5] But such comments, even if true, are crudely irrelevant. Behind the elaborate account of the work's origins is something more important—the function of the novelist as almost passively open to the tortures and obsessions, the agonies of the particular place and time of America today. The "them" of the title is not primarily the poor, the underprivileged, for whom most of us variously feel pity, compassion, anger, or derision. It is the "them" that may without warning invade our sheltered and static vision of our selves. Explicitly in her "Fer-

5 See, for example, L. E. Sissman, "The Whole Truth," *New Yorker*, December 6, 1969, pp. 238, 241–42.

nandes" stories some years later and implicitly here in *Them* is a radical Yeatsian view of the artist. The "borders of our mind," wrote Yeats, "are ever shifting, and . . . many minds can flow into one another, as it were, and create or reveal a single mind, a single energy."[6] It becomes the function of the artist to suffer and articulate the energies that drive and define his age. Here, Oates is suggesting, the minds of "Maureen Wendall" and "Joyce Carol Oates" overlap and flow together with something akin to Yeats's single energy. "I am writing to you because there is something like me, in you," writes Maureen, overwhelmed by the shock that "the books you taught us didn't explain" the "jumble" of people and things that make up her life. "All those books? Why did you tell us they were more important than life? They are not more important than my life" (T, 329, 333). In her longest letter, which in its intensity and clarity certainly seems to flow with a single energy with the prose that surrounds it, she comments on the shocking coincidence of event and yet the dislocation of feeling she perceives: "I am going to fall in love. Tomorrow night I'll see the man I have picked out to love. He is already married; he has three children," she writes. Then, the pattern of life is seen explicitly as the making of fiction itself: "I am telling you these things even though you are a married woman and would not want any other woman to take your husband from you. But you are a married woman, I think, who would not mind taking someone else's husband, so long as it happened well enough, beautifully enough like a story" (T, 336). It is true that we often enjoy fiction partly because we are afraid of the experiences it evokes, destroying our own fictions, and it may be the writer's role to exorcise these demons for us — but, as *Them* proves, the violence, randomness, pain, destruction we fear and attempt to deal with through art is as real a fiction as any art. *Them* is an attempt to make us face the shocking fiction which is reality.

6 W. B. Yeats, *Essays and Introductions* (London: MacMillan, 1961), 28.

In Oates's earlier (and, now we may say, after *Expensive People*, less critically self-conscious) novels, we saw her developing her art out of the classical Flaubertian tradition, attempting to intensify realism to the state of a parable of feeling, capturing the spirit of living in America rather than using America as a backdrop. She herself was probably always clear about her intentions, noting at one point that she was "not content with reporting events" but wished "to evoke their psychological reality for the reader, through the use of sensuous details and symbols." *Them* takes something of the subject material of, say, *A Garden of Earthly Delights*, but into its writing has come much of the sophistication of *Expensive People*. Although the events in the book, particularly the Detroit riots of 1968, have a basis in history and despite Oates's basing the novel on a student's recollections, *Them* is distinctly different from the fashionable "non-fiction novels" of the sixties and early seventies. One of the most interesting developments of the period was the merging of fictional techniques with journalism: Norman Mailer, John Hersey, Tom Wolfe, Truman Capote, and others took historical events and placed themselves either as reporter or participant in their midst. The essential quality of our age, Mailer suggested, "cannot be developed by the methods of history — only by the instincts of the novelist." Mailer has stressed the committed, essentially subjective, vision through which he argues, cajoles, and moves his reader in such books as *Miami and the Siege of Chicago* or *Armies of the Night*. Capote, by contrast, presents *In Cold Blood* as an objective re-creation of a murder, although as Tony Tanner pointed out, he did essentially the same as his greater fictional forebears, Stendhal and Dostoevsky, who assumed that "to explore the latent significance of the grim, silent facts, the most valuable aid is the human imagination."[7]

7 Joyce Carol Oates, "Background and Foreground in Fiction," *Writer*, LXXX (August, 1967), 13; Norman Mailer, *Armies of the Night* (New York: New American Library), 84; Tony Tanner, "Death in Kansas," *Spectator*, March 18, 1966, pp. 331–32. For a recent discussion of the "non-fiction Novel," see John Hollowell, *Fact and Fiction: The New Journalism and the Non-Fiction Novel* (Chapel Hill: University of North Carolina Press, 1977).

Them certainly has certain common concerns with Capote or
— to take a book also written about Detroit in 1968 — Hersey's
The Algiers Motel Incident. But where they take public, recorded
history as their subject, Oates takes a set of incidents from what
she would regard essentially as "private" history. The book is
a tripartite account of two generations of the Wendall family,
whose lives never make newspaper headlines but are nonetheless darkly determined by the limiting, hostile environment of
Detroit. We see a process of almost ritualistic disintegration as
marriages break, relationships fail, and as private history connects with the public world; cities are burnt and political and
personal discontents erupt into violence. In other words, the detailed events reflect the subjective chaos of the minds experiencing them — and here is the most crucial distinction between
Oates and, say, Capote or Hersey. In *Them* we are invited to
participate in events as private, felt, and nevertheless (or *because*
of this fact) of enormous significance. Hence we get neither a
central protagonist (Mailer's "the Candidate," say) nor an objective authorial voice (as in Capote or Hersey) attempting to
provide a perspective of objective re-creation. In *Them* the events
are frequently juxtaposed randomly, their seeming incoherence
re-creating in readers the fragmented and dislocated apprehension of reality perceived by the characters. *Them* records how
Detroit feels to its inhabitants. The story employs the usual ul-
tradramatic surface of Oates's gothic parables: murder, rape,
insanity, industrial accidents, arson, prostitution, violence of all
kinds. The opening scenes, in particular, shock the reader into
asking just what degree of heightened reality we are being thrust
into. Sixteen-year-old Loretta dresses dreamily for a Saturday
night with her boyfriend Bernie; her brother Brock adds to her
excitement by pulling a gun from his pocket; by the end of the
evening, Loretta has made love with Bernie, maybe thereby conceiving Jules; and she wakes in the morning to find next to her
Bernie's dead, bleeding body, shot by her brother. Hysterical,
she searches out the local cop, Howard Wendall, who comes to
investigate. Appalled, angered, he screams at Loretta and then

rapes her. While they struggle, she thinks of her dead boyfriend, realizing as he pulls up her dress, that "she had loved him and he was dead and she would never see him again. Never would he come to her the way Howard was trying to come to her. . . . He was dead, it was over, finished, that was the end of her youth. She tried not to think of it again" (T, 50). Pregnant, she marries Howard Wendall and settles into a life of depression, economic insecurity, and deprivation.

As we settle into the story, we become aware of the way in which Oates is dealing with the social and economic roots of the characters. We move from a rural background, something like Eden County, into rundown Detroit, with its poverty, violence, patrol cars, garbage, predatory sexuality, unemployment, and psychic as well as economic insecurity. "To Whose Country Have I Come?" is the title of Part 2 of the novel, and it seems we are essentially once again in the world of *A Garden of Earthly Delights*: Carleton's rage at dispossession of land and family has become the dominant mood of the frustrated Wendalls. Loretta, Maureen's mother, is sunk deep in the "sad limits" of her flesh, "locked" in her body as her family is locked in the economic determinism of Detroit. Her grandmother is similarly "baffled at the failure of her body to keep up with her assessment of herself" (T, 99), just as the Wendall men are preoccupied with work they hate and sullen with the daily efforts of their bodies, "so sluggish and stubborn." Like Oates's characters elsewhere, the Wendalls are haunted by dreams of autonomy or power, but their high desires find only the crudest, dullest materializations — merely "the freedom of trucks and trains and planes" or, more limiting, the apparent autonomy of material security. Life, as opposed to the dream, is crude, deceptive, and violent. "A certain number of boys must grow up to die in the electric chair" (T, 91) is the resigned belief of Jules's school principal, and behind such fatalism is the acceptance that impotence and futility can be escaped only — and then temporarily — by violence.

When one of "them" does attempt to struggle above her violent and restrictive life, then once again the dream is expressed solely in terms of money and exploitation. Like Clara, for instance, Loretta is bewildered by the lure of owning a house, by marriage, by domestic comfort, above all by the power of money. Loretta's wants fix continually on things, but unlike Clara's, her life never affords her the space for decision or opportunity for clarity or control. Her sharpest recognitions are negative, that "the world was pulling into two parts, those who were hopeless bastards and weren't worth spitting on and those who were going to get somewhere" (T, 18). Even when she acts decisively — going on the street, or leaving her husband — lacking ingenuity or drive, she bungles her attempts at autonomy and relapses for most of her life into a foul-mouthed, vacillating, sordid shrew. Money continually haunts her and just as surely eludes her all her life.

Throughout the novel, money is the symbol of all that is ugly, oppressive, and yet alluring. The psychic pressures of the Detroit of the novel are rooted in the crisp, cool cash that in *Expensive People* had made Cedar Grove and Fernwood so delectably relaxed. But here, in the Detroit of *Them*, money is brutal, exploitative, soiled — "the rumpled, soft, filthy feel of bills" that Jules earns for his mother. His sister Maureen's dreams are haunted by the question "*How do you get money?*" (T, 192). Money, all the Wendall family know, is "the secret." A man picks her up, takes her to a hotel room; through her bewilderment, indifference, and misery, what keeps her together is the thought of money. The act would "take a certain passage of time. A few minutes, several minutes . . . but he would give her money. That fact kept her from breaking into pieces" (T, 202).

Jules Wendall grows up, more aware of his opportunities as a male to acquire money. His family and friends continually gripe about money; Jules determines simply, eventually to "get it," and to "float upon it." He sells himself in another way for a more obvious kind of independence. He gets hired as a gangster's driver and is immediately overwhelmed by the fierce and sudden power money can have when he is handed a check for one hundred dollars and then is told by his employer, "Drive straight ahead. I want to think. I have got to plan the rest of my life this morning" (T, 244). At this point, the reader perhaps starts to question the realism of such a statement. But it is true to the level of significant feeling Oates is trying to evoke. Jules experiences the remark upon his nerves: "Planning the rest of his life that morning! . . . And why couldn't Jules plan the rest of his life too that very morning? Wasn't he free to make nearly anything happen?" (T, 244). It is the tone, the excitement and apparent autonomy behind such remarks that is communicated to us, an impression heightened when another check, "for groceries," is for two hundred dollars. "'And now we must get started. I have a busy schedule this morning.' . . . Jules drove off. He felt giddy from the surprise of this second check. It lay beside him on the seat, and he glanced down at it to make sure it was real" (T, 245).

In the crude, exploitative sexist society of the American city, this new financial euphoria lets Jules indulge in the exploitation of which his sister has become the victim. He stops the car outside a house in Grosse Pointe to watch a girl climb out of a blue station wagon. The girl is about sixteen or seventeen, dressed in all the accouterments of the characters in *Expensive People*. She is beautiful, casual, unconsciously provocative, and "unassailable" (T, 248). "So this" muses Jules "is the way life happens: a sudden ballooning upward" (T, 251).

The success of *Them* is built on the way Oates manages not just to depict the pervasiveness of materialism in Detroit's and America's social fabric (commonplace enough) but—as the development of her fiction to this point makes clear—on her power to evoke in her reader the pervasiveness and brutality of such basic human drives. She is writing not only about "them" but about *our* feelings. A useful contrast is perhaps with Dreiser's *Sister Carrie*. As Carrie approaches Chicago, Dreiser prepares us for her eventual downfall by a series of succinct, objective, moralistic comments, sociologically apt but totally external to the event. We are urged to feel compassion and some understanding of Carrie's plight, but Dreiser's moral perspective, even though it is compassionate and complex, is never lost sight of. With Oates, we are never provided with a firm moral perspective; instead we are taken directly into the maelstrom of feelings, motives, and drives of the participants and invited to see them as mirroring our own. Insofar as a moral perspective arises within the novel, it arises directly in relation to the vitality with which Oates's characters pursue their dreams and are seized by Jules's sense of "suddenly ballooning upwards." We are in a world of intensity, not a world of moral decision.

Where Dreiser sets his observations within a recognizable history, Oates's insights, however they seem to arise within a recognizable setting, are really rooted in a transhistorical world: her subject is not Detroit and its effect on people but Detroit as a symbol of a process that lies deep within all of us. History is not a matter of public forces and public cause and effect but, more fundamentally, personal growth and response. "The only kind of fiction that is real" is "personal history," she states in her Author's Note, and in her letter to the author Maureen Wendall pours scorn upon Oates's professional judgment that fiction is somehow an ordering of life: "You said, 'Literature gives form to life,' I remember you saying that very clearly. What is form? Why is it better than the way life happens, by itself?" (T, 338). What we experience in the chaotic, unpredictable world of *Them* is that however painful being thrown into the world may be, contingency is a necessary condition of spiritual freedom. One of the crucial emotional experiences of *Them* is the fear and challenge of contingency, which is insistently present to Maureen as she grows up. She broods about how she can tell "what would last and what wouldn't? Marriages ended. Love ended. Money could be stolen, found out and taken." Such things simply happen. The world she and we inhabit is ordered only randomly: "Objects disappeared, slipped through cracks, devoured, kicked aside, knocked under the bed or into the trash, lost. Nothing lasted for long." The tiniest arbitrary act always contains in it the possibility of cataclysm: "Maureen thought of earthquakes opening the earth in violent rifts, swallowing city blocks, churches, railroad tracks. She thought of fire, of bulldozers leveling trees and buildings. Why not?" (T, 212). Personality is fluid, open, at risk — or it solidifies and the person dies. The members of the Wendall family are involved in struggles against external forces — the Depression, poverty, an overcrowded family, violence in the city and in the family — but they are locked in a more important struggle within themselves. At the book's start Loretta, Maureen's mother, has been plunged into immediate trauma, and for the rest of her life Loretta withdraws into a cowered materialism, the hope of her beauty and sexuality battered into cynical submission. Her security becomes defined in terms of stasis. Any change or challenge must be resisted. And yet her experience of life is nothing but "all these changes, this geography of change" which Loretta simply "could not keep up with" (T, 151).

With Maureen, personal autonomy seems as deterministically defined by material desires as in her mother's life, and her instinctive youthful sense of adventure, "as if she had safely crossed a boundary line" is directed unconsciously towards the kinds of material security that have destroyed her mother and which seemingly motivate her brother. When Maureen turns to Jules for affection he offers her money, and, without knowing why, she feels "something was happening, something terrible — she was losing Jules or had already lost him . . . was losing something or had already lost it" (T, 168). Like the world around her, she becomes deliberately hard, as if a "shell were shaping itself out of her skin." The money men give her seems to justify no more intimate connection between people than the violence and degradation she experiences with her mother and which her brother, too, seems to offer. A man, she thinks, "was like a machine: one of those machines at the laundromat where she dragged the laundry. There were certain cycles to go through";

"she could not understand the weight, the force that drew men and women together, of their own free will. What she could understand was the money in her purse, and the money in that book" (T, 209, 211). But unlike her brother, she experiences no sudden ballooning upward: her money is discovered and she is beaten up by her stepfather. Shocked, cowered, she takes months to wake from the horror to which life seems to be reduced. Life has been consistent only in its accidents, and her dreams, like her mother's, have become immobile, frozen.

In the struggles of the Wendall family we see a tightly knit group of individuals driven by neurotic wants and confused values. Even Jules, the most selfish and autonomous of all the characters, realizes himself only potentially. In Maureen, the evolutionary constructive urge toward realization is warped into a grasp for material power and then for domesticity; in Jules, partly because of his sex, his desire for autonomy is a more constant part of his character and upbringing. Dreaming is built into his character and "all his life he would close his eyes upon a landscape of absolute distance, luring him forward as if he were tottering on the brink of a perpetual delirium, a child still trapped inside his adult's bones" (T, 73). His teacher and parents, suspicious of such energies, "always thinking, sifting, judging, preparing" (T, 92), prophesy a disastrous end for him. They have had to submit to society: so must he. As a number of readers have suggested, Jules resembles Stendhal's Julian Sorel, torn between his own ego and his family and communal ties.[8] Both characters, too, are intended as prototypical of the struggles and tensions of their generation. Their inner history constitutes the real history of their age.

Oates's story of the Wendalls, then, operates on two interacting levels: one is a story of conflict, tension, and material degradation; the other, continuously interwoven, is a story of spiritual aspiration beyond the suffocating violence and determinism

8 See, for example, Martin, "Towards a Higher Consciousness," 159–61.

of Detroit. And it is Jules who develops most fully into Oates's symbol for this challenge to the stifling despair of America. At one point in the story she stands aside to comment on Jules's typicality. His life, like everyone's, is a mixture of order and tedium, she says, made up of the usual irrelevant or shameful details of life. The real importance of his story is his spiritual development and, like the rest of us, Oates suggests, he thinks of himself as searching not for good or evil, but for significance, which arises from the spirit exclusively: "pure spirit struggling to break free of the morass of the flesh. He thought of himself as spirit struggling with the fleshy earth, the very force of gravity, death." This is what motivates him throughout his life, and despite a pattern of experience which appears to be arbitrary lunacy, "*a story imagined by a madman*," its coherence is a search "as an American youth," is to break "out into beauty, in patches perhaps but beauty anyway." Then, in this important parenthetical passage, she makes a statement which, we can sense, is crucial to her fiction as a whole. "All of Detroit" she writes "is melodrama, and most lives in Detroit fated to be melodramatic" (T, 274). The shift from symbolic narrative in this passage to brooding authorial commentary reminds us of the self-consciousness of *Expensive People*. Oates seems to be deliberately inviting us to consider Jules's life as representative and yet as only one of a myriad of possible representations: all lives in America are symbolic, "transparent" as she calls Detroit itself, in their own subjective way.

In relating the significance of the Wendalls' struggle for autonomy, Oates focuses on two recurring symbols. They stand for the desires of the external and internal worlds which provide the dark visceral elements of life through which the characters must seek their authenticity. They are Detroit itself and the characters' sexual drives. The passage just quoted continues, in the same brooding tone, to comment on the typicality of Jules's melodramatic life. Restless, ambitious, struggling, Jules embodies the startling and inherently unpredictable quality of the American dream. Oates describes him as repeatedly falling "into astonishing shrill spaces of craziness, all of it overdone physically and aborted spiritually, but somehow logical." Again, it is not the trivial data of childhood or adolescence which are significant, however surprising or melodramatic they may be — the "glancing knowledge he had of hoodlums and sub-crooks, petty thieves, con-men, pimps, men with no incomes and no jobs and no futures." The things that are closer to Jules's spiritual development relate to his inner life, to his dreams and his love affairs. "For love," Oates notes, anticipating her analysis in *Do With Me What You Will*, is "a delirium and a pathological condition," and it "makes of the lover a crazed man; his blood leaps with bacteria that shoot the temperature up toward death" (T, 274). There are two sides of Jules here: there is the Jules of the melodramatic Detroit of "hoodlums and sub-crooks," and there is the Jules of the delirium of love. The dualism points to a related distinction behind all the book's experiences, and to the dual pressures, external and internal, which mold their lives.

As Jules grows up, the felt pressure of Detroit's streets and buildings and people that amazes him as a child becomes a territory that he has to conquer or be overcome by. As a male, he is somehow emotionally akin to this world and thereby able more easily to survive. He senses the defeat he is struggling against within the women of Detroit. He finds them "bewildered, confused, fearful. . . . A woman in a laundromat in Detroit only appears to be in control of the machines! A woman in a car only appears to be in control! Inside, her machinery is as wobbly and nervous as the machinery of the car, which may have been slammed together by someone as mutely angry as Jules's father, now on the assembly line at Chrysler" (T, 102–103). Nothing could better illustrate, in miniature, Oates's fictional intentions than such a passage. Our emotions assimilate a barrage of symbols: the women, the laundromat, the car, and the assembly line. We are not being provided with a sketch of an historical or sociological background but are drawn into the sense of living and feeling in the angry, confused, threatening muddle that is the felt presence of Detroit in all the characters. Detroit is not primarily a place but a collage of feelings. The Sheraton-Cadillac Hotel, Grosse Pointe, Tiger Stadium, all become experienced as pressures of feeling, not as concrete objects in a Dreiserian description. For Jules, Detroit is a "smell," "a kind of stretched-out hole, a hole with a horizon" (T, 232).

The horizon (the image reminds us of Lawrence's insistent images of breaking limitations in *The Rainbow*) is represented within the individual by sex. The radical surprise of sexuality is a challenge to the materialism of Detroit, a means of getting free, people working "*themselves out of other people*" (T, 236). When Jules first sleeps with Bernard Geffin's mistress Faye, he seems replete with the sensual excitement of sex, but beneath sexual satiety is an enthusiasm with which he will seek his goal far beyond the intermingling rooms and golden chimes of Grosse Pointe and "the fragrant softness of a woman's secret body" (T, 265). It is this spirit of buoyancy that provides him a drive toward a transcendence undreamt by his family. He meets Nadine — beautiful, rich, wayward — and again, he apprehends her first in terms of her price. Her beauty seems beyond him, yet somehow accessible: "He had faith in an automatic upward swing, once he got really on the bottom" (T, 297). She runs away with him as far as Texas. When he is struck delirious by a bout of influenza, she leaves him in disgust — and "that seemed to him the end of the story of Jules and Nadine." There is a fated, melodramatic aspect to their passion, partly born of the way in which Jules has long determined that his true nature would someday be expressed through luxurious cars and beautiful women. However, despite the crassness and chauvinism of his conception of her, there is within his lust an intensity that drives it beyond the possessive: what she represents is the spark of the transcendent that will eventually fling him from Detroit and what it embodies. They meet again after her marriage and recommence a violent love affair. Into the convulsive physical confrontations between

Jules and Nadine, Oates pours the book's pent-up passions, as if the violence, anger, aspiration of all of Detroit were focused in the two lovers as they fight with images of each other, groping for some kind of relaxed fulfillment. Making love, vowing eventually to marry, they feel "as if the two of them were fated for some final convulsion, locked in each other's arms, their mouths fastened greedily together in a pose neither had really chosen" (T, 364).

Yet through the violence and darkness of their affair, there is something irresistible. Anticipating the magnificent climax of *Do With Me What You Will*, Nadine (a first sketch of Elena) muses how "a woman is like a dream. . . . She lives in a dream, waiting for a man. There's no way out of this, insulting as it is, no woman can escape it. Her life is waiting for a man. That's all. There is a certain door in this dream, and she had to walk through it. She has no choice. Sooner or later she has to open that door and walk through it and come to a certain man, one certain man. She has no choice about it. She can marry anyone but she has no choice about this" (T, 367). In *Them* Oates's focus is less on the woman caught in such a relationship than on the male drive of romantic love. Jules is a man fated to leap at the impossible and, sometimes, gain it, and all his dreams have been embodied in women — in his grandmother, in his teacher Sister Mary Jerome, his sister, and his romanticized, neurotic mistress. Though they may fail his idealism (his grandmother gets sick, his teacher looses her temper, his sister goes on the street, Nadine abandons him) they nevertheless draw out of him the imaginative vision by which Jules represents the hope of the novel. Making love, "his mind flashed to him an image of himself and Nadine, entwined together, a woman's long, pale arms lashed about his body, and Jules's strong back arched over her, in a grip of death. Hadn't he always put his faith in such bizarre images? Jules risking this, Jules leaping to that, Jules plunging in?" (T, 393). Like Nadine, as they struggle together, he feels that through, not despite, their lacerations and pain a gravitation toward unity in this fashion would bring him violently through the horizon of Detroit's limitations. Love is like art: "We're in a painting," Jules broods at one point, a painting which "had seemed, then, to hold a secret for him — the way out of Detroit." Now, with Nadine he is reminded of the same possibility: "He had gone beyond himself. He was being in a painting, embracing a woman in a painting. Their love, so sweaty and violent at its height, had exploded into a thousand clean glimmering dots and golden leaves" (T, 384).

Love of this intensity develops a hyper-realism that takes it far beyond Jules's adolescent daydreaming. While he has a lover's inability to "quite believe in all this beauty, this gift of beauty, this perfection" (T, 382), their affair contains the essential Lawrentian elements of otherness, of wrestling, like the lion and the unicorn, for the crown of fulfillment: "He did not think of this woman as someone else's wife and therefore practised in love, but as the deepest, essential Nadine. . . . He could not remember any other woman, was not certain that he had ever done this before" (T, 381). Each gives the other the overwhelming sense that, as Nadine puts it, "a man's love creates a woman's love. You've made me the way I am. I'm certain of that." Then, the typical Oates irony intervenes, as Nadine continues: "There are men who are permanent in a woman's life, everything in them is permanent, and terrible, nobody thinks about them *That's something I set out to do*; there's no choice about it. You love me and I love you, I don't have any choice about it" (T, 371–72). The affirmation of their love is through the violence and anger of the city that surrounds them, not despite it — even when Nadine cracks under the pressure and finally tries to shoot Jules in an effort, seemingly, to avoid facing the realities of his permanence for her.

This violent culmination of the second phase of their relationship (a third phase, of reunion, is suggested as the book ends) is brought about because, like so many of Lawrence's lovers, Jules and Nadine are having to fight through not only the destructive element of Detroit but through their own inner sicknesses. Nadine, in particular, is characterized by a peculiarly contemporary brittleness which typifies an Oates heroine. She has a passivity before others' manipulative pressures which makes her vulnerable and alluring — and which might hide a vacuum, an absence of any real self. She is formed by the brutal affluence of Detroit that we have already seen in *Expensive People* and its effects in her are brought out in the way Jules experiences something volatile and experimental about her which frightens him. Early in their relationship she fastens on the accidental quality of their meeting, as if such fortuity were commensurate with the unpredictability of a world which justifies her lack of commitment to him. Only through the violence of their encounters can she sense any kind of authenticity, and her attempt to murder Jules is a distorted but (Oates wants us to think) eventually purgative acknowledgment of an authentic passion invading and re-creating her.

Detroit represents the deterministic limit of the dark corruption through which the Wendalls must seek transcendence, and sex is the most immediate and perhaps final means to the necessary authenticity. Another recurring symbol is the American dream of mobility. "As long as he had his own car he was an American and could not die" (T, 400): here Jules's kernel of selfhood is built upon a drive "to live a secular life, at all costs" which would "expand" him "out to the limits of his skin and the range of his eyesight" (T, 105). His desire is focused on California, the novel's symbol for an unspecific hope of autonomy, just as Detroit symbolizes an all too specific material limitation.

They mythic dimension I have depicted in considering *Them* becomes crucial in the novel's final pages. On the surface, the novel seems to reassert its realistic basis as Detroit hurls itself into the 1968 riots, as Maureen wrenches her lover from his wife and children, and Jules screams for Detroit to be destroyed and finally sets out for Los Angeles, determined eventually to marry Nadine. But beneath the surface action, we sense how the novel's feelings also culminate on a more apocalyptic level. The significance of the ecstatic tone of the final fifty pages or so can perhaps be shown by two comparisons — with *The Great Gatsby* and *The Rainbow*.

Like Gatsby, Jules is searching for riches, autonomy, glamor, and, above all yet almost indistinguishable from these, the "peculiar translucent, uncanny beauty" (T, 355) of a woman. Like Gatsby, he submits himself to violence and corruption to win her; to reach the "frontier" he feels must lie beyond Detroit (and which he identifies with California), he will fight, kill, and burn. Yet what distinguishes Jules is that his fight for Nadine, which James R. Giles has suggested has echoes of Gatsby's green light at the end of Daisy's pier,[9] involves his whole self, not the series of false selves and social roles he has played with throughout his life. Even toward the end of the book, when he drifts into the revolutionary subculture, he retains a sense of autonomy and selfhood which has kept him apart from the stream of destruction around him. Unlike his sister, who attempts to escape poverty, bigotry, and exploitation only to end in the safe haven of domesticity, Jules persists in his more dangerous search for the authentic. Oates may seem to be sentimentalizing him, but she wants him to stand for an affirmation of hope in the midst of determinism, a buoyant romantic affirmation alongside the despairing passivity of the rest of his family.

Another useful comparison with the strong, passionate ending, which moves from the fearful chaos of the Detroit riots to Jules's departure for California, is its similarity with the ending of Lawrence's *The Rainbow*, where Ursula Brangwen fights through a series of destructive experiences to a fragile but real hope. Lawrence evokes the process through repeated images of barriers which must, like a seed's husk, be burst through, lest they destroy the life within. Jules, like Ursula, has submitted himself to a process of risk, discovery, and error. Yet through-

9 James R. Giles, "From Jimmy Gatz to Jules Wendall," *Dalhousie Review*, LVI (1976–1977), 718, 724.

out, he has retained a hard, irreducible core of being that is never subordinated to the determinism of Detroit. Near the book's end, like Ursula, Jules is cut adrift — from his family, a job, his mistress — but he is a man not merely in perpetual motion, but waiting in hope: "He was perpetually waiting for something to happen — anxious that it might happen and that it might not happen. He had no idea what it could be." Once it was the priesthood, then marriage, now it was connected vaguely with the mystery of dreams, "those disturbing dreams that seemed to belong to another man but had to be his own." His friend Mort describes him as "a depression baby. Not necessarily the *historical* depression" but rather "a permanent depression of the spirit" (T, 426). He drifts into casual, mechanical sex where his overwhelming feelings are of indifference — "What did that mean, to be a woman's lover? What difference did it make?" (T, 477). Equally indifferently, he drifts into the radical politics associated with the Detroit riots, arguing for revolution and violence with a similar impersonality: "Let everything burn! Why not? The city was coming to life in fire, and he, Jules, was sitting in it, warming to it, the flames dancing along his arteries and behind his seared eyes" (T, 488). Finally he gets into a fight with a policeman, and shoots him, virtually in cold blood.

How do we read this sequence of events? Certainly, Jules seems to descend into further degradation and violence. Yet we might recall Oates's insistence, in an essay on Dostoevsky, that violence is always an affirmation, since it is a decisive act making possible (though not certain) a further growth. She notes, too, that Dostoevsky's novels (like her own) are built upon a long preparation, then a decisive consummation in violence (EOI, 6, 96). We note that Jules's real development also seems to be moving onto a new, transcendent plane. The riot and revolution are inevitable outcomes of the dynamic of Detroit itself and not a part of the essential Jules, who through such violence is reaching beyond Detroit's horizon. Although Jules submits himself to the stream, he is, like Lawrence's Ursula, retaining an indestructible essence, which takes him through the experiences which surround and threaten to destroy him. Throughout he is open to a more autonomous future. He feels himself as somehow apart from Detroit. The sky above the city "looks to him as if he were staring out through a piece of rotten fruit. . . . He himself was a man inside a piece of rotten fruit. . . . He had become truly invisible. . . . Impressions flowed through him. Nothing caught hold. He was safe from his own past, kicked free of his own past" (T, 445). Leaving Detroit, he is purging his false self, and the final farewell with his sister is the divergence of two ways of life, one going into subordination and acceptance, the other towards hope. She goes to the safety of domesticity, he to California and then "maybe when I've done better, gotten on my feet, when I come back here and get married — I want to marry her anyway, that woman the one who tried to kill me. I still love her and I'll make some money and come back and marry her, wait and see" (T, 507). Jules has nothing more than hope, but it is after all that quality which has taken him through his childhood, his wanderings, the surging violence of Detroit, and which continues to beckon him towards the horizon. Perhaps California, and Nadine Greene (if he returns), will prove to be like Gatsby's green light, but in the terrifying dream which is Jules's America, hope is the indestructible core which may bring him through. He is no longer one of *them*. "Everything in America is coming alive. It's breaking off and coming alive. . . . Fire burns and does its duty, perpetually, and the fires will never be put out" (T, 502). In *Them* the fires are still the fires of riot and destruction; in Oates's next novel, the fire will be of a more lasting, although even more painful, passion for which Jules as yet has only the hope.

SIX

Wonderland, Do With Me What You Will

Oates's dream of the obsessions of America was given a particular direction in her novels in the early seventies. Two in particular, published two years apart, are concerned with the grim struggle of the human personality to transcend the brutality of American (and in a wider philosophical context, Western) materialism. *Wonderland* (1971) traces the deterministic and radically disconnected life of an orphaned boy who becomes a successful surgeon and who seeks, but cannot achieve, any transcendence of his limiting and discontinuous life. Nothing, including changes of identity and sexual love, gives him a strong or growing sense of his own individuality. The second novel, *Do With Me What You Will* (1973) is, by contrast, the story of a pair of lovers who look back, having in Lawrentian terms, "come through" pain, anguish, the stultifying oppression of seemingly deterministic worlds, to a transcendent hope.

"Sunk helplessly in flesh, as in the turbulent uncontrollable mystery of the 'economy', the human being with spiritual yearnings becomes tragic when these yearnings are defeated or mocked," Oates wrote, introducing Harriet Arnow's *The Dollmaker*, which she depicted as treating "the subjecting of ordinary people to the corrosive and killing facts of society" (NHNE, 99, 109). This tragedy, as we have seen in earlier novels, is based on the inescapability of the world of deterministic material facts, their power over the individual reinforced by the cultural and philosophical assumptions of Western materialism. Western man believes himself to be trapped, within history and within the material and the illusory nature of the ego. *Wonderland* and *The Assassins* (1975) dramatize the profoundly depressing determinism of contemporary Western subjection to the world of history, fact, and ego. They render more explicitly than elsewhere what she has described as the death throes of the egocentric Renaissance consciousness, with its insistence on a division between mind and body, higher and lower consciousness, self and others, conscious and unconscious.[1] *Do With Me What You Will* represents the other extreme of her vision, an intense and ultimately hopeful belief in the possibilities of transcendence inherent in human love.

II

In the epigraph to *Wonderland*, Oates quotes Borges:

We . . . have dreamt the world. We have dreamt it as firm, mysterious, visible, ubiquitous in space and durable in time; but in its architecture we have allowed tenuous and external crevices of unreason which tells us it is false.

Borges' remarks stand as ironical commentary upon the novel's action. The world of *Wonderland* is once again built upon

1 Joyce Carol Oates, "New Heaven and Earth," *Saturday Review*, November 4, 1972, p. 52.

Oates's primary symbols of the facticity of American life—
money, food and eating, cleanliness, the struggle for success and
social respectability—and, beneath these surface manifestations
of contemporary affluence, violence. *Wonderland* is divided,
like most of the novels, into three parts, and it relates the history
of Jesse—successively surnamed Harte, Vogel, Pedersen, and finally again Vogel. The first book, "Variations on an American
Hymn," re-creates a familiar world of oppressive American materialism; the second book, "The Finite Passing of an Infinite
Dream," concentrates on Jesse's struggle to assert the power and
autonomy of the mind over the material; the final part, "Dreaming America," intensifies the split between mind and matter, as
Jesse struggles for control of his daughter, Shelly. This spiritual
drama is, typically, played out through an intensely evoked historical and local setting which becomes eerily transparent as the
novel progresses. As a child, Jesse is orphaned when his bank-
rupt father shoots the rest of his family and then himself; he is
brought up, educated, and formed by a succession of influences
—his grandfather, a boys' home, then the brilliant Doctor Pedersen, the University of Chicago, postgraduate medical school,
and then his marriage, wife, and children. Through all these
rapidly changing environments and experiences Jesse constantly
fights to discover and develop his sense of self. His tragedy is
that he can sense no alternative to being defined by externals.
Late in the novel, his wife Helene describes his possessiveness in
terms of his inner insecurity. "He is a jumble of men," she says.
"There are many people in him. . . . And he wants more. He
wants his daughters, and he wants me. . . . He wants to be us. I
can't explain. He wants to own us, to be us" (w, 449). Molded
by such radically dissociated influences, continually under pressure to achieve status, stability, relatedness, he needs a sense of
the coherence of his own identity. Otherwise, each successive
experience is "a blur, shapeless, a dimension of fog and space,
like the future itself" (w, 49). And yet all he encounters is the
brutal flux of history into which he has been thrown.

One thing, in its sinister pervasiveness, links Jesse's successive worlds — the affluence of contemporary America. Money stands in *Wonderland*, as it did in *Expensive People* and *Them*, as the symbol of an attempt for spiritual autonomy which ends in frustration and death. Here, it is the lack of money that drives Jesse's father to murder and suicide. As his father drives him home from school for the last time, the display window of Montgomery Ward's with its "galaxy of gifts" is a threatening mixture of temptation and apparent possibility. Everything is "too expensive. They have no money. . . . He wants a shotgun but there is no chance of getting it. No, no chance. There is no money. . . . Who can afford such things? Where are the people who can afford such things?" (w, 47–48).

For Jesse and his family selfhood seems only realizable in terms of affluence. Personality is definable not in terms of inner serenity or strength, but simply in terms of the graspable security of the material. Uneducated, unemployed, overwhelmed by the depressing struggle for survival and taunted by such scenes, Jesse's father explodes with frustration into murder and suicide. Jesse is left orphaned and drifts until he is discovered by Doctor Karl Pedersen, who systematically tries to mold him according to a set of theories which sound like a sinister parody of third-force psychology, positive thinking, and evangelical religion. In his attempts to control Jesse's life he becomes just as destructive as Jesse's own father. His own children have been brought up by a "secret philosophy" like the one he uses on his patients: "Once a patient has come to him, he believes the patient is *his*. . . . He owns the patient, he owns the disease, he owns everything" (w, 186).

With the Pedersen family Jesse discovers something of the power of human striving and autonomy. But he also discovers the destructiveness of affluence and the material freedom it apparently brings. The Pedersens, "with their soft, gelatinous bodies," are horrifying caricatures of affluent consumers. They are all gross, stuffed "like pale sausages" yet possessing nevertheless a religion of rarefied spiritualism. Alice C. Martin has suggested that the relationship between Pedersen and his wife illustrates the nineteenth-century dichotomy of nature and consciousness, with Pedersen's possessive mental control of her symbolic of the nineteenth-century ego's "possessive manipulative relationship with the earth." "The nineteenth-century ego, fearful of nature's chaos, attempts to conquer the nightmare of an entropic dissolution into matter by imprisoning it within a mental superstructure that recognizes the power of the natural world as destructive to man's autonomy and thus tries to subdue it."[2] It is an interesting suggestion, bringing out Oates's examination of the philosophical background of modern schizophrenia, in order to show (as in Lawrence's work) the tragedy of separating the mind from the body, the higher from the lower consciousness. The Pedersens epitomize their society's split between the rhetoric of spirituality and the materialism of their actions. The central symbol of the Pedersen's life is eating, which becomes a sacred act, an obscene mock-Eucharist:

The lips parted, the mouth opened, something was inserted into the opening, then the jaws began their centuries of instinct, raw instinct, and the food was moistened, ground into pulp, swallowed. It was magic. . . . Hilda watched her father covertly and saw how his nostrils flared with the exertion of eating, his face slowly reddened, a handsome face, sharply handsome inside that pouched, bloated encasement of skin, his eyes sharp and glistening as the eyes of skinny, devilish birds. (w, 138–39)

Here we see the familiar ingredients of Oates's parabolic structure, as through the very accumulation of detail she takes us beyond mere realism. The greed of the Pedersens reveals not just a waste of material resources but a destruction of personality. Similarly with that allied fetish of the American way of life, cleanliness: fixed to the ultimate and sole reality of the material, we have tried to scrub, cauterize, deodorize, perfume the body, in a

2 Alice C. Martin, "Towards a Higher Consciousness: A Study of the Novels of Joyce Carol Oates" (Ph.D. dissertation, Northern Illinois University, 1974), 233–34.

frenetic attempt to have it assume the role of the spirit that we have, in reality, abandoned. Jesse finds himself "contagious" (w, 289); he obsessively washes; he "remembered with disapproval the years of his life he had been dirty, his hands crawling with germs. Now he understood how the invisible world of germs ruled the visible world, how there were friendly bacteria and unfriendly bacteria, and how it was necessary to control them as much as possible" (w, 101). Again, behind the obsessive materialism lies the vocabulary of the spiritual, as the bacteria become the good and bad angels of the contemporary world.

Oates's observations on the fetishes of our world are, once again, not especially original; but she uses them as starting points for something more interesting — to analyze the ways the whole personality may be cheapened, distorted, or shattered, and above all defined for us from outside. Such a concentration on money, food, and hygiene represents a fantasy world foisted upon us, giving us apparently tantalizingly easy access to just those products and experiences which seem most easily to fulfill our desires, make us more beautiful, admirable, free. Their very ease of access is at once a distortion of personality and an invitation by which we are led to believe in the absoluteness of the glittering surface of Wonderland. The basic materialistic surroundings of contemporary affluence — supermarkets, consumables, money, cleanliness, success, marriage, motherhood — are all heightened into the material of gothic parable. Wonderland is revealed as Wasteland: surrounding ourselves with the paraphernalia and the superficialities of affluence, modern Americans are still guiltily aware of an inner darkness our neon and strobe lighting barely illuminate.

Wonderland is a society of schizoids: its inhabitants define their goals in the rhetoric of idealism — the integrity of the individual, the promise of the future, the freedom and uniqueness of the personality — but it acts as if these great goals of the Renaissance and Enlightenment, Bruno's or Nietzsche's dreams of human autonomy, are graspable only in the most immediate material forms. The constant pressure to growth, to discovery, is defined in idealistic terms — "life is a movement into the infinite . . . or it is a shrinking back" (w, 120) — but it is experienced only in terms of economics, ego-expression, and exploitation. The struggle to assert one's individuality ends in being subject to the terrifying determinism of constant material competition and destruction. So Jesse, the hero of *Wonderland*, finds that in "forcing his future into place," his contemporaries and surroundings, his present (as opposed to his future), are all experienced as threats. Frustration and insecurity, Oates suggests, are not merely urged upon us by the consumer society, which conditions us to crave more, newer, bigger consumables; more fundamentally, they are at the very root of our contemporary consciousness and result not just in our physical dissatisfactions but in the destruction of the very autonomy we strive for. Grasping for the freedom of the supermarket, we become more and more subject to its demands. Striving for autonomy, Jesse finds "even his spirit was become automated, mechanized. It worked perfectly for him. He had only to direct it and it responded" (w, 208).

The survival of the personality caught in the flux of desire and history had been one of Oates's constant concerns in earlier novels. The human soul here who is caught in the flux of time is a man of exceptional ability, will, and strength, a man whose partial comprehension becomes a means of intensifying not alleviating his tragedy. On this subject, as we have seen in earlier novels, Oates becomes more than just a penetrating commentator on the all too observable drives of contemporary life. Like Updike's anatomy of New England suburbia, *Wonderland* offers a parable of the condition of twentieth-century man. Unlike John Updike, Oates has no theological *parti pris*, no nostalgic harking back to the specific ideals of the founding fathers. What seems to be her main philosophical target is, specifically, the frightening plausibility yet spiritual inadequacy of the modern material account of the self.

Jesse's constant problem is to define his inner being in a society that simultaneously cultivates individualism and yet is increasingly deterministic. As a substitute for the traditional belief in a mysterious yet real inner self, Wonderland offers the apparent security of facts. Technology—another of Oates's repeated symbols of contemporary America—offers him a way out of his fears of life's mysteries. If, as Jesse learns, "the definition of life . . . was only one of behaviour" (w, 208), then he must conclude that "the personality is an illusion. . . . It is just a tradition" (w, 360). What, then, will satisfy him is personal and professional predictability—ambition, success, well-defined and achievable material goals. And the great lesson he learns is "control": "If he had control of himself, Jesse Vogel, then nothing else mattered in the universe"; "life had become predictable. He was forcing his future into place" (w, 211, 207). Jesse progresses through a succession of names, identities, roles, toward an increasing belief in pure science's power to give his discontinuous life some order and meaning. As a medical student he becomes depressingly like Pedersen, intent on "the great lesson" of silence, and of control—"What else mattered?" (w, 211). He comes under the influence of Dr. Benjamin Cady, whose rationalism is another version of Western technological tradition's division of man into mind and body. Martin points out how his lecture on scientific philosophy paraphrases David Hume's positivistic views of human nature: "*The world is our construction, peopled by us: it is a mystery. All we know of the world, even our more precise laboratory findings, rests on the perception of the senses, but this very knowledge cannot reveal the relations of the senses to the outside world*" (w, 211).[3] By marrying Cady's daughter Helene Jesse attempts "to become that man," and embraces a rigidly dualistic, positivistic philosophy of consciousness. As his career develops, he comes under the influence of the brilliant surgeon Roderick Perrault, and like Perrault, starts to

3 *Ibid.*, 240.

work on the secrets of the brain itself. Once again, a traditional source of man's spiritual insight and power is rendered as measurable, controllable, definable. Examining a patient, he forces himself to learn something that "Perrault seemed to know by instinct and would never have thought of explaining: that the human brain was not sacred. It was not sacred, it was touchable. It was matter. Like anything else. . . . Once dead, it was dead permanently" (w, 335).

Jesse's obsession with material certainty, with defining himself by externals, is presented as an American paradigm, as he progresses from a poor, hardworking rural schoolboy to a famous neurosurgeon. His life is the epitome of the work ethic, and yet it has been achieved not by personal dynamism operating against or using weaker forces but by a series of reactions to the conditions and initiatives of others: his father's poverty, Pedersen's power and ambitions, the opinions of his professors and peers. He is essentially formed by externals. "It distressed Jesse that he must always exist in the eyes of others, their power extended in him though he did not choose them, did not choose them deliberately at all. They were a pressure on him, in his head, a pressure he loathed" (w, 166).

However subjected to change and challenge, the integrated personality is one that senses a continuity with a remembered past, not one that successively inhabits disconnected worlds. In her novel, Oates is also examining the effects of discontinuity on the personality. Jesse's struggle for survival necessitates not just denying at each stage the older set of habits and surroundings but in making a conscious attempt to create a new self—for in an obsessively materialistic world the self becomes increasingly identified with its tangible surroundings. Thus Pedersen gives him a new name, focuses his attention not on the past but, as a scientist, on the present and "the future that belongs to both of us" (w, 91). On the one hand, the human personality atrophies unless it develops; on the other, the past cannot be denied without radical distortion.

Late in the novel, Jesse's wife Helene describes to a friend how she had "found some scribbling of Jesse's . . . just pieces of scrap paper with strange designs all over, resembling human faces, and the word *homeostasis* written over and over again, maybe a hundred times" (w,450). *Homeostasis* is the scientific expression of the novel's main concern, introduced to Jesse by Pedersen. "The living being," he argues, "is stable." It must be so in order not to be destroyed, dissolved, or disintegrated by the colossal forces, often adverse, which surround it. By an apparent contradiction it maintains its stability only if it is excitable and capable of modifying itself according to external stimuli and adjusting its response to the stimulation. It is stable because it is modifiable — the slight instability is the necessary condition for the true stability of the organism. Homeostasis is what the metaphysical problem of the personality has been reduced to, and for Jesse inner integrity degenerates into the fight for material stability. Outwardly successful and materially free, a surgeon with a growing reputation, inside him something essential is constricted. Life too often appears a confusion of pieces, of limbs, books, blood, and glass — in his father's house, in the hospital operating theaters, in the university's experimental pathology farm, and eventually in the room in Toronto where he discovers his daughter amid a group of junkies. In order to overcome this threat of discontinuity and destruction, Jesse is obsessed with finding an order to his life from outside. "As far back as he wanted to remember," he muses, "as far back as he had been Jesse Vogel — he had made his way through the tremulous packed streets of this life by fastening his gaze firmly before him, minding his own business, and if the pavement were to shrink suddenly to the width of a tightrope, he would have kept on in this steady, firm, unimaginative way, knowing that salvation was won only by hoarding the emotions" (w, 255). Such control of his surroundings defines his essential being — until into his life comes Oates's constant symbol of the frightening yet often saving unpredictability of life, sexual love.

As I suggested in Chapter Two, Oates frequently uses the phrase "permanently married" to describe, with some irony, the mixture of apparent stability and constant newness seemingly inseparable from the American ideal of marriage. Jesse's concern with stability and permanence, with his homeostatic condition, is ultimately challenged by an unforeseen vulnerability in the most apparently permanent aspect of his life, his marriage. Into the middle of Jesse's successful career, apparently so well regulated and controlled from without, walks the unpredicted figure of Reva, a young blonde woman to whom Jesse instinctively responds as if she embodies something in himself revolting instinctively against its repression. She reminds him, somehow, of his past, even perhaps his mother, to whom she has a physical resemblance. Most importantly, she opens up in him an aspect of himself that his technological thoroughness has taught him to ignore — a mysterious depth in his personality. When he faces her, he is embarrassed and speechless. Feelings are unquantifiable. "Somewhere", he feels, "there were words for him, for Jesse, the exact words that would explain his life. But he did not know them. He used words shyly, crudely. It remained for someone else — a woman perhaps — to draw these sacred words out of him, to justify him, redeem him as Jesse — he could not create them himself. Not alone" (w, 374). Reva mysteriously brings back the sensuality and power of femaleness he has repressed since childhood. As a boy, he had peered at graffiti in the school washroom, seeing the drawing of a woman in which the pubic area is shaded to look like a black door, and the arms drawn so as to make the figure like a box, "something you could walk into and lose yourself in, all that empty blackness" (w, 38). Years later he stares at the supine body of Mrs. Pedersen in a hotel bathroom, "exaggerated, swollen to the shape of a large oblong box. . . . Jesse felt it pull at him, tug at him . . . as if confronting one of the terrible secrets of the world" (w, 172). Reva seems to bring back the fascination and fear of female sexuality. She is charming and beautiful but, as well, something

forbidden, "primitive, barbaric, and huntress" (w, 368). He becomes caught between fear of the past she mysteriously recalls
for him and excitement at the rediscovery of the unpredictable
and unmeasurable aspect of the personality. In the story "The
Heavy Sorrow of the Body," the narrator muses that "before
falling in love, I was defined. Now I am undefined" (MI, 394).
Reva similarly brings a sense of unprepared-for lack of defin-
ability into Jesse's life. She strikes him as an image of the wholeness he has never found in his adult life, represented in her name
suggesting both physicality and thought, idealism and reality:
"a puzzling name. He did not know if it was ugly or not. It was
soft, soothing, and then hard as a clamp; it was girlish and then
abruptly masculine, airy and then heavy as dirt. . . . An opening
and then a closing, as if jaws were clamped together. *Reva Denk*"
(w, 339). Reva herself suspects, probably rightly, that he would
smother her and insists that if he lives with her he give up his
present life — "everything new. A new start" (w, 400). So heavily conditioned by a belief in the materialism of the human personality, his spontaneity and excitement disciplined for so long,
Jesse overreacts to her invitation to visit him and, having plotted
for so long to see her, he pursues her from Chicago to upstate
Wisconsin, until finally, after she has promised to come away
with him, he is preparing for the ultimate liberating leap into
unpredictability, when he cuts himself with an unguarded razor
blade:

What if he cut himself . . . ? But he had to shave, he had no choice. . . .
And then lightly, timidly, he scraped the blade against his skin and
blood spurted out at once.
   He stared at his own blood.
   Then, again, as if hypnotized, he drew the blade against the other
side of his face.
   More blood.
   He was fascinated by the sudden streaming of blood. . . . Nothing
could stop it. He brought the blade down against the top of his chest
and drew it against his skin — such soft skin, shivering beneath his
touch.

Finally, "he stood there, bleeding from a dozen places, streaming blood so lightly, experimentally, giddily." The violence of his past, the violence beneath the perfumed, close-shaven cleanliness of affluent America has surfaced. "In the end, impatiently, he decided to put his clothes back on over the bleeding. He drove to Chicago that way" (w, 403–404).

The novel's final book, "Dreaming America," is perhaps slightly anticlimactic, although it unfolds the next, inevitable part in Jesse's tragedy. His failure with Reva still haunts him, but we now see him against his daughter, a freaked-out, drop-out, affluent teenager, representing perhaps an inevitable reaction against Jesse's obsessive work ethic, for whom "history is dead and anatomy is dead. Passion is the only destiny" (w, 429). Rejecting her father's ideology and schizophrenia, she is attempting to move beyond his obsessive materialization of the self. Jesse is nostalgically drawn toward her; she reminds him of Reva and his lost glimpses of freedom, and yet his love is a desperate possessive desire to dominate her, to subdue and smother her with his despair. Again and again, the central problem of homeostasis recurs: for one so conditioned by such a view of the human organism, the deterministic mobility of America means that failure involves death. In love with, afraid of, desiring, the freedom his daughter has achieved, Jesse pursues her to Toronto, and there he finds her.

With this climactic scene of the novel, we must consider an important textual problem: Oates has written two separate endings. In the original version of the novel, originally published by Vanguard Press, Jesse finds Shelly ill, possibly dying, in a junk-littered room, and he buys her back from her lover, Noel, for the price medical schools pay for a corpse, five hundred dollars: "She was sick, dying, he could smell the stench of death about her" (w, 512). Then, again instinctively returning to the destruction of his own father, he rows obsessively out along Lake Ontario with her:

"All of you . . . everyone . . . all my life, everyone. . . . Always you are going away from me and you don't come back to explain . . . ," Jesse wept.

He embraced her. He clutched at her thighs, her emaciated thighs, her legs. He pressed his face against her knees, weeping.

The boat drifted most of the night. Near dawn it was picked up by a large handsome cruiser, a Royal Mounted Police boat, a dazzling sight with its polished wood and metal and its trim of gold and blue. (w, 512)

Determinism, accidents, have together shattered the homeostasis of Jesse's life.

In the revised ending, however, written for the paperback version published by Fawcett, the sale is omitted, Shelley does not die, and the novel ends on an ambiguously hopeful note as Jesse finds and, apparently, rescues his daughter:

"Nobody is going to die tonight," he said alone. . . .

"But you are still the devil," Shelley said faintly. She pressed her hands against her face. He said . . . he said you were the devil and I believe him . . . I . . . he said you were the devil and I . . . I think you are the devil . . . come to get me to bring me home . . ."

"Am I?" Jesse said. (w-f, 479)

It is once again an image of control, the power of a stronger personality determining another's life from outside. Which of the two endings best fits the book and its impact upon us? Oates herself has had mixed feelings over the two. The Vanguard Press ending, quoted first above, was written at the request of her publisher. She later regretted the decision to revise what had, in fact, been her original version and the Fawcett paperback, and subsequent editions include the ending written first. However, she has looked back at the whole novel in general terms and expressed unease at its lack of catharsis, almost an immoral quality, regardless of which ending it has. "It's the first novel I have written," she notes, "that doesn't end in violence, that doesn't liberate the hero through violence, and therefore there is still a sickish, despairing, confusing atmosphere about it."[4] Consis-

4 Joe David Bellamy, *The New Fiction: Interviews with Innovative American Writers* (Urbana: University of Illinois, 1974), 23.

tently, as we have seen, Oates stresses how violence may make possible cartharsis in our lives. We come to knowledge and fulfillment through pain and anguish; violence makes possible our calm and fulfillment. But the refusal or impossibility of cathartic violence may also be as significant a revelation of the emotional drives of our world as its consummation. Again, we are required not to trust the teller, but the tale. Oates may have felt that the impact of *Wonderland* on its readers was disturbing and so worrying to her—but that, needless to say, is a sign of its power. Certainly, to read it may be a profoundly disturbing experience. Yet, again, it displays her admirable ability to bring out a reader's own potential or actual neuroses, surrounded as we are by the paraphernalia of Wonderland, its affluence, its insistence on increasing material security, its insidious insistence on the unreality of our deepest, most mysterious, but nevertheless fundamental realities.

III

In an essay on John Updike, published in 1975, Oates wrote of Updike's special insight into the attempted spiritualizing of the flesh which, she suggested, for many in our time "may be all that remains of religious experience." In *Couples* Updike wrote of how adultery became "a way of giving yourself adventures. Of getting out in the world and seeking knowledge." A crime, a breach in civic and individual order, becomes a means of achieving transcendence—"Eros is equated with Life itself . . . usually concentrated, and very intensely indeed, in terms of specific women's bodies; when they go—everything goes!" In her own novel, *Do With Me What You Will*, infidelity becomes a means to authentic life. Updike views the sexual strivings of his characters against a Barthian context of human self-deception and God's judgment, and, ultimately, in the context of a cosmic comedy where the descent into flesh becomes "a form of rebellion against 'fate'—enjoying the very absurdity of his position."[5] By

5 John Updike, *Couples* (New York: Knopf, 1968), 429; Joyce Carol Oates, "Updike's American Comedies," *Modern Fiction Studies*, XXI (1975), 459, 465.

contrast, Oates roots the significance of sexuality both in and somehow beyond the personality itself, in a way analogous to what Lawrence termed "getting beyond" sex. Indeed, a major ideological force behind the novel is the Lawrentian concentration on sexual encounter as transcendence; a possibility that is hinted at but tragically never developed in *Wonderland* and in her next novel, *The Assassins*, is the central affirmation of *Do With Me What You Will*.

On its most obvious level, *Do With Me What You Will* is a rapturous, intense tribute to the transforming power of romantic love and to the graspable if difficult possibilities inherent in the Western affirmation of the body. It celebrates the power of love, through pain, violence, and destruction, to remold the human personality and to transform human personality and to transform human relationships. It is the story of Elena Howe, the prototypal American beauty — blonde, passive, molded from outside herself even more radically then Jesse Vogel, by her parents, her husband, and her lover — who learns through involvement in the pain of sexual encounter to pare away her facticious surface and discover the possibilities within and beyond herself. More than with any other novel, Oates seems to strike a rapturous note of hope in this one. In an essay written about the same time, she called for a literature to transform America, "one that will climb up out of the categories of 'rational' and 'irrational' to show why the consciousness of the future will feel joy, not dread, at the total rejection of the Renaissance ideal." It should also "dramatize for us the complexities of this epoch, showing us how deeply we act out, even in our apparently secret dreams, the communal crises of our world." Oates then categorized herself as living in the overlap between the confused existential world of the present and the coming transformation: "I still feel my own place is to dramatize the nightmares of my time, and (hopefully) to show how some individuals find a way out, awaken, come alive, move into the future."[6] *Do With Me What*

6 Joyce Carol Oates, "New Heaven and Earth," 52–53.

You Will dramatizes in psychological, erotic, and social terms this overlap of two modes of consciousness. As at the end of Lawrence's *Women in Love* a new concept of love—a realm of transcendent experience somehow beyond love—is affirmed to redeem the infidelities, pain, and violence through which it has been created. The book's final dialogue as the now-married lovers look back on their pasts contains an uncannily Lawrentian note of hope and realism:

> *Did you forget everything else?*
> *Almost everything.*

Reviewers were generally skeptical about Oates's apparent change of tone; comments ranged from the usual imperceptive remarks on Oates's realistic settings to claims that the work was liberationist propaganda. A few saw beneath the detailed depiction of Detroit to the mythic battle being fought out, a battle that repeats much of the struggle for selfhood of *Wonderland*, but which ends more positively, not in the certainty of fulfillment but in hope. On this level, the book operates like a serious romance, an expression of profound wish fulfillment where we, the readers, are exhorted to grasp our freedom as Oates's heroine does, to seize upon our deepest desires and make them true. The "pulsation," the "demand," that finally brings Elena to take her lover from his wife and child is born of the excited realizations of her own autonomy: "Never in her life," she realizes, "had she conquered any territory, achieved any victories. Never. Never had she been selfish, never evil or adult. And now if she wanted Morrissey she would cross over into adulthood to get him." Her autonomy is then expressed explicitly in terms of overcoming an outside conditioning—"extending her freedom, as men do, making a claim" (DWM, 546).

The novel centers upon the struggle of yet another of Oates's typical heroines. Behind *Do With Me What You Will* is the demand for autonomy and respectability of Clara or Maureen and, as well, the fragile, neurotic beauty of Nadine. Oates's most important and (paradoxically, despite her passivity) affirmative heroine has affinities with the women of Doris Lessing's novels, and with Constance Chatterley, brought to an awareness of her own female vulnerability and power through the anguish and joy of sexual touch. The novel's setting, too, is Lawrentian in its fierce contrasts — just as the industrial mines threaten the mystery and natural growth of Mellors' cottage in *Lady Chatterley's Lover*, so the lovers of *Do With Me What You Will* are surrounded by the hostility and mechanism of Detroit and the cool impersonal power of the law. Oates's familiar symbols recur — Detroit, with its violent economic contrasts, its harshness, and yet encompassing the freedom of the minority who reach beyond the apparent limits of the human spirit; California, here no longer the green light glittering for Jules but concrete and actual in the possibilities of autonomy it offers transcontinental lovers.

To these familiar ingredients of her fiction, Oates adds a symbol which gives her novel an unexpected strength in its intellectual structure as well as a new emotional clarity — the law. If romantic love is a disruptive but ultimately religious force in American life, it is nevertheless confronted by tradition in the form of the law. The novel consists of three parts. Part One is "Twenty-eight Years, Two Months, Twenty-six Days," which is the span of Elena's apparent legal innocence from her birth until she meets the man who will eventually become her illicit lover, Jack Morrissey. Part Two is an assemblage of scenes, entitled "Facts, Events, Fantasies, Evidence Admissable and Inadmissable," which brings Jack's life to the same meeting beneath the statue *The Spirit of Detroit* in front of Detroit's City-County Building. Part Three, "Crime," is an account of their love affair. The final part, "The Summing Up," deals with each of the major participants and visualizes a future for the lovers, their love taken beyond and yet made possible by the law.

Few, if any, reviewers of the novel saw its most important structural device. For *Do With Me What You Will* is built up as an interwoven account of their pasts by the two lovers, Jack and

Elena, presumably now remarried to each other. For the most part we are swept along on the narrative line and barely notice how they are describing their own pasts to each other. At certain crucial moments intensely voiced comments and questions, observations and arguments, intrude.

> "I don't know about his life."
> "You don't?"
> "Why are you asking me about this?"
> "Why don't you want to talk about it?"
> *Fierce and hard and half-joking, always this poisonous sucking at me. You were sucking at my lips, my heart.*
> *You were saying: Love me, only me! Love me!*
> *You were saying: You're too beautiful. Or not beautiful enough. Or the word itself is not a serious word but a joke, spat around too often. So you are a joke yourself. Other people laugh but you cannot.*
> *You were saying* (DWM, 377)

Once we grasp this all-important narrative device, the novel acquires an extra dimension of intensity: we are witnessing two lovers who fought through pain, contradiction, estrangement, and other commitments to reach each other. The novel becomes a passionately realized expression of Lawrence's "look, we have come through." As well, the very titles of the work's three parts make up an extra dimension of tenderness — the "Twenty-eight Years, Two Months, Twenty-six Days" of Elena's life until she meets Jack; the appropriately legal language of Jack's "Miscellaneous Facts, Events, Fantasies, Evidence Admissible and Inadmissible," and (from the future perspective) the ironic title of the third part, "Crime." Paradoxically, the crime of adultery becomes their means of liberation.

The other crucial aspect of the book's structure is the two acts of crime with which it starts and ends and which uncannily echo each other. The book's initial act of conscious crime is Elena's passive acquiescence to her father's love, as she leaves school to fly with him to California. He persuades her, she hesitates, and then as he insists "Obey me, Elena. Obey me. Yes, like that, yes, don't be afraid — crawl under — crawl under —," she does so: "And the child crawled under the fence" (DWM, 10). At the book's end, the act is recapitulated, except that Elena is no longer passive. It is her deliberate realization that she must seize Jack to gain her fulfillment: "She would do it. Utterly calm, even with that familiar taste of panic, utterly still, waiting, frozen, she knew even before he appeared how he would look — having held himself back for so long, stubborn and despairing . . . with the dark abrupt impatience of Jack's that seemed always to be propelling him forward against his will. Elena understood: she felt it herself, years ago, centuries ago, it seemed, scrambling beneath a fence someone held up for her, not knowing why she was doing this but knowing only that she would do it, that she must" (DWM, 562). Both acts challenge the law by which Elena and Jack have had the external structure of their lives defined.

The book's action is enveloped in an atmosphere of legal procedures, and the suggestion pervades that the law embodies not just an agreement for society's self-regulation but a whole attempt to order and direct the individual's psychological and emotional experience. Elena grows up essentially directed from outside her undeveloped self by the pressures and desires of others and the embodiment of these forces in the law. Her parents separate when she is a child, her father kidnaps her from school and takes her to California, and her mother, vigorously craving financial security and glamor, is always threatening or avoiding litigation. The law is a constant pressure on Elena: it stands as a limitation of her own inner life, threatening her when she attempts to develop any autonomy. After a spasmodically successful career as a model, she is introduced at eighteen to the ruthless, successful lawyer Marvin Howe in a Detroit nightclub. Howe and his beliefs about the law come to dominate Elena's life. Their marriage becomes another of the external pressures forming Elena, this time explicitly externalized in a bond, a contract, "not . . . between two people, but between two people and the law" (DWM, 108).

Howe epitomizes the solid American belief in the absoluteness of law. Vaguely reminiscent of a rumbustious figure like
Richard "Racehorse" Haynes or F. Lee Bailey, he has an almost
metaphysical belief in the law. The law is power, certainty, a
force from which we are never free, however innocent or uninvolved we are. It is an involuntary agreement into which we enter by virtue of being born. It is the nascent force of order which
makes everything accountable and thereby less threatening. Civilization is built upon the enforcement of coherence upon the
conflicting forces from which it is made up, upon the imposi-
tion upon individual minds as well as the instincts its own definite gestalt, in order to protect itself from the dark forces from
without and within. The concretely formulated body of law is
only the iceberg's tip; for the sake of holding back the feared resurgence of antediluvian powers, individuals must be considered
as bundles of predictable needs and computable virtues. Thus
Howe asserts that "there are no guilty people under American
Law, not until someone finds them guilty"; since "things move
from invisibility to visibility. . . . everyone is innocent until the
crime he has committed is given a name" (DWM, 91, 93–94).

Paradoxically, Howe's refusal to believe in law as inherent in
the nature of things is coupled with a ruthless acceptance of that
law as ultimate in human society. Our age is one where so many
metaphysical certainties have vanished that the very rigidity or
status quo of the law, regardless of its equity, comes to stand for
the inviolable security we all seek. "We need the law because the
law is what's left of divinity," Howe remarks. "We need what's
holy. . . . It will never be destroyed because there is no salvation
outside it" (DWM, 124–25). Throughout American history, indeed, there has been uniquely combined the secular autonomy
of society's self-determining order with the absolute of an established religion. The law may be circumvented, but it cannot be
overthrown because it is the closest we have come to an agreed
metaphysical basis. We sense something of Howe's power when
the narrative goes back and we see him when, as a rising young

lawyer, he takes on a murder defense and systematically molds the evidence of the accused's fifteen-year-old son. The lawyer creates in the boy's mind a story that is never wholly false, but is a convincing ordering of the probable facts, the product of an artist or, as the boy feels, of a kind of god.

The boy whom Howe so molds and awes grows up and, some fifteen years younger, also becomes a lawyer. His name is Jack Morrissey. Undoubtedly fascinated by the power of the law because of his meeting with Howe, he develops however into a very different kind of lawyer. The second part of the novel merges into Jack's account of his childhood to Rachel, the woman he eventually marries. They are working for the NAACP–ACLU in Mississippi. For Jack, law is a means of social change—not an instrument for revolution, but for organized, coherent reform. He attempts, unsuccessfully, to persuade local black leaders into pressing charges against state troopers, he argues passionately with Rachel on the power of law to change history, and when they return to Detroit—"unknown . . . a poorly paid, poorly connected man from Detroit, with an undistinguished law school behind him" (DWM, 301)—he dedicates himself to defending the victims of a rapacious society: the poor, the blacks, illiterates, murderers and rapists of a class far below Howe's affluent clients. Morrissey and Howe operate in entirely separate spheres of the law—and yet there is a bond between them. Both believe in the absolute structure of the law, and in the seemingly necessary belief in the godlike power of the lawyer over a confusing and seemingly disordered society. But unlike Rachel, who argues that the "law itself is rotten" (DWM, 294), Jack believes fervently in the potential inherent in law. They quarrel about whether she should testify before a citizens' grand jury on drugs. "Goddam it," Jack cried, "you're going! You have a summons, it's the law, it's a rotten unconstitutional law but it's on the books, so you're going!" (DWM, 286). On the opposite side, Rachel feels degraded: "I don't have to recognize any power outside my own conscience," she protests. When she speaks of a deep hunger for something beyond a law whose "moral power is dead" Jack is angry, frustrated, unable, like a traditional Catholic, to conceive of salvation outside the law. Just like Howe, despite not being a reformer and deliberately not seeing beyond each case — "My clients are not ciphers, they don't represent anyone except themselves" (DWM, 122) — Morrissey is committed to the absolute demands of the law.

In developing her two main male characters, Oates conveys their affinities beneath their surface differences. But her main structural conflict is not between a corrupt conservative lawyer and a frustrated reformer. It is between the law itself and a different dimension of experience that radically challenges it. As civilized men, as a people of law, we feel compelled to limit and clarify our personal lives. The law dare not acknowledge the individual as the particular center of the universe, but must regard him as an abstraction of rights and duties. Within these limitations, an individual may often experience the law as a preserver of energy, a lubricant. The law, however, may be not merely a protection, but a sanctification of the status quo. We abide by the law because we are shocked by what we might do if it no longer constrained the passions it rouses. The law, represented in the work of Elena's husband and her lover, may constrain and confine, but it has also repressed those individual powers that are humanity's most potent resources, turning our energies aside, making us unable to discover the true nature of our fundamental longings.

Yet we are unable to escape the law. The law represents the dark, visceral nature of our very mortality against which we measure ourselves. A lawbreaker challenges the law while recognizing its hold upon him. Thus Elena's father, kidnapping her, recognizes his status and danger. Nevertheless, his act has been done out of love, reaching out toward a desire he conceives, perhaps wrongly, to be more fundamental than the law. In a tavern in northern Nevada he argues with some strangers: "Look: if a man is driven to extreme acts, he isn't necessarily guilty. The laws don't cover everything. Can they cover things that haven't happened yet? — if a man has seen a certain vision in the world, a vision of evil, and has to cleanse himself?" (DWM, 27–28). In his anxiety he is trying to formulate an element of human experience beyond the good and bad of law, a psychological dimension that is fundamentally untouchable by the law, even if the law must deal with its consequences. "What is the relationship between the law and evil?" he asks. "The law exists only in our heads. We all agree on that point. Lawyers are the first to agree on that point. It's an *agreement*, the Law" (DWM, 28). But the dichotomy which is set up, first announced in Elena's father's exclamation to her: "What has the law to do with love? — you and I transcend such declarations, don't we?" (DWM, 13), is a more complex one than simply between the law and love. It is rather between two basic ways of apprehending and judging experience. On the one side is the law, but as well the regimentation, predictability, and safety in our lives, the conventions and securities of family ties; on the other hand there is the unpredictable and the risky — dreams, emotions, drugs, meditation, experiences beyond the self. Not all of these experiences are of equal value, but they are commitments to live by the dream of hope rather than fact, by the power of the possible rather than what appears to be actual. Law represents civilization's recurrent, and all too often successful, attempt to control us, to make us safe at the cost of allowing us to reach for transcendent fulfillment.

Except for Jack's experiences in Mississippi and some of Elena's early life in Pittsburgh, Cleveland, and New York, most of the book's action is set in Detroit. As in *Them* we are given an intensely concrete evocation of the city, although of a more affluent segment than in the earlier novel. Once again, however, Detroit is evoked as a spirit of place rather than a mere backdrop. It is the embodiment of the ideals, ruthlessness, and power of the law. For Howe it is *"pure energy. This city is pure energy. The world is pure energy and must be respected"* (DWM, 161).

Morrissey himself, like Jules, is "a real Detroiter, a son of Detroit," the son of a man who, driven to murder, senses the con-
vulsions of society as something natural. Elena at one point looks
out of Jack's car across the Detroit river towards Canada and
wonders "at the people who might live there, in those houses
that looked so distant, so safe, in a foreign country and safe from
Detroit—as if anyone could be safe from Detroit, anywhere"
(DWM, 382).

Two contrasting parts of Detroit society, Grosse Pointe with
its private clubs and the seedy downtown and suburbs where
Morrissey lives and works, share the same violence and operate
within the same sinister legal power structure. Left-wing radi-
cals, private police, rightist bigots attacking "Maoists and left-
wing liberals and Jew-lawyers and nigger lawyers" (DWM, 400),
the mounting homicide figures almost being willed upwards—
"It seemed a kind of disappointment; 690 and not a round 700
would go on the books"—all create a seething presence of power,
violence, and corruption. "What a city! What a place! Jack said"
(DWM, 409). Structurally, at the novel's fulcrum and standing as
the central symbol of Detroit, at "the end of Woodward Avenue,
the tip of Detroit," is *The Spirit of Detroit*. Elena's and Jack's
narratives converge upon the statue on April 12, 1971. Elena has
been to the "Mentally Handicapped Children of Wayne County
Fundraising Luncheon" at the Detroit Athletic Club, and pauses
by the statue, five minutes' walk from her husband's office. Her
watch has stopped at 1:45. The statue itself is a huge, somewhat
disproportionate man, holding in one hand an object, supposedly
the sun, in the other a family group. The statue's inscription
is from the Epistle to the Corinthians, "Now the Lord is that
spirit and where the spirit of the Lord is, there is liberty." The
inscription then adds a gloss: "*God, through the spirit of Man
is manifested in the family, the noblest human relationship*"
(DWM, 162–63).

Much of the novel's essential symbolism is summed up here.
In the figure of the statue can be sensed the materialism and the

dream of Detroit and of the whole human city. The inscription, with its stress on the spirit of the new covenant (rather than the rigor of the law) looks toward both the lovers' transcendence of the law and also to the one central figure of the novel outside the lovers and their families, the radical Mered Dawe. The misapplication of the inscription, too, connects with "the noblest human relationship, the family" from which Elena must wrench Jack, and which she has been denied by her own marriage. She stands contemplating the statue, with her watch stopped at 1:45. Like the statue itself "she stands without moving. Straight, poised, the posture unbreakable; backbone like steel," feeling somehow that "everything has come to rest, in perfection it comes to rest, permanent. 1:45. Stopped. Permanent. 1:45. Stuck. She does not move." Then, suddenly, the unexpected accident breaks in. "'Mrs. Howe?' someone might say. A stranger's voice, and a stranger's hesitant hand on her arm, 'Mrs. Howe . . . ?' But if she hears she will not reply, will not even glance at him. She is beyond anyone's touch" (DWM, 163).

In *Them*, her previous Detroit novel, Oates had used the images of travel and horizons to symbolize the characters', especially Jules's, desire to break through the sense of limitation and powerlessness created by the city. In *Do With Me What You Will*, partly because travel does not present such an insuperable and mythic significance to the characters — Howe, for instance, is constantly traveling to clients all over the United States — the symbol is used less extensively. Liberation occurs within the psyche, not in breaking out of a limiting environment. But on two occasions journeys are crucial in the novel's development. The first is the journey Elena takes with her father to San Francisco, kidnapped from a school which is described as "heavy and protective and exciting as a prison" (DWM, 3). It is a journey made across borders, against rules and laws, and motivated by a crazed passion for another person. The second journey occurs later in her life. When she is sent by her husband to a friend's home near San Francisco, Elena is driven by a sudden urge to telephone Detroit, to summon Morrissey across the continent to her. It is a moment of great significance in the novel, the second meeting of the lovers, and like their first meeting beneath *The Spirit of Detroit* it focuses much of the novel's meaning. The motives and the consequences of Elena's sudden, seemingly irrational desire for Jack are hardly understood by either of them and the apparent unlikeliness of their meeting is conveyed in her tension as she waits for him, but their mutual smiling in amazement at their accomplishment anticipates the "look between them of pure kinship, of triumph" (DWM, 563) of their meeting at the novel's climax, when Elena herself makes her first independently willed journey, from her husband's house in Maine to claim Morrissey in Detroit.

The book's title is a rough translation of the legal term that, oddly enough, became famous during 1974, the year after the novel was published, by its association with the conviction of Spiro Agnew, then vice-president. Howe introduces the term into a conversation about tax evasion:

"If God Himself brought suit against you, what would you do? Plead *nolo contendere* and hope for a very sharp ax. That's my advice."

"*Nolo contendere* . . . ?"

"Absolutely," Marvin said, thrusting his chin upward as if to bare his throat. "'Do with me what you will.'"

Indeed, the whole of Elena's life has been lived according to one sense of this phrase: by her father's kidnapping, or her mother's exploitation of her as a child-model, where she learns her passivity, that "*everything went away if you were careful*" (DWM, 39). She becomes fortified inside herself because "nothing will happen. . . . as long as you keep quiet. Innocent. Invisible" (DWM, 161 – 62). She is a "doll" to everyone. As a model, "she could sit under those hot lights for half an hour, not seeing anything, not moving her face, not even sniffing, hardly breathing; she was a little doll. 'You really are a little doll,' people agreed" (DWM, 53). She drifts through her youth and into her marriage, protected from a world where girls had "bad posture or bad skin or hems that were not even, their shoe-boots stained with salt from the sidewalk, people who picked openly at their ears and talked loudly to one another, ugly people, all of them ugly and real" (DWM, 67). Her life is constantly "prepared" for her. She is sheltered, passive, manipulated, belonging to others. When she marries, her husband keeps his work and most of his life away from her; she is a statue, a reminder of passive, ideal beauty, uncontaminated, a merely visible woman.

Elena's marriage brings her wealth, comfort, and the prestige of being married to one of the city's most powerful lawyers. But socially her role is essentially a decorative one, while individually her passivity is even more limiting. Her mother has brought her up to absorb men, to accept herself as a doll, a statue, to be submissive to her husband's wealth and desire. Sexually, she has remained unfulfilled, feeling nothing in her passive frigidity. Throughout her life she has lain undeveloped, acceding to but uninvolved by touch. The closest emotional tie her husband offers is the advice: "Don't allow anyone to cry in your arms. If a man cries in your arms, you're stuck with him for life. If you try to push him away or escape him, he'll want you to die" (DWM, 117). Elena is to discover the limited truth of this: both her husband and her lover do, in fact, cry in her arms, but the emotional depth which her marriage never opens for her comes eventually to challenge her defenses in a radically more painful way.

Elena's development is based, as Rose Marie Burwell puts it, on a need to either "synthesize her personality or accede to her own disintegration."[7] Her restlessness leads her initially to allow Jack to drive her home and, although she does not for some weeks call the number he scribbles on a card, she is aware that he has awakened something volatile in her. Her eventual desire to call him arises not from a desire for him so much as from a sense of incompleteness in herself: "*He would do* . . . a need to be fulfilled: he must fill it" (DWM, 344).

7 Rose Marie Burwell, "The Process of Individuation as Narrative Structure: Joyce Carol Oates's *Do With Me What You Will*," *Critique*, XVII (1975), 525.

Although the roots of Elena's dissatisfaction in her marriage are clear enough, it is less easy to see why Jack's attraction to her goes eventually beyond a mixture of curiosity and revenge. She is, of course, ethereally beautiful in an enigmatic, passive way. To her father, her face had been "a miracle, yet terrible. . . . Because it existed, the universe was not at peace, would never be at peace; but it was beautiful, miraculous. . . . It was a face to be dreamed over, cherished" (DWM, 7). Her mother's friend, Mr. Karman, is equally struck: "It is amazing, a miracle . . . how the flesh can be arranged on the bones . . . the effect is one of such beauty . . . it is such uncanny beauty that almost one does not want to look into it" (DWM, 53). Throughout her life, Elena is an object, an "it" in such a manner. Staring at her in a friend's adult education class, Jack similarly "had an impression of her being very pretty but not believable" (DWM, 258); when he learns she is married to the man who years before had saved his father, he finds that she excites a strange mixture of envy, lust, fear, revenge, which in turn brings out an insecurity in his own marriage and creates a radical discontent where there had previously been only the most normal tension. His wife is an intelligent woman who, even if she is impatient with Jack's belief in "the absolute structure of the law," deeply shares his belief in social change. But there is a whole side to Jack which Elena alone seems to bring out. John Updike writes of how sexual love is fulfilling so far as it satisfies a man's nostalgia for his lost eternity: "What is it that shines at us from Iseult's face," he asks. "It is our own past, with its strange innocence and its strange need to be redeemed. . . . A woman, loved, momentarily eases the pain of time by localizing nostalgia . . . elusive glints of original goodness that man's memory stores toward the erotic commitment."[8] Again, without Updike's theological context, Oates is suggesting something beyond mere sexual attraction — it is an essentially ecstatic experience of the transpersonal, an instance of Lawrence's "beyond" in sex.

8 John Updike, *Assorted Prose* (Harmondsworth: Penguin, 1965), 187, 189–90.

Looking back on the surprise and daring of their meeting in San Francisco, the lovers realize something of the unstated and unknown implications in their relationship. Life is lived forward, but understood backward, as Kierkegaard remarked. On the one hand, they can recall: "*What did you think of? Not love*" (DWM, 342), and Elena's thought as Jack enters the hotel exactly echoes Jack's as he first approached her in Detroit — "*He would do.*" On the other hand, there is the inescapable triumph of their meeting: their very willingness to commit themselves even this far is an unspoken acknowledgment of their relationship. She is amazed by their daring and the strange reality of their actions: "What did this mean? Had she committed a crime? Adultery? Was it real? . . . Oh very real. . . . What had happened was real, even if she herself were not real. . . . 'You were really here, waiting for me,' he said, in a kind of triumph" (DWM, 347).

Their affair starts, then, out of an acknowledged restlessness in each of their lives. Chapter 5 of Part II of the novel ends with Elena back with her husband, believing "she would never have the need to see him again" (DWM, 353). Then immediately, with a typically dramatic transition, Oates thrusts us into the extremity of the lovers' affair:

> *What are you thinking? What are you remembering? Why were you late? Who were you with? Where are you going now? Where are you now?*
> *I want from you this —*
> *And this —*
> *I want —*
> *I —. . . .*
> *I want from you this I want this and this*
> *But not that*
> *I want you to do this and think this*
> *But you must not think that*
> *In fact I forbid you to* (DWM, 353)

We are thrust into the doubts and agony of the affair, the juxtaposition of love and hate, excitement and anxiety of their adultery. Elena is initially quite able to divide her life; Jack's more intimate and fulfilling marriage makes him more vulnerable and anguished. He works in a daze, he is often miserable, "sleepless with guilt, actually twitching with guilt as he lay beside his wife" (DWM, 359), and his love for Elena is forced out of him, by negatives, in angry ejaculations of misery and pain. The maturing of their love, which both try to deny in their different ways — Jack by angry aggression, Elena by passivity and wordlessness — emerges indirectly: in small, almost domestic details, and above all in their very actions in returning again and again to each other. Their love is forged through doubt, pain, and secrecy — all aspects of life from which Elena has been sheltered. It is a lesson that Jack has always known: "Nothing is real but pain"; "this was real life: the pressure people exerted on one another, as tangible as the heat everyone had to walk through. You had to accept it, to breathe it into your lungs, or you couldn't live" (DWM, 429, 225). Elena has to learn to survive in this dark, muscular world; in his turn, Jack must struggle with the broken promises, moral and legal, of his past commitments.

Any adulterous relationship between intense and serious people is tested by predictable experiences, any of which can destroy it: physical conflict and sexual confusion, guilt, deception of self and others, quarrels, the constant exhaustion of analyzing the strength of the new relationship, even the feeling that death would be the easiest conclusion. What makes such a relationship authentic is often an unrecognizable thread of commitment to discovery, the sudden (even if transient) intensity of joy, the emergence of aspects of the self which had lain unknown or dormant. In Lawrence's terms, the relationship must offer each the hope of a purer, single being. With Jack and Elena, their affair shatters what from the outside seem to be fixed, essential aspects of themselves — Elena's doll-like uninvolvement and Jack's dogged belief in absolute obedience to law in both his public and private life. For Jack, the affair itself is extra-legal; it is a breach of trust and commitment, and it involves him in the guilt determined by the law by which he believes society can be ordered. For Elena, the change occurs on a deeper level. In her sexual relations with her husband and initially with her lover, Elena is essentially passive, her deepest sexual drives unawakened. As the affair develops, she becomes aware of being the object of demanding, restless men. She inspires similar feelings in each man—Jack looks at her, making love as if she were breakable: "Her husband did this also: that quick, almost furtive checking of her to see if she was damaged" (DWM, 384). Howe uses her as a model on which to display his wealth; Morrissey admires her as a mysterious and valuable gift. Essentially, neither knows her in her essential being: each wants her for himself, as an ornament, possessed and worn.

Through the violence and anxiety and the very need for commitment of her affair, however, Elena discovers a raw physicality which is new to her, "a minute maddening pulsation of her blood" (DWM, 387) which, lying awake beside her sleeping husband, she urgently associates with her lover. In the early hours of the morning, obsessively "she could almost feel the smallest veins and capillaries of her body, tendril-like currents of her finest, most secret blood, waking, waking slowly and terribly, pulling her up to consciousness. . . . She wanted him here with her, closer to her. She didn't want just the idea of him, this floating, impersonal, disembodied lover of hers" (DWM, 387). Elena's awakening to the autonomous drives of her sexual being and her need for Morrissey is the turning point of her life. Like Ursula in Lawrence's *The Rainbow*, she becomes unattached and restless, at once afraid of and afraid of losing the surging feelings she has never before discovered. She finds the admiration of her husband and lover trivial alongside the energy generated within her. She pretends to be pleased by Jack's admiration for her expensive "junk"; but "something flashed immediately through her mind: *He wants my husband's wife not me*" (DWM, 392). Indoctrinated with the beauty of flesh, jewelry, created as a "beautiful thing," Elena is experiencing "a kind of pregnancy of the spirit" (DWM, 405) that neither of her men, obsessed with possessing her, enters into. Dislocated, she wanders, dazed with despair, obsessed with death, her own and her lover's. The parallels between Ursula and Elena gain in significance as Elena's tensions increase — the half-understood physical restlessness, her desire for death, her dislocation from her body, and above all the deep countermovement in her being, *"pushing its way to life"* (DWM, 407), always in motion. And just as Ursula feels that her ever-widening circles of material experience become, in fact, more constricting, so Elena's final barrier lies in her own willingness to suffer and be possessed. She is "a reservoir of darkness . . . her acquiescing to him, her body used as a vessel to accommodate him" (DWM, 444). Her willingness is a kind of chastity, a spiritual virginity which in turn drives her lover wild with desire and rage, neither of them understanding the mental barriers they have erected before the power of their passion.

The violent climax of their struggle occurs as Jack and his wife make plans to adopt a child, an event which if carried out, Jack feels, must force him to stop seeing Elena. The scene is perfectly proportioned; as in Lawrence's great symbolic climax in *The Rainbow*, Oates has her novel's culmination occuring simultaneously on two levels. The lovers are driving furiously along the freeway; Jack is demanding that she must choose, either to break with her husband or accept that Jack and his wife will adopt the child. But for Elena the real development is taking place on another plane altogether. It is not a conscious decision, not a matter of law — to divorce or not to divorce, to adopt or not to adopt — but another change entirely. Jack's misery and anger, reflected in the traffic, the winter road, and their highly charged confrontation, explode as the car, nearly out of control, bounces onto the shoulder of the expressway. He accuses her of what he, her husband, and the whole culture have made her: "You're so deadly, you're so virginal," he shouts. "You're really dead. You're dead. In yourself you're dead. And you want death for everyone — I can understand that — you're so dead yourself, so frigid, certainly you want the rest of the world to die, don't

you? You're such a virgin, a sweet perpetual virgin! You're so
perfect that you turn other people hard as ice, like you, and they
want to die too — you draw them to you — you draw men to you
— and then you feel nothing, nothing! Your insides are as dead
as the rest of you, aren't they? You're so pure, such a gift! You
are really a corpse!" She cannot respond to his outburst. She experiences him like her husband, as part of "the pressure of the
entire world, screaming to get inside her." Inside herself she
feels him *"like a stranger . . . a lover . . . a lover who does not
dare believe. . . ."* (DWM, 466 – 67). Immediately the narrative
fades to a scene where, like one of Howe's grateful clients, Elena
is prostrate, distraught before him, as he reveals the photographs,
tapes, and films he has of his wife and her lover. Law and its
power of compulsion, discovery, guilt, and justice seem triumphant: Morrissey will adopt a child, return to his wife, and abandon Elena; Howe performs "a sacred ritual"; and impersonal
judge, he burns the evidence of his wife's infidelity. Elena survives, ill, distraught, unfulfilled. Only the summing-up remains.

The emotional power of *Do With Me What You Will* has so
far rested on the frustrated struggles of a dimension of experience somehow beyond the law. The law has stood for the impersonal, powerfully deterministic element against which any
drive for individual autonomy must fight. It is reiterated in the
power of Howe, the anxious manipulations of Morrissey, the
drive and prestige of Detroit. Every challenge to the law seems
doomed — Elena's father's love, Jack's desire, his wife's revolutionary anger. There is only the law, beyond which there is no
salvation. The most radical challenge to the law is that of one of
Jack's clients, Mered Dawe, a hippie with a gift for gentle ora-
tory and a spirit of contemplative peace which the law will finally abuse, distort, and destroy as he is convicted on a trivial
and trumped-up offense and ends writing unanswered appeals
to his judge from a mental hospital. Elena visits Dawe with Jack
and, much to his annoyance, strikes up an immediate relationship. Mered embodies just the degree of nondemanding, unas-

sertive love that Elena needs to balance the demands of her lover.

It is in the hope offered by Mered Dawe that the novel reflects most tantalizingly Oates's emphasis on a spiritual revolution in the American consciousness. Behind Dawe's conventional mystical revolutionism lies a quality akin in one sense to Lawrence's insistent goal of love beyond sex, an impersonal bond with the spiritual pulse of the universe where the pulsing egocentricity of the "I" is subsumed into a cosmic spirit. Of course, Dawe's mysticism is, in one important sense, at the opposite pole to Lawrence's. He is antimaterial; what Elena's mother, interviewing him on television, patronizingly terms "your campaign against 'matter'" (DWM, 329) is a way to fulfillment directly opposed to the Lawrentian affirmation of the flesh: "*There is no material but only mind-stuff . . . the old beliefs are just structures of pure thought we must obliterate*" (DWM, 422). Oates is offering Dawe as the prophetic voice of the future, a spirit of hope, a call to Western man to free himself from the domination of the body-mind split that has so haunted the struggles of characters in her earlier novels. In *The Assassins*, Eastern dissociation from the body and from history will be one alternative to the bondage of materialism; here Dawe represents a noncombative alternative to the determinism of the law. Dawe refuses to acknowledge the law as the necessary repression of his and others' fundamental longings. The law gives us no chance to face either the destructiveness or the vast energies of renewal that lie within us, beneath our conventions and duties. It rejects the commandment of life, the commandment to grow into no-one-knows-what. But as Dawe's fate shows (and Oates's own views concede), if a new world is waiting to be born, its time is not yet come. Harassed by the police, persecuted by the law, Dawe is cruelly condemned by the justice on which American society is built. What he lacks is the recognition of the dark, painful deviousness which survival in the world demands. Jack's anger at "whatever the hell mystic crap he believes in" (DWM, 372) is that of a man who knows deep down that, as he had mused years before, "there was love in the world, but you had to be not on trial" (DWM, 216). But how? Can a love maintain its inner integrity when it can only be established through dislocating qualities — pain, deception, lies, illegality? Jack knows that Dawe "represents a new voice, a genuine new voice" (DWM, 414), but he knows too with an equally burning passion the omnipotence of the law. Love, openness, forgiveness, and creativity are, it seems, not possible through the "sterile logic of the Law." "What is the Law, that it renders us into totally separate beings?" (DWM, 492). How can this be resolved?

The answer — and it is with her, not with Dawe that the novel's most realistic hope exists — lies in Elena. In a world where it is impossible to escape the law — "as if anyone could be safe from Detroit, anywhere" (DWM, 382), we recall — what Dawe offers can as yet be experienced only in the body and in the world. Elena's instinctive warmth for Mered brings a "freakish joy, a festivity her lover was almost acknowledging — but he did not yet acknowledge it" (DWM, 457). Mered's unpossessive spontaneity seems to be the antithesis of Jack's possessive, demanding love, and it provides a prophetic vision of the eventual goal for which the lovers must struggle. Dawe is destroyed, and Elena knows that "she might risk no more than five minutes" (DWM, 460) of the peace she senses in him; nevertheless, he provides her with an experience that she might eventually combine with the dark obsessive sensuality of her lover to bring about a final transformation of their love.

In the novel's final section Oates deals with each of the main characters in turn, coming closer to the central conflict. We again encounter Elena's father, her mother, Mered Dawe, Marvin, and then finally the two lovers themselves. The initial tone is cool and rational, and suddenly we are confronted with the familiar mixture of ugliness and tragedy, and then the intensity of an ecstasy that could be born only of crisis and pain.

The law, as represented by Howe as he listens to a tape of his wife and her lover, is unambiguous. "*Extra ecclesia nulla salus*

. . . he had to make no arguments personally, since his wife's lover had made every possible argument. Everything was there. Every plea, every self-incriminating remark, every acknowledgment of misery, shame, guilt" (DWM, 497). According to such evidence, the status of the lovers under the law is clear. Duty, concern, justice, security, responsibility, the ordered society, all condemn them. The responsibility, the authority, and the numinous power of the law also convince Morrissey of their guilt inside the mind. Their affair ended, he becomes the dutiful servant of "*the Self-Starting Self-Stopping Word Machine*" (DWM, 500), a derisive title presumably given by the lovers themselves as they look back at this crisis in their love. To conceive of men as machines, as answering automatically to external pressures, is the least disturbing and efficient way of escaping the resurgence of anarchy: "Was that good or bad, to be insulated? Loving Elena had disrupted the Machine, had used up too much of the voltage" (DWM, 507). Meeting an attractive woman at a party, held (disturbingly) in the house where his father's alleged crime had been committed, "he wanted to tell her *Thank you, you're very beautiful, yes, but I tried one of you once and it almost killed me.*" If all "he had to pit against his terror was a woman's body" and the fear and risk through which he had gone, it was "mad, it could not be endured. He wasn't going to endure it again" (DWM, 513, 519). Morrissey puts his marriage back together. His wife, after all, represents security against inadequacy and terror: "They had been married a long time. Inside their long, comradely marriage was a short, brutal hallucination of a marriage, Jack and Elena's, which seemed to have contaminated the permanent marriage. No excuse" (DWM, 504). Life might be mechanical, but worse might befall him. We are back with *The Rainbow*, with Ursula's apparent capitulation before Skrebensky's determination that she shall marry him.

Here it is that we see how the law, in its guise of obligation and security, is finally destructive. As Werner Pelz remarks, it "idealizes and deifies work which prevents us from thinking too much of our fundamental longings and from realizing too poignantly the threat of our mortality, the fear of ultimate disappointment. It exalts the institution of the family and the concept of duty to give us security. It imbues the organs of government, industry and commerce with pompous dignity in order to persuade us — and itself — that it can procure for us what we need to keep alive."[9] And yet finally what will save Jack and Elena is a more fundamental commandment which has been inherent in their relationship, and which is now tragically repressed — a demand upon them to go beyond the law and to grow into no-one-knows-what. Paradoxically the lasting things are those sudden glimpses, fleeting moments found precisely through the deliberate denial of the law and all its obligations. Law is neither the last nor the best answer to life's real quest. Once again cosseted, nursed by her husband, Elena knows that "in her there was that same infinite, unknowable space, not an emptiness but a mysterious substance that could not be controlled" (DWM, 498). She loves her husband in the sense of being grateful to and dependent on him. "Obligated to him, spiritually she belonged to him. . . . She loved him for his patience, for the infinite busyness and complexity of his life . . . she loved him for his existence, the fact of his existence" (DWM, 531). But there is more: deeper in Elena is a sense of hope and inspiration without which she cannot live, holding before her a fullness of experience that, like Jack, she had despaired of, making her turn away from the seemingly never-quite-attainable. Like Ursula at the end of *The Rainbow*, the decisive act that makes the unattainable attainable involves a radical reorientation of the whole being. Once she has realized what she desires at the deepest level of her being, matters of law, obligation, affection, duty become irrelevant.

The book's final decisive act is depicted first from Jack's and then from Elena's point of view. At the end of the section dealing with Jack, we find him in the midst of his relaxed domestic

9 Werner Pelz, *God is No More* (London: Gollancz, 1964), 100.

life; the doorbell rings and Jack immediately knows who it is
and that he is helpless before Elena's demand. He closes the door
on her, hoping maybe she will go away. He stands surrounded
by the accusations of his wife, the bewilderment of his son, and
his own terror. The narration then switches to Elena, re-creating
her struggle, her awareness that only with Morrissey could she
achieve more than survival, and that she could have him only
through further pain. We are thrust into their retrospective
dialogue:

> *You didn't love me?*
> *How could I have loved you!*
> *Then why . . . ? Why all of this . . . ? Why?*
> *Why do you ask?*

As she recalls him, she remembers him as "a difficult, troubled
man, not very likable. Physically he was attractive, from the
outside; but she did not remember what he looked like, really.
She remembered him from the inside. And she remembered the
fighting, the struggling." Most important of all, in the development of her autonomy, what she must do is outside the law, the
given: "And he wasn't free, either. She would have to hunt him
down, she would have to take him away from another woman,
and from his son. This was hateful to her: she did not want to
be a criminal, like everyone else." But she knows something beyond the law. Whether, specifically, she "loves" him or not she
does not know. But she does know that "if she wanted love, she
could love only Morrissey; but she half-doubted that she wanted
love again" (DWM, 543, 544).

So she leaves her husband and, with almost ritual concentration, comes to Detroit. Looking back later, the lovers remember:

> *Didn't you love me? You looked at me without love!*
> *Was that love you brought me, Elena?* (DWM, 560)

Inside Elena, now acting decisively and with the full force of her
personality for the first time in her life, is a claim she makes not
only for herself but for both of them — that when Jack comes

out of his apartment to her, she has acted for both of them in an affirmation that fulfillment is greater than obligation, that challenge is greater than security, and that love transcends the law. Life is growth, change, challenge; the law may be more humane, more conciliatory, simply asking of us that we conform to a given, general righteousness. But Elena now knows, and Jack is made to see, that men and women have within them something that is at once more vulnerable and yet more fundamental than law. The law cannot transfigure us. Pain, exile, unhappiness, and cruelty may be the price they pay for our challenge to the law, but their committed togetherness will become their freedom. Beyond the law there may be no salvation and Mered Dawe's fate may be a savage warning, but salvation ultimately can be imagined, if at all, only as risk and commitment:

When he appeared, exactly as she had imagined he would — dark-haired, in a rush, a man in his mid-thirties — she was not prepared for their sudden, surprised smiles. They smiled as if seeing each other for the first time, a look between them of pure kinship, of triumph: and in that instant they forgot everything else.

Did you forget everything else?

Almost everything. (DWM, 563)

SEVEN

The Assassins: A Book of Hours, Childwold

T HE ASSASSINS: A Book of Hours was published in 1975 and seems to have taken
Oates four agonizing years to write. As we
have seen, the early seventies was a period
of distinct transition for her. After *Wonderland*, she wrote that she had come "to
the end of a phase of my life" and wanted
to "move toward a more articulate moral
position, not just dramatizing nightmarish
problems but trying to show possible ways
of transcending them. . . . Blake, Whitman,
Lawrence and others have had a vision of a
transformation of the human spirit. . . . I
want to do what I can to bring it nearer."[1]
Do With Me What You Will certainly shows
evidence for a newer vision of hope. But if
The Assassins shows evidence for such a

1 Walter Clemons, "Joyce Carol Oates: Love and Violence," *Newsweek*, December 11, 1972, p. 77.

transformation it does so only by forcing reaction to the deterministic world it surrounds us with. It is probably the most concentratedly grim of all of Oates's novels, focusing on death, murder, and the spiritual destructiveness of a family obsessed with prestige, power, and political aspirations. Like the Pedersens in *Wonderland*, the Petrie family in *The Assassins* represents the extreme of the obsessive and dualistic materialism of Western culture. The ultimate judgment on the Western experiment of defining individuality in measurable terms is in the way death is perceived as a threat to the ego. Instead of death being seen, as Heidegger puts it, as a boundary against which the seriousness of life may be measured and finitude faced as ultimately illusory, death becomes a touchstone of the ego's fear of the future, and of the imagining of the future without the self. As Oates wrote on Kafka, "it is not the higher life that knows good or evil or dread, but only the self in its fear of ascending to the higher life, as if, in releasing itself even from fear, it would suffer a tremendous loss" (NHNE, 297). Of all the novels, *The Assassins* has the most affinities with Kafka. Like *The Castle*, it articulates a fear of life, a sense that material existence is imperfect and continually threatened, a desperate and incessant struggle against flux, ambiguity, and absurdity. As well, the novel expresses something of Kafka's—and, for that matter, Lawrence's—search for a transcendence beyond the mere personal, beyond the self-obsessiveness of the ego. In *The Assassins* death is the ultimate threat to the autonomy of the ego, whether that of the individual or the collective ego of history—in this case represented by the Petrie family, "petrified," "trapped in stone" (A, 4), within the self and within history.

The central character of the novel is Andrew Petrie, a powerful right-wing political philosopher, publisher, and former senator, who has just been assassinated. Each of the novel's three parts concentrates on what at one point is called his "revenge" —the effects of his death on his brother Hugh, an impotent, paranoid cartoonist who lives in New York, on his young second wife Yvonne, and on his isolated, religious younger brother Stephen. Death haunts the novel: Yvonne has had premonitions of her husband's death, the murderers are continually being investigated, and we are told of previous attempts to assassinate Andrew; as well, Hugh attempts to kill himself, and Yvonne herself is hacked to death in a scene probably more horrific and arbitrary than any earlier violence in Oates's fiction. There is throughout the book the sense that "everyone was doomed" (A, 561), and yet that death is frighteningly arbitrary—"*this sort of arbitrary, whimsical death . . . death by accident, almost . . . It's very American and very frightening*" (A, 560). The novel's fundamental material reality is conveyed in a conversation between Hugh and Yvonne:

> *He was a good man and he died horribly.*
> *We all die horribly, Yvonne.* (A, 378)

The Petrie family, "famous for the transactions viciousness can make with civilization" (A, 4), is a close-knit, vindictive clan, built upon a tradition of power, money, and self-righteous morality. We are saturated with details of the Petries' lives, past and present, their property, political and social power, and above all the genius of the murdered Andrew. Each member of the family, however he may reject it, is formed, and deformed, by his part in its dynasty. Yet beneath the prestige of the Petries is the despair that history, seemingly the ongoing justification of individual acts and ambitions, is nothing but "a joke . . . an assemblage of lies" (A, 95). The members of the family—including the patriarchal father in a Catholic rest home in California, Andrew's brothers, wife, ex-wife, and son, and a waspish assemblage of cousins—all experience his death as calling their own fragile egos into question. Yvonne buries herself in his unpublished papers, continuing his battle for a place in history through his words; Hugh feels cheated of the opportunity to hate his elder brother who had for so long humiliated him and seeks a perverse revenge in an obsessive pursuit of Yvonne through letters, calls, visits, and a feeble attempt to drug and then seduce her. Andrew's cousins and relatives, variously appalled and fearful before the fact of death, all try to perpetuate Andrew's presence. The dead senator had seemed to possess the only hope of defeating the deterministic materialism of history and thus of preserving their own sense of permanence. Even his wife "does not mourn *him*. She is mourning his absence, the loss of his power. His name, his prestige. His essence" (A, 334). That he could be killed is a final shuddering reminder of the fragility of the ego's attempts to transcend itself and the traditions and customs which at once created and annihilated them. Yvonne broods at one point, trying to make herself realize his absence: "He was dead. Permanently dead. If she heard his voice again it would be only in her imagination, and she could not direct her imagination, could not will it to re-create him — she could not force it — was helpless" (A, 252).

The novel's three parts are held together by three structural concepts through which the book's intellectual patterns emerge — the world, the flesh, and the spirit. The most insistent presence is the sheer brutality of the physical world, the *dinglichkeit*, the thingness of the world — or perhaps equally relevant, the definition of the ego in terms of things. As in the central episodes of *Wonderland*, we are submerged in a world of facts, things, property, prestige, power, and the wills that clutch at them. The characters constantly move from one unsatisfying thing to the next. Their bewildered, suffering egos obsessively cling to the factitious surfaces of their lives, desiring the world to give back a truth and satisfaction that no material thing can ever afford. Where the grasping egos of *Wonderland* strive for more basic desires, of economic security and status, the affluent, securely established Petries of *The Assassins* are more complex and destructive in their passions and ambitions. Their world is determined by the values which historically have formed it: they make up a family both at home in and driven by the world of lies, publicity, status, political appointments, tax exemptions, and a continual background of violence. It is as if just because their world is one where control and manipulation are paramount, impulsive violence and "haphazard circumstances . . . a rent in the cosmic fabric through which all sorts of ugly things poured" (A, 103) seem more likely to threaten them.

Oates overwhelms us with the cloying factuality and threatening unpredictability of this world. Some months after her husband's death, Yvonne Petrie attends a conference in the Yaeger Institute, and we are immediately assaulted by a list of some five hundred distinguished visitors whose photographs dominate the institute. Together they constitute an image of the world of status and clashing individualism in which the Petries have flourished. Oates juxtaposes these exhaustive lists of the solid public world with scenes of despairing grasping for another kind of fulfillment through the violence of sexuality. As we are bombarded by hundreds of names, titles, and roles—"Robert M. Hutchins; Professor E. McNamara of the Harvard Business School; J. McCormick Topping of the Federal Communications Commission; Edward P. Murphy of the U.S. Army Defense Biology Laboratories at Ford Detrick, Md.," and so on, we are suddenly confronted by: "Harvey labored over her, his eyes closed, his hands now shut into fists on either side of her head, his body raised slightly from her—and relieved of his weight she felt her mind drift and spin and dart—mixed in with the air hammers and Harvey's strained gasping breath and yet freed of them, soaring away from them" (A, 415). Such relentless, violent juxtapositions force upon us the traumatic realization that no object or activity can ultimately satisfy our needs. We probe, penetrate, grasp, and find only further anxiety and frustration. Even the flesh, the focus of possible transcendence in both *Them* and, more hopefully, *Do With Me What You Will*, is a blind alley. Love, represented in *The Assassins* most poignantly by Yvonne, is merely another form of suffering attachment to the perishable by grasping at unrealities (what Buddhism terms *tanhā*).

Love, too, is essentially directed toward death. The marriage

between Andrew and Yvonne, *"utterly devoted to each other"*
(A, 109), as one of their relations coos, and then the "insatiable
curiosity" about the widow, as well as her desperate, dislocated
attempts at sexual fulfillment are all essentially tied to the unreality of time. Love's reality is represented gruesomely in Hugh's
drawing of "a copulation-crucifixion," his "personal revenge
upon the Angel of Death and the Woman—the Angel crucified
on a ludicrous fleshy cross" (A, 203). Love is experienced as pain,
as a series of neurotic demands of quantification and grasping—
pawing, teasing, caressing, mauling. Yvonne thinks of her lovers
and pursuers together: "*Love* was the word they assigned to
their need, their ephemeral, egoistic need; she was the accidental
object of that need and might easily be replaced by another object" (A, 293). In this way Yvonne, just because she is the beautiful, youthful wife of the dead seer Andrew Petrie, becomes a
sexual focus of the psychic pressures which her husband had
embodied. Lovers drift through her consciousness, seeking in
her body the power and mystique of her husband. "What do you
want from me—all of you?" she cries at one point (A, 325), and
the answer is frustrating and destructive: they had all sought her
passive acquiescence to their own fantasies, needs, and insecurities. But ultimately, she senses that whether she is manipulated
or free, there is a grim indifference in the universe which renders
all human commitment meaningless. In her turn, "she had loved
him, had worshiped him—and he had probably loved her too"
—but that had "made no difference" (A, 431). All humans seem
doomed to search for transcendence through the flesh just as her
lovers grasp at the dead Andrew Petrie through the agony of her
body: "Her cousin-in-law claimed to be obsessed by her, but
now, making love to her, she suspected he was hardly aware of
her, had no concern for what she might be feeling or whether
she was feeling anything or whether he was hurting her. . . . So
many deceptions, so many lies . . . misstatements . . . rumors"
(A, 419). Even in love, despairingly grappling in mankind's most
frenzied attempts to achieve serenity, we are overwhelmed by the

horror that our deepest and most fragile experiences of passion cannot be a means to nirvana. Love is an unreality, "a sweaty, impassioned struggle" (A, 526). Like the rest of life in the body, love is nothing more than a "blur of motion" (A, 553).

The most persistent of Yvonne's pursuing lovers — who include cousins, family connections, her husband's lawyer and editorial assistants — is her brother-in-law Hugh. The long first section of the novel (223 pages) is devoted to the disintegration of Hugh under the impact of his brother's death. Emaciated, embittered, despising and yet needing his brother in order to envy and despise him, Hugh is a despicable and weak character whose parasitism and paranoia become increasingly malicious. He draws cartoons of political leaders sanctimoniously disemboweling each other. His theory of art is "to grasp the perfect deformity, and thus reveal the very essence of a personality" (A, 75) and this seems indicative of his own warped, grasping nature, truthful only in so far as it reveals the death of his spirit. Hugh's attempt at transcendence throughout is futile. No less than the politician or lover, the artist is trapped in his body and his warring desires.

Hugh's plan to seduce Yvonne is conceived as a confused mixture of revenge, exploitation, and sheer childish perversity. He observes her at the funeral, sick and in terror. She is "very easy for the Artist to imagine — that shy stubborn social manner turned inside out. If a man can be reduced to whimpering sniveling terror, why not a woman?" (A, 87). She is youthful, boyish, and isolated — and her very arrogance provokes such meditations in him. After the funeral, he attempts clumsily to attract her, pursuing her by phone calls, visits, letters, although as much in his fantasy as in reality. Indeed, with the narration filtered through Hugh's mind, we perceive only his frantic self-obsession. He fantasizes that "she accepted me. In spite of what the evidence suggests" (A, 45). At other times he implores his relations to disbelieve malicious rumors spread about his relations with her. What ameliorates Hugh's vindictive and exploitative pas-

sion a little is a small but genuine attempt to reach beyond himself. He, like all of us, is groping for transcendence, and we respond sympathetically as, out of his self-obsession, he attempts
to articulate an appeal to her. "I spoke to Yvonne," he records,
"hoping — silently begging — that inasmuch as beauty of such
heartbreaking authority does exist in the world — the maligned
material world — inasmuch as we two are alive — living . . ." (A,
69). Yet as his dream meets the material world, it becomes distorted, acquisitive, and impotent. He experiences no genuine
desire but "only the angry memory of desire, the idea of desire"
(A, 131), and finds himself to be, as he later sardonically broods,
"omnipotent in the head. In the body less so" (A, 132). He slips
a drug into her drink, takes her to her apartment, and tries unsuccessfully to seduce her, collapsing (despite a series of frantic
after-the-event fantasies) into impotence and nausea. When he
finds himself with the simple physical courage to carry through
the seduction, he is haunted by his dead brother's presence and
backs off in hysterical disgust and shame. When Yvonne comes
to confront him in his apartment to accuse him of raping her, he
confesses his inability in a pathetic display of weakness. "I un-
snapped my pajamas — groped for my penis — feeble, limp, tiny
creature like nothing else on earth — a joke, yes — it was a joke
— must have been a — I shoot it at her, toward her, trying to
laugh again, again with some minimal success: couldn't she see?
wasn't this proof? A joke, a joke — I was never anything but a
joke" (A, 215).

What intensifies Hugh's tragedy is the near-possibility of a
connection with Yvonne that would not be grasping and exploitative. Later, we read an account of the scene from her viewpoint. Even while we know that he is lacing her drinks, she is in
fact sensing a humanity in Hugh that he himself cannot recognize. She thinks "He's real, he's living. He's like myself. He's
real, a human being, a man. . . . Hugh was revealed to her as
something quite different from the person she had assumed him
to be. . . . A *human being, a man!*" (A, 371). But because of the

anxious grasping ego, the possibility of a free, unexploitative relationship never materializes. Mingled with Yvonne's thoughts during this same scene are reminiscences of similar puzzled, friendly, and unreciprocated sentiments she once had about Hugh's younger brother Stephen. Caught in their egos, people never connect. Suffering is intensified by the bondage of attachment to the uniqueness of the self. Hugh's agony ends in a final impotent assertion of his existential self as he shoots himself, and even as he does he feels that the unique importance of his suffering self will be misunderstood. As he points the revolver into his mouth, he draws back: "Not the mouth, not the mouth!" Suddenly it occurs to him that someone will misunderstand him —that one of his psychoanalysts will interpret his act as "symbolic and not real—deathly real—will place a degrading and perhaps even obscene 'meaning' upon it—And so you press the end of the barrel against your forehead and pull at the heavy heavy trigger and—" (A, 223). Even in his confrontation with death, Hugh cannot emulate Andrew. He lies in a coma, visited in hospital by the family, a Petrie who could not live up to his brother's prowess.

In *Wonderland* the mystery of the individual personality in its fragility was constantly bombarded by the crude materialism of time and space and yet remained the final realm of human meaning. In *The Assassins* Oates suggests, more radically, that the Western emphasis on the reality of the personality is an illusion, as much a material snare as roles imposed by the world of medicine, law, politics, or even art. Whereas in *Do With Me What You Will*, the lovers' struggle toward authenticity, however painful a process, was made possible because romantic love contained the seeds of its own transcendence, in *The Assassins*, no activity, however temporarily fulfilling, can do anything but fragment us. "The neurotic," Hugh Petrie is told, "is continually frustrated, thinking about what he wants to do while doing something else, thinking about something else when he does what it appeared he 'wanted' to do, half here, half there," and above all "pleading and cajoling with himself, -self, -self" (A, 73). Even Stephen Petrie, of all the family the least dragged down by a preoccupation with ego, panics before the possibility of total self-surrender. As a child, he has pored over an old map and sensed the impermanence of anything recognizably personal and historical. He sees the seemingly unchanged natural features of an apparently familiar world — rivers, lakes, mountains — but "everything that belonged to a specific moment in history, everything specifically human" is impermanent and unreal. "There were modern cities indicated in parentheses, as if they were ghostly, mere ideas or premonitions," and then as if, desperate to fix himself, to give permanence to himself, he sees how one of his ancestors had put a tiny mark in black ink beside Albany, the family hometown. He supposes it to be a child like himself, marking "the spot upon which he existed at the moment he marked the spot," as if to stop history. Stephen takes a pen and makes the mark firmer: "*I am here*," he says. "*I was here*." And then the thought breaks in, "*Someone was here*" (A, 490–91). As Stephen grows, he struggles to learn to abandon such reliance on the idea of a permanent, fixed self. He alone knows, even if fitfully, of the terrible unreality of the material world and the grasping egos which inhabit it. What alone seems real are the fleeting experiences of escaping the entrapment in the flesh, in the ego, in any kind of connection with the world: "Not existing, not wishing to exist, he lived a life of constant surveillance; his host was *Stephen Petrie* and he was forced to dwell within that host, sharing a common bloodstream, common organs, a skeleton, a dim reservoir of memories" (A, 446).

What vision of the universe is Oates offering us in *The Assassins*? Initially, we are faced with a paradox. The world the Petries have inhabited through their history is a world of fact, materialism, cause and effect. And yet, beneath this hard, rational, competitive world we are forced to sense that somehow another level of reality operates. Events occur without apparent reason or cause; the world seems locked together by "certain patterns, certain non-causal events" (A, 160), where the concept of the "cause" of a violent death may be irrelevant to the real spiritual reverberations that surround an individual's death. A sense of premonition, a sudden emptiness of personality, may be truer reflections of the ultimate reality of things than the usual account by cause and effect. The "assassins" are, in the everyday world of fact, causality, and material reality, an unknown group of murderers; the real assassins may equally be those grasping, destructive egos with which we are burdened and with which we collide. On the spiritual level, we are all assassins. Andrew Petrie "provoked someone into killing him" (A, 4), broods his brother, and we sense that Yvonne, too, is a victim of her own as well as her husband's spiritual destructiveness. We are in a world of accumulated spiritual violence, distorted energy, and thirsting egos so that violence, even apparently random, becomes seemingly the inevitable outcome. The gruesome death of Yvonne, hacked to pieces by some unknown assailants, possibly those who killed her husband, seems to be a manifestation, causeless and yet at the same time determined, of the distortion of a universe from which she cannot escape and which she is both a victim and a willing participant. Oates eerily draws us into a view of the world which, it should be noted, has been implicit in her fiction from the beginning, but which only in *The Assassins* is given what almost amounts to an explicit philosophical backing. The world, Hugh's psychiatrist suggests, is "so constructed . . . that there is a network of relationships invisible" unless one is enabled to wave aside "the mists of what is known as 'common sense'" — and so discover "certain patterns, certain non-causal events" (A, 160). The events of *The Assassins* provide us with such a pattern, "a rent in the cosmic fabric through which all sorts of ugly things poured" as Andrew's cousin Pamela puts it.

How do we find meaning in such a universe? At one point Hugh broods that "when there is no meaning to events, we are surly, dissatisfied, deathly," and then immediately balances his feeling by the observation that "when there is too much meaning, we are terrified" (A, 100). Does the world have a given meaning? Are our grasping egos so frightened by the possibility of meaninglessness that we must find or impose a meaning to justify our uniqueness? The possibility that Andrew's death had "*No meaning to it*" terrifies his brother: "merely things that happened, to him and to others bound closely to him. Stray formless events — whispers that never rise to coherence — repugnant to me" (A, 112). For the Western mind, trained and guided by rationality and causality, there must be "a reason for everything. Nothing without its reason." Otherwise, we panic: "Causality: sanity. Chaos: unsanity" (A, 238).

In her book on Lawrence, Oates comments on the revolutionary implications of Lawrence's poem "Fish":

... my heart accused itself
Thinking: I am not the measure of creation.
This is beyond me, this fish.
His God stands outside my God.

Oates argues that "calm and matter-of-fact as this statement is . . . it is a total rejection of that dogma of the West that declares *Man is the measure of all things*" (NHNE, 79). Only the personality-bound ego must project its own need for justification upon the universe. We may be seekers of meaning, but we inevitably find that meaning comes to us; it cannot be created or willed into existence. "The universe," wrote Lawrence, "is like Father Ocean, a stream of all things slowly moving," with "each other, living or unliving" streaming "in its own, odd, intertwining flux." "Nothing," he goes on, "not even man . . . nor anything that man has thought or felt or known is fixed and abiding." Our life consists not in desiring to be everything, not in conquering and achieving power over the material world. The power over the world such as that sought by the Petries is, in Lawrence's words, "a platitudinous bubble." The true way of discovering meaning is "not to *have* all . . . not to *grasp* everything into a supreme possession," but to achieve a pure relationship of acceptance and change with the circumambient universe.[2]

How paradoxical it is, in both Lawrence and Oates, that a passionate concern with integrity, singleness of being, and commitment, should lead to a no less passionate celebration of a mystery beyond personality! Lawrence, says Oates, "allows this experience — whatever it is — to take possession of him; he does not attempt a false possession of it" (NHNE, 62). In the third Petrie brother, Stephen, Oates offers us another figure, like Mered Dawe, who exists as a corrective to the fiercely combative and possessive wills of the rest of his family. Stephen is a strange recluse-like religious fanatic, who is regarded by his family as deluded and crazy, "absolved . . . from ordinary life," as Andrew patronizingly puts it. His life is constantly dislocated by intense visitations from a realm of experience beyond himself, which he apprehends as God. At Andrew's funeral he senses the presence of death in Yvonne, "flooded now with a spacious warning sensation, a sensation of light, an almost physical knowing . . . he must keep away from her. He must never approach her. She was death" (A, 463). "Transparency" we are told "was Stephen's single talent" (A, 446); the term recalls one of the crucial features of Oates's whole fictional world — the "transparency" of the material, revealing a more fundamental level of existence. He embodies an intense yet curiously disconnected sense of the spiritual world that is not merely beyond but a negation of the world in which he lives and which has formed him. Andrew tells him that *the real business of governing the world falls to responsible men* (A, 542). Stephen has simply "surrendered the rest of the world to people like his brother, who turned and turned it in their hands and could not comprehend it" (A, 472).

What kind of God is Stephen's? He does not know, and Oates

2 D. H. Lawrence, "Art and Morality," in *Phoenix: The Posthumous Papers of D. H. Lawrence*, ed. Edward D. McDonald (New York: Viking Press, 1972), 525; D. H. Lawrence, "Democracy," in *Phoenix*, 707.

offers us no explanation, although she is clearly fascinated by this dimension of nameless mysticism somehow entering human experience—what she terms, again writing on Lawrence, the proclamation of "the impersonal and the divine within ordinary men" (NHNE, 40). In what ways, we might further ask, does Stephen apprehend this God? Not primarily in affirming experiences of joy, relationship, or personal transcendence. Although Stephen knows God in and through the world, he perceives him through pain and agony, as the negation of the world and especially of the history that has created him. He knows "the essential absurdity of the exterior world," where "fragments daily did battle" (A, 494) and where people are trapped "*in bodies they can't recognize are diseased*" (A, 500–501). He has cast that world away—and yet because he is Stephen Petrie, the brother of Andrew Petrie, he fights against losing that identity and the sense of self that is formed by it. What Stephen comprehends and what he embodies in the novel's pattern of meaning is that to surrender oneself to God is to have no self, no strong center of consciousness, no being-toward anything. The true self is a realm of absolute negation, a void.

Stephen's vision embodies a radical denial of all that the American dream has been built on. We are reminded throughout the novel of the ironical interpenetration in the history of America of the mystical and the material and, above all, of the exclusion of the mystical from the ruthless pragmatic control of civilization represented by the Petries. Stephen is, according to Hugh, "moved by 'religious promptings'—which no one was cruel enough to assign a more clinical term to" (A, 17). In the same way the visions of the Jesuit martyrs, the Indians, and the spriritual strivings of the original Petrie, a seventeenth-century nonconformist emigrant from England, have been dismissed as superstition or reduced to crass materialism. At one point Andrew has been asked whether the Manitou, the spirit-god of the Indians, still haunts the mountains around the family land. "*Absolutely not,*" he says. "*The Indians are gone from the moun-*

tains and with the Indians are gone their devils; we live here now" (A, 354). What we see, however, is the return of what the Manitou, and all other manifestations of the spiritual, stand for. Distorted, violent, and destructive, the spirit, which the Petries have denied, nevertheless reasserts itself.

I have paralleled Oates's exploration of spiritual presence in contemporary America with Lawrence's. Equally apposite — and, indeed, the connection might be made with Lawrence too — would be comparisons with Eastern, especially Buddhist, philosophies. Stephen's experience of God seems to draw much more on Eastern than Western sources, in its suggestion that evil, suffering, and materialism itself are manifestations of the same underlying spiritual alienation. As well, Stephen's conception of God is close to the Buddhist doctrine of *annatta* or *nirātina* (non-ego) whereby negation becomes the means of overcoming the bondage of desire and egocentricity. By such a doctrine, the human personality itself becomes negated: no kind of self-assertion, even self-understanding, can offer peace. The pain, evil, and crime that so overwhelm the novel are judged as the inevitable manifestations of the ceaseless desires and ego-assertions of mankind, and the self in its unreality must be got rid of, not cultivated.

As we move toward the end of this grim, deterministic novel, we might be struck by a similarity between its judgment on the world of material fact to the celebrated self-abrogating Zen koan which takes the form "If you do X, I shall do Y; if you don't do X, I shall do Y; if you do nothing, I shall do Y." Such sayings, aiming to nullify or abrogate the reliance on the rational, analytical faculties, embody in their contradictions the futility of material existence. None of the book's characters escapes the endless circles of this world. Andrew Petrie is dead, Hugh prostrate with brain damage, Yvonne dead: everyone is doomed. Even Stephen, with his vision which allows him to accept the world as unreal and deceptive, can find no way of relating that vision to the world in which he is thrown. Stephen travels over the surface of American society separating himself from the guilt and futility of material existence, but unable to change or ameliorate it. It is a grim vision. The hopes of transcendence, through the integrity and self-reflection of the personality, or through love as in *Do With Me What You Will* is nowhere felt. Instead, we apprehend the traditional Western account of the self as futile and deceptive; above all, sexual love has become the most unreal, because most ambitious, attempt at transcendence.

The Assassins is Oates's most forbidding novel to date. It seems to mark a crossroad in her vision of America. She has progressed from observing and evoking the tragic irony of the dislocation between dream and materialism in America; here, the dream is not only deceptive but unreal. The only reality is renunciation, and yet modern America cannot escape the bondage of its history. *The Assassins* seems to reach this despairing conclusion: We are bound to a world into which we have been thrown, a world measured by the "hours" of the novel's subtitle, and from which there apparently is no escape.

II

Childwold (1976) is on first reading a curiously retrospective novel. It returns to the setting of many of Oates's early stories and novels—to Eden Valley, to its oppressive towns and derelict farms. Its characters, too, seem familiar—strong but defensive women, self-lacerating intellectual men, relationships that explode into arbitrary and decisive violence. *Childwold* focuses on the love between Fitz John Kasch, a middle-aged recluse living in Yewville, a small town like so many in Oates's Eden County, and Laney Bartlett, a fourteen-year-old girl from the nearby hill country. Kasch's obsessive passion develops into an agonized but deeply affectionate love as he finds in the puzzled and only partly responsive girl a surrogate daughter, a reminder of his own youth and broken marriage, and a focus of lost, forgotten needs and desires. Eventually Kasch becomes fascinated by Laney's large and chaotic family and out of a mixture of self-torture, altruism, and affection, meets and plans to marry her mother, Arlene. One of Arlene's many previous lovers, Earl Tuller, encounters Kasch during a visit to the farm and — in a confrontation so typical of Oates's emphasis on the randomness of decisive events in human life — Kasch accidentally kills him; out of horror and guilt, he becomes insane, declares himself dead, and lives on, isolated and even more distraught than when he started, refusing all communication with any visitor. Like *Do With Me What You Will*, the novel lyrically celebrates the surprising joys of love, but its conclusion is devastating, its violence as unredeeming as that in *The Assassins*.

Published ten to fifteen years after her early Eden Valley novels and stories, *Childwold* seems to mark the end of a phase of Oates's development. Probably more than with any of her other novels, reviewers were impatient with what they saw as its incoherence and repetitiveness. Many saw the affinities with more radically disjunctive kinds of fiction and were confused by what amounts to an important redirection in her handling of fictional form.[3] The Eden Valley, Yewville, Port Oriskany, and Childwold are certainly reminiscent of their counterparts in, say, *A Garden of Earthly Delights*. But probably more than in any previous novel, setting is evoked overwhelmingly to reveal psychological, emotional, and spiritual states, and as in *The Assassins* the overbearing factualness of material existence does not appear simply to provide social or historical background but becomes, again, strangely "transparent."

The lives of Arlene and her children are buried in the oppressiveness of material trivia just as the Wendalls' lives are in *Them*; equally, Fitz John Kasch's life has, at least in his past, been built upon solid middle-class values — literature, art, affluence. But social distinctions, like the whole material world, exist within the novel only as foci of underlying feeling: the material is real only as it is perceived by the mind. Regardless of the characters'

3 See, for example, Carol Pearson in *Library Journal*, November 15, 1976, p. 2394, or Joseph Hendin in *New York Times Book Review*, November 28, 1976, p. 8.

backgrounds or status, what we encounter are the confusions and overlapping of minds and feelings, wordless collisions of incommunicable realities and perspectives. At times the novel merges the half-articulated confusion of characters' responses to a shared event; actions seem to overlap or occur without motivation or completion. "So much, so many things, what did they mean" (C, 86) is therefore, as in so many of Oates's earlier novels, a recurring question here. One kind of response which we have seen Oates use repeatedly in earlier novels is also found here — the technique in *Expensive People* and *The Assassins* for example, of juxtaposing jumbled lists of surroundings with a character's inner confusions in order to convey radical dislocation. We are bombarded with the factual and material world — "Grain elevators, chain-link fences, barges, tugs, cattails, knotweed, chicory, blacktop, telephone posts, Coulos Auto Service, Honey-Bee Drainage Service, Lake View Motor Court, traffic lights, moonlight, Lone Lee's Take-Out, barbed-wire fences, water towers, chimneys, No Trespassing, concrete, North Oriskany Car Wash, bulldozers, cranes, gas tanks. Mamma Mia Submarines, ramps, underpasses, Diesels, Greyhound buses, railroad tracks, Lots for Sale, Chuck's Harbor Inn" — and then asked to assimilate the list with an ejaculation of confusion — "What is this place, Vale asked, I don't know this place, who are these people?" (C, 256). We may become somewhat impatient with Oates's repetition in this novel, but as compensation we are given two not entirely unprecedented but unusually moving perspectives on the action. One is provided by the unusually self-conscious brooding nature of Kasch himself, which gives the novel unusually explicit meditations by which his struggles may be judged. The other is the dense, occasionally confused but typically intense and demanding narrative structure of the work, which shows just how complex and sophisticated a technician of fiction Oates has become since her early work.

More than any of Oates's earlier novels, *Childwold* relies on fragments of interior narrative and revelation, on partial and dislocated understanding held together largely by an atmosphere of intensity. All the major characters have their own narrative voices: an objectified "you" for Laney as if a narrator were providing the confused, semiliterate girl with an articulate voice as she looks back at the events; the direct and obsessive "I" of Kasch, also remembering what he announces in the book's first paragraph to be "that final year of my life"; and a host of voices that swirl around — confusing, violent, voices of the present or the familial past, all of which seem to bear down upon the central actions. We are given glimpses of people and events in the lives and ancestry of both Kasch and Laney — Irish and German immigrants, Laney's grandfather and her brother Vale, a violent, predatory Vietnam veteran, rural superstitions, Kasch's parents and family. Overwhelmingly we sense that every incident in the present is subtly and unconsciously determined by people and actions of our pasts — our ancestors live through our apparently autonomous actions and dimly grope and battle within us. The book's overall atmosphere is therefore one where motives and intentions dissolve under the pressure of a multiplicity of intangible or unknowable factors, where obsessive leaps at freedom are at once the only authentic human actions and yet those most rigidly predetermined.

The novel opens with a brief and unexplained reference to "that final year of my life," presumably by a man (soon identified as Kasch) who is recalling his dreams of "Evangeline" (who we later know as Laney) "in her attic room"; then follows a swirl of voices mixing pain, domesticity, violence, and family quarrels. Then we are thrown into the intensity of Kasch's meditations on his inner foulness and his speculation on whether to kill himself or, possibly, someone else:

Horrendous stink. Eyes rolled back into the head, swollen black tongue protruding, neck raw-rubbed, broken, its rope burns aswirl with insect life, teeming in the heat of late August of an endless summer, unrecognizable face aswirl, ateeming, humming with activity, swarms of flies, colonies of maggots, unrecognizable creature, no one's corpse, stink of rot and excrement, no no no, hanging from the beam, dead weight, weight of the dead, heavy as concrete: no no no no NO. No one's corpse.

Six days' beard. Melancholia. Filthy bare feet. Liquor, stale rye bread, peanut butter. Suicide impractical in this heat. Endless summer, endless Augusts. (C, 13)

We enter the diseased world of Kasch's mind. Rejecting suicide ("wouldn't be found for days. Horrendous stink. No glamor"), he contemplates killing someone else: "A full sized creature impractical. Better a child? A child. Boy, girl: no matter. Perhaps a girl. Girl. Kasch delirious with excitement, ecstasy-pain, oblivion" (C, 14). Then he rears back from his perversity with a quotation from Pascal and we realize we are encountering a peculiarly intellectual perversity, even if as yet we do not quite see it Kasch's way as an "Experiment. Spritual. Retreat from desire. Experiment in progress" (C, 15). Slowly, Kasch's background and nature become clearer, however. Once a poet and something of a philosopher, divorced, middle-aged, he has returned to his childhood home of Yewville because he "wished to live deliberately, to retreat from history, both personal and collective . . . to live deep and suck out all the marrow of life . . . to drive life into a corner and reduce it to its lowest terms" (C, 15). We pause, perhaps, over the contradictions in the images here — but either way, Kasch seeks life at its most private and intense, in contemplating death, violence, sexual perversity, the great mystics. He, Kasch, is a short-sighted, weak, dirty, forty-year-old, his face increasingly "a blur, rapidly receding. . . . Middle of the journey of what is known as life. Obstacle course. Series of experiments" (C, 20).

Halfheartedly seeking a victim — although clearly it is the thought of violence rather than carrying it out that excites Kasch — he wanders through Yewville and observes some children playing. "Wanting only a voyeur's pleasure" — "the pulse of, the throb of" — "not a hero's" (C, 22), he backs off when he sees a girl being bullied. Wanting "no involvement. No rebaptism in the waters of the world," he determines to slip away. Instead "he hears himself shouting . . . actually running," rescuing the girl: "He is daring all. Risking all. Kasch the poet, Kasch the pervert: now Kasch the hero. In the forty-first year of his life. In the middle of the journey of. He runs. . . . *Come along with me*, Kasch will whisper. *I can take care of you. . . . Come*" (C, 23–24).

In this way begins the strange relationship between the idealizing, short-sighted, poet-pervert and the tough fourteen-year-old hillbilly schoolgirl, "permaturely aged, dirtied, used, wise," a "serious cynical frightened little girl" (C, 48, 81). By means of her radically impressionistic narrative technique, Oates prevents us from judging the relationship except through Kasch's and Laney's own reactions. Violent passion, typically, takes us into an area of experience that is beyond moral judgment, where the intensity of joy or corruption is its own explanation. We observe the predatory, exploitative obsession Kasch has for the girl, but we also sense the increasingly lyrical, compassionate dimension of the relationship. Kasch the pervert can gloat that "I hurt her didn't I. Hurt her badly. Made her acknowledge me. Oh the grief of it, the nausea of triumph, the afterhurt of pleasure squeezed from another's body" (C, 60); but there is more. What starts partly as a voyeuristic jealousy of youth's passionate innocence and as a self-destructive urge to degrade himself deepens into a fixation with "paedomorphosis: the shaping of the young" (C, 83), a fixation of his own lost youth as much as hers. Kasch broods on "the queer, ugly, disturbing, maddening, marvelous depravity of the young. . . . So many of them, and so young! Mine is the fairest of all, I want none other, but they are nevertheless everywhere, aren't they? Marvelous. Terrifying. . . . Murderers, and so innocent. So lovely. So purposeful, squeezing us out" (C, 82–83). As an evocation of the rhythms and instinctive urges of perverse obsession, Oates's characterization of Kasch is superb. He follows Laney, spies upon her, and frantically broods on his "soiled angel. I reached up into your small tight body, didn't I, I jammed myself up into you, didn't I, and we are bound together forever, forever, forevermortal, the two of us" (c, 60). We are taken into the intensity of his agonized, lyrical brooding over the contradiction between "forever" and "forevermortal" through the obsessive rhythms of Oates's prose — repetitive, irrational, rhapsodic, self-concentrated. Laney, merely an ordinary teenager, with a neat attic bedroom and a collection of glass figurines, becomes a living symbol of Kasch's lost youth — "could not have loved her then. Not as I do now" (c, 128) — and also a desperate possibility for present rebirth and regeneration as the gentler, more compassionate lover or father he might have become. Oates makes us extraordinarily sensitive to the complexity of Kasch's perversity, to a man's maddened desire and passionate idealism, directed not merely at the girl but at his own past and possible future transcendence.

Laney lives, she tells Kasch, in the rural settlement of Childwold. The very name, of course, suggests more than a small village, population 800; it becomes in Kasch's ecstasy, an image of lost innocence and youth, a pastoral respite from his own sordidness. "*Childwold*, the girl said, her voice low, almost hoarse, throaty. . . . *Childwold*, she said." The image of what she stands for in his experience teases him and at night he hears her voice echoing in a litany, "a sacred chant":

Childwold
Childwood
Childwide
Childworld
Childmold
Childwould
Childtold   (c, 48 – 49)

Such litanies echo throughout Kasch's continuing passion, as he tries to create in words the intensity of his love. He keeps a journal. At first it is merely voyeuristic reportage, but increasingly it becomes lyrical, taking up phrases and the tone of Kasch's litanies. A little like Nabokov's Humbert Humbert, Kasch is attempting to change the really rather ordinary features of a surly schoolgirl into a rapturous, permanent creation of his own making. In his despairing attempt to turn his vision of a "brattish scrawny fourteen-year old" into a permanent unalienable vision, he comments with some self-directed irony: "One invents wildly. Small breasts prominent. A cheap Orlon sweater, dark blue, and the usual blue jeans, faded and soiled. Nostrils pink-rimmed; a bad cold. Lips refusing to turn up in a smile though I smiled with love." But through his mind, his fiction, she will be transfigured: "I will transform her: I will invent her. I will write about her with devotion" (C, 111).

There is, of course — as in *Lolita* — a tragic paradox here. At the same time as Laney is being fixed into the stasis of Kasch's imagination, she herself is growing, changing. And it is Kasch's mixture of lust and kindness to her that is the instrument of that change. Both glorifying in Laney's very ordinary youthfulness and yet with his very actions ensuring she grows out of it, he makes her his "own invention, my own treasure" (C, 129). Nearly six months after he meets her, he examines his journal entries, seeking in the concentrated way most Oates characters pursue some kind of given meaning in their lives, for a pattern in his records. What he encounters is in fact not the fixed stasis of art but the creativity of unpredictability, and he comes agonizingly to realize the futility of seeking any single key for the meandering complexity of life. He realizes that "there is no single moment of comprehension, no key to one's relationship with anyone at all, such ideas are theatrical, hysterical, deadly." And yet love and the vision it affords have often tempted men, as it tempts Kasch, to make their experience "permanent," fixed. "A common misconception I once wanted to write about in depth," he notes. "Therefore I want no false unity in my life . . . because it would be a lie. I have lived too long with lies" (C, 138). Katch experiences the agonizing paradox of any middle-aged idealization of youth, perverse or not — celebrating Laney's inexperience, her weakness, ignorance, and unsophistication, he wants to preserve her as he has found and created her; and yet by his very involvement with her, as well as through the simple passing of time, she will inevitably change. Childwold, the pastoral paradise, slips away from Kasch even as he celebrates it. Only within the significant fiction of his mind, can Laney, his own Evangeline, be made permanent.

Like *The Assassins*, therefore, *Childwold* is a book of hours, thrusting at us the eerie fear of the ultimate unreality of time, the body, the personality itself. Kasch apprehends himself as "pure consciousness trapped in time, in a body" (C, 126), and he is torn between the enjoyment and surprise of the present that his love for Laney opens to him and his fear of its final unreality. "How real the world strikes us, the world of the present moment. . . . Tactile, it is; palpable. Demonstrable (Aquinas: Knowledge begins with the senses.)" (C, 128). Kasch knows, intellectually, that "*existence involves changes and happenings*" (C, 129) and yet he is deeply aware too that "the body must be an error. . . . Nothing can explain it, that we are trapped for a certain period of time in a fleshly vehicle. Cruel, cruel. Capricious" (C, 225). These two contradictory intuitions (deeply felt, if not so explicitly articulated, by many characters in the novel) are epitomized in juxtaposed quotations from Saint John of the Cross:

> The soul that is attached to anything, however much good there may be in it, will not arrive at the liberty of divine union. For whether it be a strong wire rope of a slender and delicate thread that holds the bird, it matters not, if it really holds it fast; for, until the cord be broken, the bird cannot fly. So the soul, held by the bonds of human affections, however slight they may be, cannot, while they last, make its way to God.

Chilling, lovely, irrefutable. I know, I know. . . . Yet elsewhere I discover that Saint John has also told us

> When the will, the moment it feels any joy in sensible things, rises upwards in that joy to God, and when sensible things move it to pray, it should not neglect them, it should make use of them for so

holy an exercise; because sensible things, in these conditions, sub-
serve the end for which God created them, namely to be occasions
for making Him better known and loved. (C, 135)

Kasch, obsessed and confused, recalls Saint Augustine's admo-
nition "that God is to be enjoyed by man and creatures only as a
means to God" (C, 135–36). Yet the saint's advice, cool and rational, makes Kasch's dilemma worse as he obsessively broods
over its words: "*Used, use, enjoy, means to God, holy exercises,
love, her face, her body, her arms about my neck, deliverance,
God, no no no no no*" (C, 136). The cool words cannot contain
the obsession with which Kasch pursues their significance within
his own life. His affirmation, attainable only in art or madness,
is to have both: "Either/Or," he ponders, recalling Kierkegaard,
"But it must be Both/And! Both/And! Both the girl and God,
both time and eternity, both beloved and daughter, wife and sister, beauty and goodness. Both! Both!" (C, 192).

Laney's response to Kasch's obsessive passion, at once crazed
and gentle, perverse and compassionate, is a mixture of puzzle-
ment, cynical acceptance, repulsion and, slowly, an inarticulate
gentleness born of her realization of her own newly found lone-
liness. Like any fourteen-year-old, perhaps, she is incapable of
being aware of the depth of anguish she stirs in her lover. She is
at first equally indifferent to his inarticulate horror that she reeks
of cheap red wine and allows herself to be touched by anyone,
including him, as she is to his obsessive desire to explore and ex-
ploit her body. Gradually, not despite but in a sense through the
extremity of his desire, she conceives a strange compassion for
him. She explains to her mother that he is strange, sweet, and
gentle. He will talk to her for hours or lend her books: "'It's
very strange, I can't explain,'" she says. "'Sometimes he scares
me and at other times he, he's just . . . he's just so funny. . . .
That book is his; he lends me books'" (C, 88). Unlike him, she
has no words for what is growing in her and which is tragically
so cut off from the rest of her external life as an ordinary teenager. The words of love Laney knows are exploitative or coyly

romanticized, where "the girl was the center of the story, yes, you were the center of the story, just kissing and sinning and going wild with love and then the disaster followed and you wept or were beaten nearly to death or had an abortion or had a Mongoloid baby as punishment for your sins. . . . There were no words available, the magazine stories gave you no words, the girls were you and yet not you" (c, 216–17). Kasch, the man of words, is painfully discovering feelings which he has either forgotten or never had; Laney, the child of instinct and illiteracy, can find no words for the strange feelings of gentleness which invade her. We should probably not allegorize the relationship between the two simply as that of experience and youth, intellect and body, but there seems no doubt that in their relationship Oates is suggesting something in the painful dislocation of our habitual Western dualism. Kasch likewise experiences his inner conflict as a crisis of self. At once he can rationalize his behavior and yet also admit the irrational power of his lusts. He is "Kasch the pawing self-pitying mess" as well as "Kasch the enlightened spirit" (c, 157). "Ah," he agonizes, "we think of ourselves as one person! We hug that delusion to our deaths. Not just the mad who are split but all of us, brains split as if with an ax, one side in authority, one side *the* self, and the other quietly waiting" (c, 157–58).

Kasch's confused and anguished dreams of permanence similarly alternate with the bitter awareness that he "must let her go: she can't make me other than I am now and must be forever, forevermore, forevermortal" (c, 157). His affection can have no real outlet because only his dream of Laney can embody all the significance he finds in her but—like so many of Oates's characters—he is forced to pursue that dream down into the material world. The Childwold of his dreams struggles to become incarnate in the small, poor village and Laney's rambling family. When Kasch first meets Laney, he learns of her family— "Hillbillies, nearly. White trash" (c, 126)—and his disgust gradually becomes a fascination, a desire to penetrate to the secret of

Laney's origins and possess the Childwold of his fevered imagination. Through the confused and frantic fragments of the later stages of the story emerges Kasch's risky intent of marrying Laney's mother. We are never able to clarify his motives; we notice Laney's brief awareness of the possibility of the marriage as if Kasch's affection for Arlene exists on a totally different plane from his own love for her. We are given Kasch's own embarrassed explanation to his elderly aunt, but we are never sure — just as Kasch, presumably, is never sure — whether he wishes to marry her for herself or as a means to love or protect Laney. "My Bride awaits. My Brides" (c, 253), affirms Kasch. In this dimly motivated action we are being taken into an area of emotional experience where conscious motives matter less than the dimly articulated drives far beneath them. We are what we act, not what we articulate. He seems to make plans to buy land, he celebrates his bride, or brides, perceiving perhaps in Arlene his younger love grown into a woman of his own age and therefore defeating time: "You hold them all in one embrace. All. Always. Forever" (c, 268).

The final, sixth, part of the novel opens with a low-key description of Arlene and a man called Wallace, apparently a new lover, at a volunteer fireman's picnic. Gradually we piece together from Arlene's reactions what has occurred. "Why dwell on the past, on unhappy things. Why ruin this beautiful day. Why, why, no sense to it" (c, 277), she thinks, musing over the kindness of Wallace, the new home the family has rented, her father's death, and the confrontation between Kasch and Earl Tuller, in which she realizes "how lives were changed, irreparably changed, in a few minutes. A certain choice made, no time to think, no time to think ahead: and that was that. If only Kasch had not been nearby when Earl showed up. . . . She would not have minded being beaten by Earl again, not even that, so long as he hadn't crippled or killed her, the bastard, the drunken loudmouthed swinish bastard" (c, 281). Then with a brief reminder of Laney and her brother Vale, we are plunged into a series of fragments, evoking the extreme guilt and agony with which Kasch has reacted to the occurrence. The surface events seem to be simply and frighteningly that Kasch has accidentally killed Tuller in a fight and he has subsequently been convicted of second-degree manslaughter (acting in self-defense, and not guilty by reason of temporary insanity). But the surface events, tragic but not, surely, necessarily without hope, belie the terror of Kasch's reactions, which are thrust at us in violent agony. How ironical that at the start of his passion he has wanted to kill, if not himself, another —to "bring someone else back to the room! Liquor, a blow to the head, the rope, the beam" (c, 14). Now, on the verge of his transcendence, of being "translated," the power of the universe's arbitrariness brings about his doom: "Accident. Essentially. A tenth of an inch's difference and no reverse, no regain. Accident: essence sprayed out onto the cinders. No scooping it back up again. Perhaps in my madness I tried? Tried to scoop the brains back up again, squeeze them into the broken shell?" (c, 286). Like so many of Oates's characters, Kasch has chosen to pursue his deepest obsessions and has been defeated not by their inherent good or evil but by the arbitrariness of the material universe. His passion is forced to descend from the dream of Childwold to the earth of Childwold; "Kasch the poet, Kasch the lover" is "battered to death by Kasch the murderer" (c, 288). Kasch's agony seems disproportionate to the events, but beneath is a further dislocation of his existence as he realizes that his plan of transcendence through marriage with Laney's mother is a betrayal of his deepest vision of Childwold. In his agony he confesses his betrayal and asks: "Laney, Evangeline, do you forgive me? Do you even remember me? I betrayed you with her; I had not the courage for you. Years pass. Our lifetimes pass. My dear, my lovely girl, my daughter, did I ruin your life, did I poison your childhood?" (c, 289). His repeated cry *"to be executed as swiftly as possible"* (c, 288, 289) is therefore a response not so much to Tuller's death but to the failure of realization of his obsessive passion. "Where are you Laney?" he cries. "Where have

you gone? I have lost you. Do you exist? Did you ever exist?
You have left Childwold, I sense that: but where have you gone?
. . . You are no longer recognizable! You are no longer mine!"
(C, 290).

From Kasch's disoriented fragments, the final pages of the
novel merge into an even darker irony. Earlier, when Laney has
realized the inadequacy of the words she has found in romantic
magazines to express her feelings for Kasch, she has voiced in
timid spontaneity something he has found only in his idealization of her. They lie together on a bed and she recalls: "Kasch,
you said, Fitz John you are saying, softly, timidly, as if the sound
of his name is outrageous, wait, please—wait—I'm sorry—I
can't help it—I love you—But he doesn't reply, he is asleep, his
breathing is strained and slow, he's asleep or drunk, he's gone,
you aren't going to see him again, you are greatly relieved, you
are sick with the loss, you are triumphant" (C, 217). The scene
is reminiscent of the unspoken sympathy of Yvonne for Hugh in
The Assassins, a moment of affirmation never communicated
which passes and is lost. Now, at the end of *Childwold*, Laney
thinks, "'I love him. I didn't love him. I wanted to love him
but I didn't know how. Is it too late? It's too late,'" even as she
had said earlier, "Momma . . . don't be such a baby! He's just a
friend, I could never love *him*" (C, 284). And, at the end, with
Kasch deliberately isolated from the world, with "*no interest in
any living human beings*" (C, 294), she attempts to visit him first
in the hospital, then in a shack where he lives totally cut off from
the world:

It's Laney, you call out to him. Do you remember . . . ?
He steps away from the window again. . . . Kasch? Is it really you?
Here? After so long? But why? Am I here, calling to you? Waiting for
you? Kasch? My love? Are you really here, are you still alive? Is that
you, hiding in there, in that ruin of a house?—hiding from me? Kasch?
Bearded, gaunt, sickly-pale, hair colorless as dead hair, eyes in shadow,
dry bitter mouth in shadow, is it Kasch, here, it is Laney, here, shading
her eyes, waiting for a sign?
A sign, a sign . . . ? (C, 294–95)

Although it continues many of Oates's typical themes and the obsessional drives of her early novels, *Childwold* is a moving and powerful indication of her growing technical skills. It is probably the most skillfully constructed of her novels since *Them*. It evokes with care and power the obsessive desire for transcendence, but it does so by seizing upon the moments and fragments in our lives when we are threatened or invaded. While *Childwold* recapitulates familiar themes from her work — the emphasis on the falsity of fixing the self, the awareness that "the interior life constitues the authentic life," and that "reality is what I am thinking, what is thinking through me" (C, 138), the tragic arbitrariness of the physical universe. But alongside *A Garden of Earthly Delights*, or even *Wonderland*, the novel is amazingly sophisticated and complex in its narrative form, continually forcing us to make connections, puzzle over motive, and participate in the obscure surges of powerful feeling that are both the book's subject and its most impressive technique. *Childwold* may well be seen as a watershed when we look back at Oates's career in decades to come. A major source of Oates's power in all her fiction, as I have tried to articulate it throughout this study, is precisely this obsessive concentration on the ever-present, inarticulate arbitrariness and violence which lie buried in our psyches and which obscurely but definitively mold our lives. *Childwold* takes us into areas of desire and terror we recognize, from which we are glad to escape, as we are glad to escape from the concentration of tragic intensity of *Macbeth* or *King Lear*. To live by obsession totally is to go mad, but — at least as Oates articulates it in her novels — except through facing and, through fiction, reliving our obsessions, we will hardly be able to face the possibility of transcendence that those obsessions yearn for. It may be that it is to the sources of this transcendence that she will turn in future fiction.

EIGHT

Conclusion

TO WRITE a critical study of any living writer
is inevitably both risky and exhilarating.
Misjudgment is obviously all too easy and
any claims of distinctive merit or stature
must be made with great caution. Yet however difficult, the struggle to articulate a
contemporary writer's significance is one
of the most challenging tasks a critic may
set himself. Living in the same era, the
writer and the reader dwell as it were in
the same emotional and mythical neighborhood. When both are attempting to make
sense of their ongoing lives the proxim-
ity may not only aid in the explication of
the writer but may help criticism escape
its recurrent charge of parasitism. The author ceases to be an object of study. Instead, he or she becomes a partner in a
dialogue, which both parties enter with

overlapping interests, even if with different means of articulating them.

As a consequence, although any attempts to evaluate a contemporary writer within a comparative or historical context are not without point, they nevertheless lose their central urgency. When we work with a developing writer we can take criticism outside academia and engage in the assessment and—in however minor a way—the creation of our age's self-understanding. "Our lives," Oates writes, "are narratives; they are experienced in the flesh, sometimes in flesh that comes alive only with pain, but they are recollected as poems, lyrics, condensed, illuminated by a few precise images" (CB, 33). It is the role of the critic of a contemporary writer to point to the significance of those "precise images."

This account of Oates's fiction has revealed—in ways that were unpredictable when the task was started—that she is able to articulate and evoke some vitally important aspects of our contemporary sensibility. What an engaged reader of her fiction emerges with is a disturbing and yet exhilarating vision, one that is both fascinated with and appalled by the emotional and spiritual determinism of our age. Like Lawrence, as I have suggested, Oates has felt it to be the writer's calling to point us towards such awareness, and to call forth our creativity to respond to it. Hers is a fictional stance that we may perhaps see symbolized by her personal situation. She is an American citizen, living and working in Windsor, Ontario. From Windsor she can gaze across the Detroit River straight into what she terms the "transparent" heart of her America. She is at once tied to the United States by birth and sentiment while she is afforded a perspective of contemplation and judgment. "The border between two nations," she writes in one of her stories about American immigrants to Canada, "is always indicated by broken but definite lines" (CB, 13). Boundaries enable us to understand as well as to be separate from. Indeed, her migration to Canada in 1968 seems to have encouraged her fascination with the very dynamics of America from which she is physically separate. Canada is thus as much a state of mind as America; Canada is the perspective of a writer who is compelled to write about the experience of being overwhelmed (or nearly overwhelmed) by America, without being overwhelmed in her own person.

When we look at Oates's fiction as a whole, we are struck by the way place, physical surroundings, and everyday personal details are made, in the word I have frequently used, "transparent," revealing, as in Lawrence, a *spirit* rather than the mere presence of place. Paradoxically, the spirit of America is characteristically made accessible through the very opposite of the spiritual—through the repeated bombardment by an obsessed concentration on detail. For Oates, a peculiarity of contemporary American experience is that insight seems overwhelmingly to arise through paradox, contraries, and extremity of feeling. Confrontations of dream and reality, spirit and material, therefore dominate her fiction. In the sudden eruption of violence, through discoveries or shattered expectations bordering on the insane or absurd, by vivid juxtapositions of nature and mechanism, we may discover ways of transcending our bondage to self and the world. Crossing borders we may find our identity lost, dissolved, unrecognizable, at risk of disintegration. Much as Lawrence does, Oates forces us to confront ourselves at the boundaries of our known and comforting experiences. We are never allowed to accept appearances as final, even though the intensity encountered beneath our surfaces may destroy us. Paradoxically, it is the very fearfulness of America which makes for the excitement of the dream which may create us new.

There are characters in her stories—Maureen and Jules in *Them*, Elena and Jack in *Do With Me What You Will*—who have come through, in Lawrence's phrase, who have survived an unpredictable and absurd set of crises and struggles. They have pursued an obsession, often by violence or the destruction of apparent order, and have triumphed. Theirs is the way of transcendent affirmation. "Life *consists*," writes Lawrence, "*in* this achieving of a pure relationship between ourselves and the living universe about us." Such transcendence is achieved through desire, through obsession. "A new relation, a new relatedness hurts somewhat in the attaining. . . . Each time we strive to a new relation, with anyone or anything, it is bound to hurt somewhat. Because it means the struggle with and the displacing of old connexions."[1]

Such a reading of Oates as I have attempted, with its emphasis on her Lawrentian affinities in both her prophetic stance and her emphasis on transcendence through struggle, pain, and the affirmation of the flesh, culminates, so far in her career, in *Do With Me What You Will*. But part of the fascination of working with a living author is the unpredictable developments that occur within his or her literary personality and vision. In Oates's work one now discerns a movement, observable in her essays as well as her fiction, towards a fascination with Eastern renunciatory philosophical modes. It is as if the violence and egocentric destructiveness which have been such tragic outcomes of Western history and philosophy must somehow be transcended by embracing the opposite vision. Of course, such a development in Oates's thinking is prefigured in Lawrence's own. Lawrence, too, came to despair at the cultivation of the uniqueness of the self which has been so fundamental to Western consciousness. As I have argued, Lawrence's vision is not unlike that of Oates in *The Assassins*, which is the first major expression of her espousal of the Eastern renunciation which seems to be entering her work in the mid-seventies. On the surface, such a development is strange in a writer so imbued with the possibilities of transcendence through the flesh. But it is indicative of the seriousness of her conception of the writer's task and indeed it would be false to the very conception of this study of Oates's novels from *With Shuddering Fall* through *Childwold* if I attempted to

---

1 D. H. Lawrence, "Morality and the Novel," in *Phoenix: The Posthumous Papers of D. H. Lawrence*, ed. Edward D. McDonald (New York: Viking Press, 1972), 528, 530.

impose a static unity on her work. It might be hoped that this study will be regarded in the future as a stimulating account of the *early* Oates. It may be that the next phase of her career as a writer will develop in surprising and uncertain directions. One might risk some predictions — such as a continuing concern with religious experience and mysticism, for instance. Perhaps, too, we may see her becoming more experimental in her conception of fictional form. Her stories — which would justify a study in their own right — have consistently been more technically experimental, and she may integrate the formal daring of some of her short fiction into the longer form of the novel.

So far as her vision of contemporary America is concerned, Oates's future writing can be anticipated with eagerness. Possibly more than any American novelist now writing, she has shown herself sensitive to the eddying feelings of living in the 1960s and 1970s. We look to writers to respond to more than the intellectual or social fashions of their age. Oates sees the cultural role of the artist as that of struggling with and articulating the underlying, ongoing movements of feeling within his or her age. It is through art that a society expresses its gradually realized sense of being a society. As readers and critics, we are, or should be, concerned continually with creating the necessary active relationship between art and our society's whole way of life. Too often in this century artists and readers alike have taken refuge — from our society, ultimately from ourselves — in an apparently autonomous aesthetic world; too often, too, as critics and scholars, we have constructed abstract and generalized world views and then triumphantly set an author within them. This, too, is a kind of escapism. For a society's ongoing life is lived in individual men and women, within their specific and changing lives — and it is the vocation of the artist to probe and capture that particularity in all its contradictions, tensions, confusions, or uncertainties.

In turn, I believe it is that role of the critic, and the teacher, to struggle with the artist, helping through dialogue to make other readers sense the importance of their own, subjective wrestling with the issues the writer thrusts before us. I have frequently used Lawrence as a companion through this study because, of all major modern writers, he can remind us most powerfully of the way the novelist meditates not on abstract ideas but on the age's changing structures of lived feeling — and also because, above all else, Lawrence's vision is thrust before us in particularities. Like Lawrence, Oates's work articulates for us both our ideological dynamics and the more complex structures of feeling which lie deeper than the surface of our age. Around the words and the structures of our idioms and patterns of thought accrete subtle, often contradictory, implications, which the great artist — a Shakespeare, a Hawthorne, a Lawrence — struggles uneasily to verbalize, knowing uneasily the problem of articulating the movement of an age while living through it. As Oates's skills as a novelist have developed, her work has increasingly evoked the confusing experience of our time and, more importantly, related our chaotic and imperfectly apprehended experiences to wider patterns of significance. Her importance for us is seen partly in the seriousness with which she sees the writer's dual, and perhaps contradictory, role of submerging herself in our age, and partly as well, in her struggle to achieve a transcendence of our time in her articulation of it. As Oates presents us, we are a people between ages, living in a time of not yet. We are obsessed with what limits us most, and yet we believe passionately that it is through those obsessions that we will transcend our limitations. She has been presenting our time of transition not as a breathing space but a time of breathlessness and struggle, where obsession, not renunciation, has seemed the only authentic means to transcendence. It may be, as she has started to affirm, that our struggles for uniqueness will be transcended by a "new heaven, new earth" of egoless involvement and compassion, where struggle will not be destructive, where fulfillment will come through self-transcendence not self-affirmation. Recently she has written, comparing our age with Lawrence's, that "our own era is one in which prophetic eschatological art has as great a significance as it did in 1916; Lawrence's despairing conviction that civilization was in the latter days is one shared by a number of our most serious writers, even if there is little belief in the Apocalypse in its classical sense."[2] As with Lawrence, it is to the apparent impasse of our civilization that Oates's fiction offers its most radical challenge. What, it asks, are the possibilities that await us, and dare we meet them?

2 Joyce Carol Oates, "Lawrence's Götterdämmerung: The Tragic Vision of *Women in Love*," *Critical Enquiry*, IV (Spring, 1978), 562.

Selected
Bibliography

Two extensive bibliographies of writings by and about Joyce Carol
Oates have been compiled, as follow: Lucienne P. McCormick, "A
Bibliography of Works by and About Joyce Carol Oates," *American
Literature*, XLIII (1971–72), 124–32, and Douglas M. Catron, "A
Contribution to a Bibliography of Works by and About Joyce Carol
Oates," *American Literature*, XLIX (1977–78), 399–414. Linda M.
Wagner is presently editing a collection of essays on Oates's work for
G. K. Hall. Readers are therefore referred to these studies for extensive
references to Oates. What follows may be more useful for the reader of
this particular study: a selective list of Oates criticism which has proved
to be especially suggestive, and — perhaps more useful — a list of works
which have been instrumental in creating the approach I have taken to
Oates's work. When one engages fully in a dialogue with one writer,
one inevitably finds oneself in conversation with others. Readers of
this book may wish to engage in the same, or similar, conversations.

I   A SELECTIVE LIST OF OATES CRITICISM

Bellamy, Joe David. *The New Fiction: Interviews with Innovative
American Writers*. Urbana: Universeity of Illinois, 1974.
Burwell, Rose Marie. "Joyce Carol Oates and an Old Master." *Critique*, XV (1973), 48–58.

——. "The Process of Individuation as Narrative Structure: Joyce Carol Oates' *Do With Me What You Will*." *Critique*, XVII (1975), 93–106.

Creighton, Joanne V. "Unliberated Women in Joyce Carol Oates's Fiction." *World Literature Written in English*, XVII (1978), 165–75.

Gies, James R. "From Jimmy Gatz to Jules Wendall." *Dalhousie Review*, LVI (1976–77), 718–24.

Hassan, Ihab. *Paracriticisms: Seven Speculations of the Times*. Urbana: University of Illinois, 1975.

Kazin, Alfred. *Bright Book of Life: American Novelists and Storytellers from Hemingway to Mailer*. Boston: Little, Brown and Co., 1973.

Martin, Alice C. "Towards a Higher Consciousness: A Study of the Novels by Joyce Carol Oates." Ph.D. dissertation, University of Illinois, 1974.

Stevick, Philip. "Remembering, Knowing, and Telling in Joyce Carol Oates." In Barbara MacKenzie (ed.), *The Process of Fiction*. New York: Harcourt, Brace, Jovanovich, 1974.

Waller, G. F. "Joyce Carol Oates' *Wonderland*: An Introduction." *Dalhousie Review*, LIV (1974), 480–90.

——. "New Fiction: Myths and Passions, Rivers and Cities." *Ontario Review*, No. 5 (1976–77), 93–97.

——. "Through Obsession to Transcendence: The Recent Work of Joyce Carol Oates." *World Literature Written in English*, XVII (1978), 176–80.

II   OTHER USEFUL STUDIES: CRITICAL, PHILOSOPHICAL, METHODOLOGICAL

Cavell, Stanley. *Must We Mean What We Say?* New York: Cambridge University Press, 1976.

Dabrowski, Kazimierz. *Mental Growth Through Positive Disintegration*. London: Gryf Publications, 1970.

Dane, Peter. "D. H. Lawrence's *Women in Love*." *Bulletin of the Auckland English Association*, III (1964), 8–12.

Dufrenne, Mikel. *The Phenomenology of Aesthetic Experience*. Translated by Edward S. Casey *et al*. Evanston: Northwestern University Press, 1973.

Frankl, Victor. *Man's Search for Meaning*. Translated by Ilse Lasch. Boston: Beacon Press, 1962.

Fraser, John. *Violence and the Arts*. New York: Cambridge University Press, 1975.

Heidegger, Martin. *Being and Time*. Translated by J. Macquarrie and E. Robinson. New York: Harper, 1962.

———. *On the Way to Language*. Translated by Peter D. Hertz. New York: Harper and Rowe, 1971.

Holland, Norman N. *The Dynamics of Literary Response*. New York: Oxford University Press, 1968.

Iser, Wolfgang. *The Implied Reader: Patterns of Communication in Prose Fiction from Bunyan to Beckett*. Baltimore: Johns Hopkins University Press, 1974.

———. "Indeterminacy and the Reader's Response in Prose Fiction." In *Aspects of Narrative*. Edited by J. Hillis Miller. New York: Columbia University Press, 1975.

D. H. Lawrence. *Apocalypse*. New York: Viking Press, 1967.

———. *Phoenix: The Posthumous Papers of D. H. Lawrence*. Edited by Edward D. McDonald. New York: The Viking Press, 1972.

———. *Collected Letters*. Edited by Harry T. Moore. 2 vols. New York: Viking Press, 1972.

Merleau-Ponty, Maurice. *The Primacy of Perception*. Edited by James M. Edie. Evanston: Northwestern University Press, 1974.

———. *Signs*. Translated by Richard C. McCleary. Evanston: Northwestern University Press, 1964.

Palmer, Richard E. *Hermeneutics*. Evanston: Northwestern University Press, 1979.

Pelz, Werner. *God Is No More*. London: Collins, 1964.

———. *True Deceivers*. London: Collins, 1966.

———. *The Scope of Understanding in Sociology*. London: Routledge and Kegan Paul, 1976.

Ricoeur, Paul. *The Conflict of Interpretations*. Edited by Don Ihde. Evanston: Northwestern University Press, 1974.

———. *Fallible Man*. Translated by Paul Kelbley. Chicago: Regnery, 1964.

———. *Freud and Philosophy*. Translated by Denis Savage. New Haven: Yale University Press, 1970.

———. *La Métaphore Vive*. Paris: Seuil, 1975.

Tanner, Tony. *City of Words: American Fiction, 1950–1970*. London: Jonathan Cape, 1971.

Tillich, Paul. *Systematic Theology*. 3 vols. Chicago: Chicago University Press, 1951–63.

Waller, G. F. "Speaking What We Feel: Shakespearian Criticism in the Late Seventies." *Dalhousie Review*, XXVIII (1978), 550–63.
———. *The Strong Necessity of Time*. The Hague: Mouton, 1976.
Williams, Raymond. *The Long Revolution*. London: Chatto and Windus, 1961.
———. *Marxism and Literature*. Oxford: Oxford University Press, 1977.